THE
National ◆SABR◆ Pastime

Baseball in the
Sunshine State

EDITED BY CECILIA M. TAN

 **Published by The Society for American Baseball Research**

THE NATIONAL PASTIME

Copyright © 2016 The Society for American Baseball Research

Editor: Cecilia Tan
Design and Production: Lisa Hochstein
Cover Design: Lisa Hochstein
Fact Checker: Clifford Blau

Front cover image: Havana Sugar Kings program courtesy of The Rucker Archive

ISBN 978-1-943816-03-3 (print edition)
ISBN 978-1-943816-02-6 (ebook edition)

Society for American Baseball Research, Inc.
Cronkite School at ASU
555 N. Central Ave. #416
Phoenix, AZ 85004

Web: www.sabr.org
Phone: (602) 496–1460

Contents

Land of New Beginnings   Francis Kinlaw   4

Spring Training in St. Petersburg
Its Beginnings and the Phillies' Experience in 1915   Robert D. Warrington   5

Black Baseball's "Funmakers"
Taking the Miami Ethiopian Clowns Seriously   Brian Carroll   17

Blurring the Color Line
*How Cuban Baseball Players Led to the Racial Integration
of Major League Baseball*   Stephen R. Keeney   23

NAPBL Gathering in Miami Gave Birth to the Caribbean Series   Lou Hernández   30

The Long Forgotten Florida International League   Steve Smith   35

The Short but Exciting Life of the Havana Sugar Kings   John R. Harris / John J. Burbridge Jr.   40

Satchel Paige: Twilight with the Marlins   Alan Cohen   45

Woody Smith
The Original Mr. Marlin   Sam Zygner   49

Spring Training, *Safe at Home!*, and Baseball-on-Screen in Florida   Rob Edelman   54

Field of Schemes
The Spring Training Tryout of NFL Star "Jerry LeVias"   Dan VanDeMortel   59

El Presidente
The Life and Times of Dennis Martinez   Danny Gallagher   64

Miami Amigos   Eric Robinson   70

One Last Season in the Sun
The Saga of the Senior Professional Baseball Association   William Schneider   74

Take Me Out to the Courtroom
A Look at Baseball Cases in the Florida Courts   Louis H. Schiff   80

The Best Baseball Story Ever?
Cecil "Stud" Cantrell, the Tampico Stogies, and Long Gone   David Krell   86

Walking It Off—Marlins Postseason Walk-Offs   Steven Glassman   89

Contributors   95

Land of New Beginnings

Francis Kinlaw

When I was a boy, 16 years old,
And the majors had 16 teams;
Mention of Florida brought refreshing thoughts,
Along with pennant dreams.

The time was 1960,
But those vibes came every spring
For sports fans spread across the land
When baseball ruled as king.

Romanticism fed my thoughts
Of carefree sites of joy;
Amid sunshine, beaches, rejuvenation and hope,
Few problems could annoy.

Optimism seemed to fill those weeks,
As news of each camp spread;
Folks eagerly awaited reporters' critiques
And news of what skippers said.

People were drawn to *The Sporting News*
And to radio interviews
For subtle facts about each team
And for emerging clues.

Twelve teams toiled under Florida's sun,
Datelines became well-known;
Places where prospects took their tests
And where much hype was sown.

The Tigers roamed in Lakeland,
Fort Myers was the Pirates' haunt;
Yanks and Cards trained in St. Pete,
Which had two parks to flaunt.

White Sox hung in Sarasota,
Bradenton had its Braves;
Orioles flocked to Miami,
Attracted by March heat waves.

Clearwater enjoyed its Phillies (as in baseball,
    not cigars),
Tampa welcomed a bunch of Reds (but not the
    Commie kind!)
Orlando hosted the Senators in pre-Disney days…
To tourists, roaming everywhere, all the world
    seemed fine.

The A's and Dodgers were based near beaches—
Vero and West Palm;
Baseball held on to center stage
With great scenery as its balm.

Cool nights in late season were distant thoughts
As the players ran their sprints;
Aching muscles produced by hours of drills
Made stars and rookies wince.

Old guys prayed for one more good year,
While traded ones adjusted;
Most reveled in their new, fresh start
With few men yet disgusted.

Disappointments would come in the months
    ahead
But, for now, the birds were singing;
As pitchers nibbled around home plate
And hitters kept on swinging.

Soon the teams would head up North
To settle pennant races;
Prepared for the summer, players made those
    trips—
Florida had put them through their paces!

Acknowledgements
Databases maintained by SABR's Spring Training Research Committee were invaluable to the author in the writing of this poem.

Spring Training in St. Petersburg

Its Beginnings and the Phillies' Experience in 1915

Robert D. Warrington

It seems obvious that Florida is an apt location for major league baseball to conduct spring training. While winter holds the north in its dark, frigid grip, Florida is comparatively sunny and warm—ideal weather to prepare ballplayers for the grueling season ahead. But as the second decade of the twentieth century dawned, Florida remained largely ignored as clubs continued to hold their spring training camps farther north and west in states like North Carolina, Georgia, Arkansas, Louisiana, and Texas.[1]

Things changed in the 1910s, however, and it had little to do with tropical temperatures and balmy breezes. The siren song of financial inducements drew clubs to train in Florida. Tampa enticed the Chicago Cubs to train there in 1913 with an offer to pay the room, board, and expenses of the 35 players on the roster.[2] St. Petersburg attempted the same gambit with the Pittsburgh Pirates, but owner Barney Dreyfuss rebuffed the overture, writing, "You must think I'm a damn fool to train in a whistle stop little one tank town."[3]

LURING A TEAM AND BUILDING A BALLPARK IN ST. PETERSBURG

Albert Fielding Lang moved from Pittsburgh to St. Petersburg in 1910, and became a successful businessman as well as one of the city's biggest boosters, in particular promoting its attractiveness as a site for a major league club to hold spring training. An avid baseball fan, Lang was indefatigable in his efforts to convince team owners that Florida provided ideal conditions for their players to undergo pre-season conditioning.[4]

Undaunted by Pittsburgh's snub, Lang approached the St. Louis Browns to hold their spring training camp in St. Petersburg. The city's Board of Trade took a critical step in laying the groundwork for a club to come by forming the Major League Baseball and Amusement Company (MLBAC). In an August 18, 1913, meeting, it identified three locations as suitable for building a ballpark, and leading businessmen purchased stock in the company to finance the venture.[5]

After extensive mail communication with Lang, Robert L. Hedges, president of the Browns, visited St. Petersburg on September 20 to listen to a presentation on the benefits of holding spring training there in 1914. Convinced, he signed a one-year contract for his team to do so. The $10,000 raised by MLBAC would be used to offset expenses incurred by 35 Browns' players plus five newspapermen from St. Louis who would accompany the team during spring training.[6]

Multiple sites were proposed on which to build a ballpark for the team to train. At its meeting on October 3, MLBAC board members voted 4–2 for the Coffee Pot Bayou location in the Snell and Hamlett subdivision.[7] Dissenting members objected, preferring the Kerr tract on Fourth Street South, which they claimed would be more accessible for people walking or driving cars. The local street car company offered its Oak Park ball grounds, pledging to spend $4,000 to build a grandstand and make other improvements to the site. Board members judged the location's distance from the city a major drawback in that proposal.[8]

A full stockholders' meeting was held on October 9 at which the Coffee Pot location was unanimously approved as the ballpark site. The deciding factor was Snell and Hamlett's offer: allow free use of the land for six years, pay the costs of removing tree stumps, fill holes and sink a well on the property, and assure proper drainage on the site at all times. Free use of the Kerr tract was guaranteed for only one year, after which MLBAC would have to buy the property for $18,000 or leave and find another location for major league clubs to train. Improving the property to make it suitable for baseball, moreover, was the responsibility of MLBAC. Costs associated with upgrading the land coupled with the ultimatum to purchase or abandon the tract after one year disenchanted investors, as did the prospect of paying to construct a grandstand that might be torn down a year later if MLBAC decided not to buy the land.[9]

COFFEE POT PARK'S LOCATION

Although noteworthy in history as the first ballpark in St. Petersburg used for major league spring training, uncertainty still attends the exact location and physical

Phillies' trainer Mike Dee hanging laundry to dry outside Coffee Pot Park. The photo shows the area surrounding the ballpark was undeveloped in 1915.

layout of Coffee Pot Park.[10] In an article written in 1965, baseball historian Fred Lieb placed it at First Street North and 22nd Avenue.[11] In his book on the history of spring training, Charles Fountain states it was located on what "is today part of a string of parks that runs along the water north of the Vinoy Hotel."[12] Jeff Mashier, who from 1923–57 covered sports for St. Petersburg's *Evening Independent* newspaper, stated in a 1963 interview that the home in which he lived at 2232 Brevard Road, NE Grenada Terrace, was positioned at the home plate area of Coffee Pot Park.[13] Another long-time resident of the city, Walter Fuller, recalled in a 1945 newspaper article it was located in what had become the Grenada Terrace residential section of the city.[14]

There is no doubt the ballpark was adjacent to Coffee Pot Bayou. Although officially named Sunshine Park, it was habitually called Coffee Pot Park or Coffee Pot Bayou Park.[15] Manatee and H.B. Plant excursion steamers would bring fans over to games from Tampa, landing customers just beyond the outfield after sailing up Coffee Pot Bayou.[16] Moreover, numerous reports covering spring training noted that players would often fish in the bayou "adjoining the ball grounds" during breaks in practice, and that the pier they used was just a short walk from the ballpark.[17]

BROWNS' BRIEF STAY IN ST. PETERSBURG

The St. Louis Browns' residence in St. Petersburg for spring training lasted just one year. An abrupt end to the relationship was attributed to a dispute over who should pay certain expenses—unrelated to room and board—the team had accrued during its stay. City businessmen refused to pay the $6,500, while team owner

Hedges insisted it was St. Petersburg's responsibility to do so.[18] The disagreement was caused in part by the lack of a formal agreement clearly differentiating expenses for which the city would be responsible—beyond room and board—versus those the club would cover.[19] The quarrel ended with Hedges declaring, "I'll promise you one thing, Mr. Lang—no other major league club will train in your hamlet."[20]

PHILLIES BECOME THE NEWEST TENANTS

Yet again, Al Lang faced the task of enticing a major league team to adopt St. Petersburg as its spring training home. This time, his gaze fell upon the Philadelphia Phillies, who had trained in Wilmington, North Carolina, in 1914 and struggled with the poor weather conditions they endured.[21] Lang concluded a deal with Phillies' president William F. Baker to train in the city in 1915—the first time the club would hold preseason in Florida.[22]

The extent to which St. Petersburg subsidized the Phillies' stay is unclear. MLBAC officials, according to one newspaper report, stated the Phillies would pay "hotel bills, transportation charges and incidental expenses," while the city would "assist in finding suitable quarters and lend aid in other directions."[23] The phrase "lend aid in other directions" was not further defined, but the accuracy of MLBAC's statement is open to question. The notoriously penurious Baker almost certainly insisted on financial concessions similar to those offered the Browns. Other reports judge the room rate for Phillies players to stay at the Fifth Avenue Hotel was offset considerably by MLBAC subsidies, as were the costs of players' meals.[24] Lieb notes the city had to furnish baseballs used in training.[25] Maintaining the ballpark and grounds was also St. Petersburg's responsibility.[26]

ADVENTURE ON THE HIGH SEAS

Spring training for some Phillies' players began on February 26, 1915, when they—along with players from the Philadelphia Athletics and Brooklyn Dodgers—boarded the steamer *Apache* in New York City for a trip down the Atlantic seaboard to Jacksonville.[27] A few hours out at sea, the *Apache* was approached by the British cruiser *HMS Essex*, patrolling America's coast looking for ships smuggling war goods to Germany, then at war with Great Britain. Eventually satisfied the *Apache* carried ballplayers, not military matériel, the *Essex* departed to resume its duties.[28]

After arriving in Jacksonville on March 1, Phillies' players boarded a train for the 256-mile trip to St. Petersburg.[29] One Philadelphia writer accompanying the players dubbed the train the "Florida Rattler" as a way of describing jolting rail journeys in the state.[30] Other Phillies players went directly by train to the city, either in small groups or individually from their homes.[31] All but a few players were in camp for the start of training.[32]

1915 PHILLIES: A TEAM IN TRANSITION

The Phillies team that took the field in St. Petersburg had changed substantially since the end of the 1914 season. That club had finished a disappointing sixth, caused primarily by the loss of six players who had "jumped" to the Federal League, enticed by the fatter paychecks the upstart league had dangled before them. Saddled with an enervated pitching staff and infield, player-manager Charlie Dooin was the first casualty of the poor finish, fired soon after the season ended.[33]

The club, moreover, was riven by factions, the two most prominent headed by Hans Lobert and Sherry Magee. A threat loomed that if either Lobert or Magee were selected as the new manager—both wanted the job—the other and his faction of players would jump to the Federal League. Phillies president Baker finessed the problem by choosing Pat Moran—a veteran catcher-coach on the team—for the job. Phillies players held Moran in high regard and endorsed the choice.[34]

But picking a new manager created a problem as well as solving one. Dooin still wanted to play, but not for his former coach. Ridding the team of internal friction that had hampered its performance meant Lobert and Magee also had to go.[35] All three men were traded before spring training, and players received in return became important parts of the 1915 team, along with a shortstop purchased from the Pacific Coast League, Dave Bancroft.[36]

When he announced Moran's selection as manager, Baker announced, "I think a change is advisable—and necessary."[37] Just how much change was in store for the Phillies players would quickly become apparent in St. Petersburg.[38]

SPRING TRAINING UNDER MORAN

Pat Moran conducted a highly organized, rigorously run, tightly supervised, and strictly disciplined spring training camp the likes of which Phillies players had never seen.[39] Of the many newspaper reports filtering out of camp, two revealed the novel and exacting nature of Moran's training regimen. Veteran sportswriter James C. Isaminger wrote:

They should call him Pat Thousand Eyes. Never have the Phillies had a tactician who watched cases closer than the Fitchburg man. In past years, inside play has always been as prominent on the Phillies as an ant at a coronation, but it is different this season. Peerless Pat runs the drill like the Czar leaving out the despotic stuff. The point is that Moran runs the practice and the practice doesn't run itself. The team spent yesterday rehearsing signs. There's a signal there will be no team in the National League knowing more inside stuff than the Phils.[40]

Jim Nasium sounded a similar refrain in his column:

We have been given a slant at things on this spring jaunt that, to the best of our knowledge, have never occurred on a Philly team before, and we've been trailing this bunch with our eyes open for quite a spell now. Never before have we seen a Philly manager call his players into a conference room behind closed doors at the hotel of an evening to discuss signals, new plays and systematic methods of committing our great national frolic, and never before have we seen said manager devoting his time on the playing field to drilling his players in the fine points of the pastime instead of confining the entire attention and training of the team to the low-brow art of slamming the pill and fielding…A Philadelphia National League club will take the field prepared to mix brains with its pastiming instead of merely committing the national nuisance by main strength.[41]

Each day began for Phillies players when they were awakened at 8AM. After breakfast, they walked two miles between their hotel and Coffee Pot Park as part of their physical conditioning, referring to the cross-country jaunts as "Tipperary Hikes."[42] Workouts were held twice daily: 10AM to noon and 1–4PM.[43] Then the players walked the two miles back to their hotel.[44]

Three Phillies, Al Demaree, Milt Stock, and Stan Baumgartner, "found a way to cheat the long hike to the ball grounds, hiring bicycles on which they make the round trip daily."[45] Lieb claims in an article written fifty years after the fact that Moran discovered the subterfuge, forbade the bicycles, and ordered the men to run six extra laps around the ballpark for each day they had ridden the journey instead of hiking it.[46] Period accounts dispute Lieb's recollection, affirming the players used bicycles throughout spring training.[47]

Tough physical conditioning was a key element of Moran's training program. One writer noted "not an individual was idle" on the ballfield,[48] while another observed that Moran's emphasis on "hard exercise" produced "sore muscles and aching limbs," especially early in spring training.[49] This is how one reporter described a typical day of practice:

Moran has mapped out a program of various forms of exercise. He had the men toss the ball around as a preliminary exercise. Then they had batting practice, and this was followed by the infielders and outfielders chasing grounders and flies. After each man bats the ball he is compelled to run around the bases in order to develop his wind.[50]

Beyond conditioning players at a demanding physical pace, Moran's focus on mastering the "mental dimension of the game" clearly differentiated this spring training camp from past experiences.[51] It was called "inside baseball" at the time and involved, as one writer put it, "instruction on what to do and how to do it at the right time."[52] Players were drilled on baserunning and shown what to do as a runner in different game situations. Marveling at the emphasis placed on the thinking side of baseball, a writer remarked, "Intelligence on the bases is a commodity that the Phils can use to advantage."[53] Pitchers were schooled extensively on the art of holding baserunners close to the bag. The morning session on March 11, for example, consisted of the following drill:

The pitchers were put on the slab and with basemen and catcher in their positions and base runners on first and second, the runners were instructed to try to get a lead on the pitcher, while the pitchers were coached in the art of picking off the runners with deceptive moves and quick chucks to the bag.[54]

Moran also dedicated significant time to turning "this bunch of brawn into a machine that works in unison."[55] He bluntly declared, "You will play together and you will have the desire to operate as a team."[56] Moran also reminded players that their continued employment depended on achieving success on the ballfield. "This is your bread and butter as well as mine," he admonished them.[57] Moran also did not play favorites among players—veterans trained just as hard as rookies—and made clear that as long as the managerial reins were his, he was running the ball club. To drive home the point, the Phillies' manager announced, "Anyone who thinks these rules are too severe can look for a job elsewhere."[58]

But Moran's managerial abilities transcended the roles of despot and taskmaster. He was personally popular with the players who respected his baseball acumen, commitment to training, and determination to be victorious.[59] Moran was familiar with all but the team's newest players, having served as the Phillies' reserve catcher and unofficial pitching coach since 1910.[60] The players recognized, moreover, the value of his tough physical conditioning regimen and unrelenting focus on "inside baseball" in claiming the pennant that had long eluded the club.[61] Outfielder Dode Paskert was quoted as saying that "he had heard more real baseball instruction and tactics talked about here in the last week than he has since he joined the Phils."[62]

Moran also was aided by an absence of internal strife on the team. As noted, Phillies' teams in recent years had been split by factions and personal animosity between some players. The new mood was captured by one sportswriter who observed:

The members of the Phillies are commenting among themselves about the different spirit which is being shown among the players on the team this season. There is better deportment among the members of Moran's squad than I have ever seen in the Phillies' training camp. The men are going about their work in a better and more satisfied frame of mind, and on all sides there is a willingness on the part of the men to assist and encourage each other.[63]

To ensure continued harmony on the team, Moran laid down strict rules to govern one of the players' favorite pastimes: gambling.[64] Shooting craps was not allowed, and card games such as poker were limited to ten-cent antes. Reading was preferred by some players, but Moran even regulated that.[65] He believed reading on trains was bad for batting eyes and forbade players from doing so for more than limited periods.[66]

In retrospect, probably the best tribute paid to the Phillies manager—or to any baseball manager—was offered by a veteran Phillies player who said, "Moran makes me do things that I don't want to do. He has my goat."[67]

THE "SECRET SESSION"

Of all the innovative steps taken by Moran at spring training in 1915, none posed a greater riddle than the "secret session." On March 16, Moran held a meeting with players in the Coffee Pot Park clubhouse to rehearse the team's signaling system, something he did repeatedly during the preseason. Then, he ordered all outsiders to leave the ballpark and its gates closed. Sportswriters—ousted by Moran's edict—were mystified. One wrote:

> This was a distinct novelty in the training camp at the Phillies. Moran has some secrets up his sleeves. These he has refused to impart to anyone but his players, and Pat doesn't propose that any prying eyes shall get wise to what is going on. Such a thing as secret practice has never been known before among the players of the Philadelphia Nationals.[68]

Players were mum about what transpired behind closed doors, and the puzzle went unsolved for decades. It was only in the late 1940s that a player let the cat out of the bag. Phillies infielder Bert Niehoff, then working as scout for the New York Yankees, returned to St. Petersburg and admitted the "secret session" was devoted to stealing other teams' signs. Moran was convinced victories could be earned employing such a tactic, and Niehoff reminisced, "Anytime we had a man on first base and less than two outs, Moran would sacrifice the runner to second. He never missed an opportunity to have a runner looking in at the catcher's signals."[69]

THE SAGA OF RAMIRO SEIGLIE

Moran was fortunate there was little personal drama at Phillies' training camp. Outfielder Possum Whitted—obtained from the Braves in an offseason trade—held out briefly after turning down the Phillies' initial $4,800 offer,[70] but the dispute was soon resolved, and all players were in camp by March 6.[71] One player, however, Ramiro Seiglie, became the object of a tug-of-war between the Phillies and Washington Nationals.

The 22-year-old Seiglie impressed observers with his blazing speed and sure hands as a shortstop in the Cuban League.[72] One of the people who saw his talents was sportswriter Edgar Wolfe, then vacationing in Cuba.[73] Wolfe recommended him to Moran, and Seiglie accepted transportation from the Phillies to report to St. Petersburg, which he did on March 3.[74]

Clark Griffith, manager of the Nationals, asserted Seiglie had made an oral commitment to Merito Acosta—a Washington outfielder who played with Seiglie in the Cuban League—to join the Nationals.[75] Griffith sent a telegram to Moran on March 5 demanding Seiglie be delivered to the Nationals' training camp in Charlottesville at once.[76] Griffith continued sending daily telegrams to Seiglie and Moran threatening dire consequences if the Cuban infielder did not report promptly.[77] To Griffith's telegrams were added those sent by Acosta and Seiglie's brother, Oscar, who worked in Washington, DC, urging him to join the Washington club.[78]

The story Seiglie told shifted over time. He first claimed to have made no commitment to Washington and would remain with the Phillies.[79] But on March 18, Seiglie left camp and traveled to Charlottesville to converse with Griffith. He explained his brother had convinced him to make the trip, but Seiglie also opined that he expected Griffith to pay him substantially more than the Phillies were offering.[80]

Seiglie signed a contract to play for the Nationals the same day he arrived at their camp. Doing an about-face from his previous statements, the infielder admitted the first offer he received had indeed come from Washington, and now he felt morally bound to join that club. The only reason he started training with the Phillies, Seiglie continued, was that their money to pay for transportation reached him before Griffith's.[81] Despite his professed pangs of guilt over moral obligations, Seiglie's expectation of a fatter paycheck from Washington was undoubtedly the reason he switched allegiances.

Moran was outraged, claiming Griffith had tampered with Seiglie. He noted the Phillies had paid for the player's transportation and expenses for three weeks, and Moran threatened to take the matter to baseball's National Commission.[82] But the manager "doth protest too much, methinks."[83] He already had decided Seiglie was not ready for the major leagues and intended to send him to the New England League for additional training.[84] Besides, Moran had future Hall of Famer Dave Bancroft to play shortstop.

The Seiglie affair proved to be a tempest in a teapot. Griffith discovered, as Moran had,

Sitting in the bleachers at Coffee Pot Park during a break at spring training. The seats were pine boards without arm or backrests. Left to right: Erskine Mayer, Pat Moran, Jack Adams, Dode Paskert.

PHOTO FROM JACK ADAMS ESTATE—AUTHOR'S COLLECTION

the Cuban infielder's need for more seasoning in the minor leagues. In early May, Seiglie was sent to the Newport News club of the Virginia League.[85] That experience apparently did not remedy his shortcomings. Griffith decided after the 1915 season that Seiglie's "uncertain quality" ruled out a future with Washington.[86] Released by the Nationals, Seiglie never appeared in a regular-season major-league game.

EXHIBITION GAMES

Preseason games against other major league teams did not have the prominence in 1915 that they do today. Part of the problem was a lack of proximity between teams. The only games scheduled for the Phillies in Florida against peer competitors were three games against the Tampa-based Chicago Cubs, and four games opposing the Philadelphia Athletics, who trained in Jacksonville.[87] No other major league teams trained close enough to St. Petersburg to make games with the Phillies geographically and financially advantageous.

The first game against the Cubs was held at Coffee Pot Park on March 8, and it was a special day in St. Petersburg. One reason for the excitement was that the National Commission had relaxed its rule that previously had forbidden teams from the same league playing exhibition games. Recognizing the popularity of interleague games at spring training, especially in drawing paying fans to ballparks, the Commission allowed intraleague games to also take place.[88]

To encourage a large turnout, all stores in St. Petersburg—except grocery stores and meat markets—closed at 1PM so people could get to the game by its 2PM starting time.[89] Announced as "Boosters' Day" at the ballpark, a crowd of about 1,500 people saw the Phillies lose to the Cubs 8–5. It was a cold day, and one reporter noted the crowd "shivered in the grandstand" while watching the game.[90]

The return game in Tampa on March 16 saw the Phillies again come out on the losing end of a 10–4 score.[91] Although only an exhibition contest, it was steeped in controversy. The Cubs used an "emery ball" during the game, which had been banned in the American, National, and Federal Leagues in 1914.[92] Its appearance coincided with Cubs' pitcher Jimmy Lavender, who had had considerable success with the trick ball until it was outlawed, entering the game. Phillies' pitcher Ben Tincup had trouble controlling the ball with its roughened exterior and walked three men in a row throwing it. The Phillies complained about its use, but the Cubs retorted that the ban only applied to regular season games.[93]

The third game between the clubs took place in Tampa on March 23. The Phillies came out on top 4–1, but the game lacked the hoopla of the first and contentiousness of the second. The contest drew only 500 spectators.[94]

The Phillies hosted the Athletics on March 12 and 13. The first contest ended in a 5–5 draw.[95] The second was called off due to rain.[96] The teams played two more games on March 26 and 27 in Jacksonville, with the Phillies taking the first one, 13–6, and the A's coming out on top in the second game, 3–1.[97] These were the last two games the Phillies played in Florida before heading north.[98]

The club the Phillies played most often in spring training—seven times—was the Havana Reds, a team comprised of all-stars from the Cuban League that was touring the United States.[99] The Phillies won all but one of the games.[100] The Reds were not the draw of a major league team in attracting fans to the ballpark. In a game played against the Phillies on March 17, the Reds' take of the gate receipts amounted to $8.03.[101]

The Phillies also played several intra-squad games, advertised as "Regulars" versus "Yanigans."[102] Competition in these games could be fierce.[103] "Regulars" played hard to avoid the embarrassment of defeat, while "Yanigans" were ambitious and eager to move up to become "Regulars" themselves. There was a fair amount of trash talk between the two sides in the run-ups to games.[104] The squads split two games, two were rained out, and the other was canceled.[105] The "Yanigans" also were dispatched to play two games against the Birmingham Barons of the Southern Association on March 10 and 11.[106]

An intra-squad game that did not occur was the annual St. Patrick's Day game between "Irish" and "Dutch" (i.e., non-Irish) members of the roster. A tradition at Phillies spring training, the team did not have enough "Irish" players to field a full team—a reflection of changing demographics on the club and more generally in baseball.[107]

Admission fees for a person to go to Coffee Pot Park to see the Phillies varied.[108] Viewing practice was free. To watch the Phillies play the Cubs, Athletics, or Reds cost one dollar for a box seat, 50 cents for the grandstand, and 25 cents for the bleachers. Intra-squad games could be attended for a flat price of 25 cents regardless of where one sat.[109] The ballpark could seat 2,000, but none of the Phillies' games sold out.[110]

BASEBALL BEYOND THE DIAMOND

For all the hours Phillies players trained at Coffee Pot Park, they spent many more away from the ballfield.

PHOTO FROM JACK ADAMS ESTATE—AUTHOR'S COLLECTION

Standing along the third base line at Coffee Pot Park. Right field is bounded by the fence in the background. Left to right: Billy Fish, Ramiro Seiglie, Eddie Matteson, Jack Davis.

Between the end of practice at 4PM and curfew at 11:30PM, players had idle time on their hands and looked for something to do.[111] In addition, there was no practice on Sundays, and only a couple of the players spent the day in religious devotion.[112] The search for entertainment led to a variety of adventures and misadventures.[113]

THE STILLNESS OF ST. PETERSBURG

For players from the north, especially those who lived in larger cities, St. Petersburg was dull. The city was dry—alcohol was prohibited—which posed an inconvenience for noted drinkers like Moran and Grover Cleveland Alexander, but one that could be overcome without too much difficulty.[114] Players complained that the city's two movie houses closed at 9:30PM.[115] The most damning comment on St. Petersburg's lack of nightlife was uttered by a player who observed wryly during spring training, "I never knew there was so much pleasure in winding one's watch."[116]

ANOTHER SEABORNE ADVENTURE

Fishing was a primary occupation in St. Petersburg, and players took many opportunities to do so off the pier at Coffee Pot Bayou.[117] For more hardy souls, two excursions into the Gulf of Mexico were organized. The first—March 7 on board the *Michigan*—was mostly uneventful. The only noteworthy piece of news, which made the front page of St. Petersburg's *Evening Independent* newspaper, involved Alexander being bitten on two fingers of his pitching hand by a 15-pound grouper he had caught. Fortunately, the wound was superficial and interfered only slightly with his training.[118]

The second excursion proved far more hair-raising. On March 21, all but two Phillies' players boarded the *Frank E* at 6AM for fishing and a trip to Fort Dade so

the "Yanigans" could play the Havana Reds for the benefit of soldiers stationed at that isolated outpost.[119] The gastronomical highlight of the day was a sumptuous noon meal at Mitchell's Beach Hotel.[120] This was followed by the trip to Fort Dade where the "Yanigans" would be dropped off while the rest of the entourage returned to St. Petersburg. The *Frank E* would then go back to the fort to retrieve those who'd been left there for the game.[121]

After the meal, the *Frank E* ventured forth in its journey to Fort Dade but soon encountered high winds and rough seas. At first treated casually, the boat's engine gave out, and the *Frank E* "was tossed hazardously in the mad surf." Grim-faced Phillies players sat below deck garbed in life preservers. Some removed items of clothing to ease swimming if the boat foundered. With the boat's pitching and rolling occurring so soon after the lavish meal, seasickness was common. Fortunately, the crew got the engine running again after an hour and the *Frank E* made its destination. The "Yanigans" were dropped off and the boat with its queasy passengers returned posthaste to St. Petersburg.[122]

SIGHTSEEING AND ENTERTAINMENT

Dances were scheduled for Phillies players. Most were held at the Fifth Avenue Hotel, but occasionally they occurred elsewhere.[123] On one occasion, pitcher Erskine Mayer was in an automobile going to a ball being held at the Hotel Scholl when it struck another automobile that had stopped. Mayer's left hand hit the windshield upon impact and was cut badly, but no bones were broken and he was able to resume pitching in a few days.[124]

Players took in the local sights, including having their photos taken by St. Petersburg's famous Shell Fence.[125] The beach was another place players could be found during their off hours. Al Lang organized automobile tours of the surrounding countryside for those players who wanted to explore beyond the confines of the city.[126] But most nights, players hung around the hotel talking in the lobby and watching minutes tick by on the clock.

HIJINKS AND PRANKS

A spring training tradition that continues to this day is practical jokes pulled by players on other players. The 1915 Phillies were no exception.

On the morning the "Yanigans" left for Orlando to play Birmingham in a split-squad game they had to arise at 6:15AM rather the normal wakeup time of 8AM. When hotel employees rang hand bells outside their

PHOTO FROM JACK ADAMS ESTATE—AUTHOR'S COLLECTION

Phillies' players relaxing on the Coffee Pot Bayou pier. Left to right: George Chalmers, Erskine Mayer, Jack Adams, Dode Paskert

rooms—the method used to awaken guests—the "Yanigans" rang the bells throughout the hotel to arouse all others present, particularly the veteran players.[127]

But the veterans had already pulled a prank of their own. The "Yanigans" had packed their luggage the night before and placed it in a storage room adjoining the lobby to expedite their departure. Billy Killefer and other "Regulars" discovered this, took paving blocks from the street outside, and placed them in the luggage. The "Yanigans" were bewildered the next morning when they could barely lift their suitcases.[128]

Another prank originated in Killefer's abject fear of snakes. Teammates put a five-foot snake—scary-looking but harmless—in his locker. When he opened the door and saw the snake, it "caused Bill to break the standing broad-jump record in his haste to get out of the dressing room."[129]

FRATERNIZATION IMPERILS PHILLIES' PLAYERS
Some players sought out female companionship at spring training. One evening, George Whitted and Oscar Dugey had dates with two local ladies. While walking along Beach Drive, the four were "pranking around" when one of the ladies fell and cut her face.[130] A rumor soon spread that she had been struck by one of the players. There was talk of going to the Phillies' hotel to teach the players a lesson. Al Lang heard of trouble brewing and raced to the Fifth Avenue Hotel to extricate the players before the vigilantes arrived. He hid Whitted and Dugey at the home of a friend in Gulfport for a few days until the matter could be sorted out satisfactorily.[131]

ROOM AND BOARD
Sleeping and eating in St. Petersburg during spring training was a disagreeable experience for Phillies

players. Baker—an infamous miser—and the MLBAC—which almost went broke subsidizing the Browns—together collaborated to house and feed players on the cheap.[132] The Fifth Avenue Hotel was rundown, and lodging there "was not living it up in the lap of luxury."[133] In fact, when the Phillies returned to the city for spring training in 1916, Moran pulled his men from that hotel and shifted them to the more upscale Edgewater Inn.[134]

The food was unappetizing. Lieb noted, "the meals were terrible, even for that period." Lunch included fried fish with the heads still on, or a roast beef sandwich with meat so tough that Alexander once nailed a slice to his shoe to use as a sole.[135] Lunches, moreover, were sent from the hotel to the ballpark by automobile and were often cold by the time they arrived.[136] Players foraged for oranges in nearby groves to supplement their meager lunches.[137]

Evidence of the Phillies' desire for a square meal was evident on March 23 after their game against the Cubs in Tampa. The team ate dinner at the Tampa Bay Hotel, and not only did they gorge themselves on the food, they took an abundant supply of it back with them to St. Petersburg to savor instead of what their hotel's menu offered.[138]

Penny-pinching practices in baseball, it should be noted, were not limited to players' housing and meals. One of business manager William Shettsline's primary occupations—often aided by Lang—was to retrieve foul and home run balls hit out of Coffee Pot Park so they could be used again in training. One reporter noted: "Shettsline yesterday played baseball for 10 minutes and retrieved 23 baseballs which went over the grand stand. As each baseball is worth $1.25, it can be seen that Shettsline earned his day's wages and board."[139]

SPRING TRAINING AFTERMATH
The Phillies broke camp in St. Petersburg on March 25 and began the long trek north toward home and the regular season. Spring training had been an overall positive experience, buttressed mostly by the favorable weather.[140] One reporter commented:

Residents, tourists and members of the Phillies who are in St. Petersburg have no cause to complain about the weather… Under such conditions the Phillies certainly have reason to congratulate themselves on being in St. Petersburg. Up to date the Phillies have been scheduled for 27 workouts and games, and they were forced to call off only one workout and one game.[141]

President Baker required little convincing to return in 1916.[142] Sent a contract by Al Lang on April 3 to continue the relationship, Baker quickly signed it and wrote in a letter:

> While the amount of money taken in at St. Petersburg was a disappointment, we were compensated in large measure in the difference by the fine way you and your associates treated our club…We hope that this pleasant relationship will continue through next year.[143]

Al Lang pitched Baker to buy the baseball grounds and Coffee Pot Park for the bargain-basement price of $17,500 in hopes of keeping the Phillies in the city permanently.[144] Baker declined, much to his subsequent chagrin. The property was valued just six years later at $500,000–600,000, and by 1950 at several million dollars.[145]

For Lang, enticing a ball club to hold spring training in St. Petersburg was an end and a means to an end. He championed the city as a wonderful place for spring training—a campaign made all the more persuasive when the Phillies won their first National League pennant in 1915—but he also used the preseason presence of ballplayers to draw tourists to the city.[146] Lang succeeded on both counts.[147] St. Petersburg evolved into a major tourist destination, and Florida became the epicenter for major league spring training within a decade.[148] By conducting spring training in St. Petersburg in 1915, the Phillies helped open new chapters in the evolution and confluence of baseball and Florida.[149] ■

Notes

1. Clubs made occasional forays into Florida for spring training. The Washington Nationals trained in Jacksonville in 1888, and in 1903, Connie Mack took his Philadelphia Athletics to Jacksonville for pre-season conditioning. Mack was a player on the 1888 Nationals, and that probably influenced his decision to return there 15 years later as a manager. Frederick G. Lieb, *Connie Mack: Grand Old Man of Baseball* (New York: G.P. Putnam's Sons, 1945), 84–85.
2. "Chicago Cubs, 20 Strong, Off for the South," *Pittsburgh Gazette Times*, February 16, 1913.
3. Dreyfuss's letter is quoted in Nevin D. Sitler, *Warm Wishes from Sunny St. Pete: The Success Story of Promoting the Sunshine City* (Charleston: The History Press, 2014), 86.
4. Melanie Ave and Curtis Krueger, "Remembering Al Lang, St Petersburg's Mr. Baseball," *Tampa Bay Times*, March 22, 2008. Additional information about Al Lang and his critical role in bringing spring training baseball to Florida can be found in Charles Fountain, *Under the March Sun: The Story of Spring Training* (New York: Oxford University Press, 2009), 23–32.
5. "Sites Available for Ball Ground," *St. Petersburg Daily Times*, August 19, 1913.
6. "Hedges Decides to Bring Browns to St. Petersburg Coming Season," *Evening Independent*, September 20, 1913. A contract for rooms and meals for the baseball players, team officials, and the newspapermen was let to Dr. J.S. Barnes at "$2.50 per head per day." "Baseball Park at Coffee Pot," *Evening Independent*, October 10, 1913.
7. The amount of land offered in the Snell and Hamlett subdivision was described as "two blocks of land" in newspaper accounts. The Kerr tract was more precisely described as 20 acres. "Say They are Running Base Ball Not a Real Estate Proposition," *Evening Independent*, October 6, 1913.
8. "Row is on Over Ball Park Site," *Evening Independent*, October 4, 1913.
9. Proponents of Coffee Pot Park provided a detailed estimate of the added costs that would be encountered by choosing the Kerr tract for the ballpark site, thereby rendering it far less desirable. *Evening Independent*, October 10, 1913. Those supporting the Coffee Pot Park location also championed its advantages by noting, "The Coffee Pot site is practically as close to Central Avenue, the post office, as close to the (street) car lines, has more hard roads adjacent to the property, sidewalks all the way, and deep water for boats." *Evening Independent*, October 6, 1913.
10. Gary R. Mormino, "Spring Training, 1914," *Tampa Bay Times*, February 21, 2014. Mormino acknowledges the ballpark's exact location "remains elusive." He writes some believe the site was today's Grenada Terrace, "which is near the northern end of the city's Old Northwest neighborhood." Others judge it was on North Shore Drive.
11. Fred Lieb, "City, Phils in 1915 Sunshine," *St. Petersburg Times*, December 22, 1965.
12. Fountain, *Under the March Sun*, 24.
13. Jimmy Mann, "Branch Wasn't All Wet," *Evening Independent*, February 11, 1963.
14. Dick Bothwell, "Ballplayers Tangled with Alligators in Early Years," *St. Petersburg Times*, March 1, 1945.
15. *Tampa Bay Times*, February 21, 2014.
16. *Evening Independent*, February 11, 1963.
17. Jim Nasium, "Phillies Battle Nine Full Rounds," *Philadelphia Inquirer*, March 7, 1915. In addition, A.W. Tillinghast, who covered Phillies spring training for the *Public Record* newspaper and was also an avid golfer, reportedly took a mashie and hit a golf ball from inside Coffee Pot Park over the left-field fence and into the bayou. James Isaminger, "Cravath's Bat Sends in Scores Enough to Down the Cuban Team," *Evening Independent*, March 12, 1915.
18. Fountain, *Under the March Sun*, 24. The author identifies the amount in dispute as $6,500.
19. St. Petersburg newspapers claimed at the time that Hedges had decided to switch the team's spring training site to Houston, Texas, because of the more lucrative terms that city offered to host the team. No mention was made that the parting was caused by a quarrel over the payment of certain bills. "Hedges Calls Off Negotiations for St. Louis Team to Come Here," *Evening Independent*, October 9, 1914.
20. Lieb, *St. Petersburg Times*, December 22, 1965.
21. "Phils to Train Down in St. Petersburg, Fla," *Evening Independent*, October 29, 1914. Difficulties the Phillies endured in finding enough good days for conditioning in Wilmington, NC, during 1914 spring training are mentioned in Thomas D. Richter, "Philadelphia Plans," *The Sporting News*, November 7, 1914.
22. Baker also considered San Diego, CA as a training location but rejected it because suitable ball grounds were not available. "Moran's Phils to Train in Florida," *Evening Independent*, October 29, 1914. States in which the Phillies had previously held spring training included Virginia, Georgia, Alabama, and Arkansas. Allen Lewis and Larry Shenk, *This Date in Philadelphia Phillies History* (New York: Stein and Day, 1979), 154.
23. "Phillies Sure to Come Here; Sign Contract," *Evening Independent*, November 2, 1914.
24. Frank Fitzpatrick, "Spring Training a Lot Different Than it Was in 1915," *Philadelphia Inquirer*, March 30, 2015.
25. Lieb, *St. Petersburg Times*, December 22, 1965.
26. Whether St. Petersburg was obliged to defray the expenses of newspapermen covering Phillies' spring training, as it had for reporters accompanying the Browns, is unknown. Five newspapermen traveled with the Phillies to spring training: William G. Weart, *Evening Telegraph*, James C. Isaminger, *North American*, Walter Dunn, *Public Ledger*, Albert

W. Tillinghast, *Public Record*, and Edgar F. Wolfe, *Philadelphia Inquirer*. Wolfe wrote under the pen name Jim Nasium, a wry derivation of the word "Gymnasium."

27. "Moran's Arrival Starts Hustling," *Philadelphia Inquirer*, February 24, 1915.

28. "Ball Players Safe on Southern Shores," *Philadelphia Inquirer*, March 1, 1915. The *Apache* was a rickety-looking vessel. It had suffered extensive damage a decade earlier in a collision with another ship. Fitzpatrick, *Philadelphia Inquirer*, March 30, 2015.

29. "Athletics and Phillies Will Get Away for Florida Training Quarters," *Philadelphia Inquirer*, February 26, 1915. The *Apache* made one stop during the journey, a port call in Charleston, South Carolina.

30. Jim Nasium, "Phils Manhandle Mack's Regulars," *Philadelphia Inquirer*, March 27, 1915.

31. *Philadelphia Inquirer*, February 26, 1915.

32. Players, primarily veterans, started arriving in camp in late February to begin exercising. Regulation practice could not begin until March 1 according to National League rules. Thomas D. Richter, "Philadelphia Points," *The Sporting News*, March 6, 1915.

33. A complete description of the Phillies' 1914 travails is beyond the scope of this article. For more information see, Frederick Lieb and Stan Baumgartner, *The Philadelphia Phillies* (New York: Van Rees Press, 1953), 102–12. Baker, well known for his parsimony in paying players, would not match the Federal League offers.

34. The threat of additional players "jumping" to the Federal League depending on who was chosen as the new manager is discussed in David Jordan, *Occasional Glory: A History of the Philadelphia Phillies* (Jefferson: McFarland & Co., 2002), 44–45. Lobert did return later as a coach with the Phillies and got to manage the awful 1942 team, which notched an abysmal 42–109 record.

35. The deep-seated animosity that had divided the Phillies is described by Lieb, who claims the worst feud was between Magee and Dode Paskert. Pitcher Eppa Rixey also hated Magee. Lieb, *Philadelphia Phillies*, 110–11.

36. For Magee, the Phillies received Oscar Dugey, George "Possum" Whitted, and $10,000. Lobert yielded Milt Stock, Al Demaree, and Jack Adams in return. Trading Dooin brought Bert Niehoff to the Phillies. Jordan, *Occasional Glory*, 46.

37. Lieb, *Philadelphia Phillies*, 111.

38. The Phillies sent head scout William Neal to St. Petersburg several weeks before the start of camp to ensure the ballfield was in proper condition for the players to train. He also worked with Al Lang on ironing out administrative details associated with the Phillies' stay in the city. Lang served as the liaison between MLBAC and the club. Thomas D. Richter, "Philadelphia Points," *The Sporting News*, January 23, 1915. Neal's presence in St. Petersburg prior to spring training also is discussed in "Head Scout of the Phillies Says Prospects for Winning Team Good," *Evening Independent*, February 27, 1915.

39. The Phillies had 29 men in camp. Moran's task was to reduce that total by eight in accordance with a league rule adopted in 1914 that capped the number of players on a roster during the regular season at 21. Thomas D. Richter, "Philadelphia Points," *The Sporting News*, April 3, 1915. The rule is also mentioned in William G. Weart, "Moran Lays Down Ironclad Rules for Conduct of His Ball Tossers," *Evening Independent*, March 4, 1915.

40. James C. Isaminger, "Havana Reds Lose Their Pepper in Second Event with Phillies," *Evening Independent*, March 11, 1915. The characterization of Moran as the "Fitchburg man" is a reference to his hometown of Fitchburg, Massachusetts. Isaminger and William Weart wrote for Philadelphia newspapers, but their columns were also carried in St. Petersburg's *Evening Independent* newspaper.

41. Jim Nasium, "Pat Moran Promises to Create New Epoch in Checkered History of the Quaker City's National League Club," *Philadelphia Inquirer*, March 18, 1915. As used in the column, "pill" is jargon for ball.

42. "Newcomers not at Phillies' Camp," *Philadelphia Inquirer*, March 3, 1915. "Tipperary Hikes" is a reference to the popular song, "It's a Long, Long Way to Tipperary," sung by British soldiers as they marched during World War I. See https://en.wikipedia.org/wiki/It%27s_a_Long_Way_to_Tipperary.

43. After an exhausting day of physical conditioning, players could use the ballpark's single cold-water shower afterwards, but most preferred to use showers back at the hotel. John C. Skipper, *Wicked Curve: The Life and Troubled Times of Grover Cleveland Alexander* (Jefferson: McFarland & Co., 2006), 42.

44. Jim Nasium, "Bancroft Looks Like the Goods," *Philadelphia Inquirer*, March 5, 1915. In 1914, St. Louis Browns' players took the North Shore street car between the Fifth Avenue Hotel and Coffee Pot Park. It was so slow-moving that adults and kids could jog along the "express" car to talk with players and get autographs. Mann, *Evening Independent*, February 11, 1963. The walk between the hotel and the ballpark transited areas where alligators resided, hence the former's nickname, "Alligator Hotel." The players were none-too-fond of the prospect of encountering these reptiles during their hikes. Bothwell, *St. Petersburg Times*, March 1, 1945.

45. Jim Nasium, "Cubs and Cold Too Much for Phillies," *Philadelphia Inquirer*, March 9, 1915.

46. Lieb, *St. Petersburg Times*, December 22, 1965.

47. Lieb identified the bicycle-riding players as Eppa Rixey and Stan Baumgartner. A reporter who covered the Phillies' camp wrote in an article they were Milt Stock and Al Demaree. The reporter also observed that both players rode the bicycles throughout spring training camp, thereby contradicting Lieb's account of Moran forbidding their use to travel between the Fifth Avenue Hotel and Coffee Pot Park. The article noted that Stock and Demaree returned the bicycles "in good shape" on March 22—just before the Phillies broke camp to head north—to the dealer from whom they had rented them. Allegedly, pedaling the bicycles had been just as beneficial for the players' physical stamina as hiking the distance. "Phils Hitting Not Up to Standard," *Philadelphia Inquirer*, March 23, 1915.

48. Nasium, *Philadelphia Inquirer*, March 3, 1915.

49. William G. Weart, "Moran's Athletes Wake Up Sore But are Put to Hard Work Early," *Evening Independent*, March 3, 1915.

50. Ibid.

51. Jim Nasium, "Phils Drilled in Inside Baseball by Peerless Pat," *Philadelphia Inquirer*, March 14, 1915.

52. Ibid. It was also referred to as "inside play" at the time.

53. Nasium, *Philadelphia Inquirer*, March 9, 1915.

54. Jim Nasium, "Three Straight for Moran's Team," *Philadelphia Inquirer*, March 12, 1915.

55. Nasium, *Philadelphia Inquirer*, March 14, 1915.

56. Jimmy Mann, "Moran was a Tactician," *Evening Independent*, February 12, 1963.

57. Lieb, *Philadelphia Phillies*, 119.

58. Weart, *Evening Independent*, March 4, 1915.

59. Phillies pitcher Stan Baumgartner commented in retrospect, "I also can say that Pat was the smartest manager I ever played for—or observed in action—in my 39 years in baseball." Lieb, *Philadelphia Phillies*, 115.

60. Mark Stang, *Phillies Photos: 100 Years of Philadelphia Phillies Images* (Wilmington: Orange Frazier Press, 2008), 25.

61. Nasium, *Philadelphia Inquirer*, March 12, 1915.

62. Ibid.

63. William G. Weart, "Phillies Working Together Now for First Time in Many Years," *Evening Independent*, March 9, 1915.

64. Early in spring training, Moran became aware of a craps game that had started one night and lasted until four o'clock the next morning. Large sums of money were won and lost among the players. Pitcher Grover Cleveland Alexander even lost his diamond ring when he bet it on a losing hand. Moran realized gambling with such stakes could cause hard feelings among players. Lieb, *Philadelphia Phillies*, 119.

65. Those ballplayers who wanted to read had to have their own books. St. Petersburg's first library did not open until December 1915. http://www.stpete.org/history-and-preservation.

66. Weart, *Evening Independent*, March 4, 1915.

67. Isaminger, *Evening Independent*, March 11, 1915.

68. William G. Weart, "Work in Secret at Coffee Pot," *Evening Independent*, March 17, 1915.

69. Mann, *Evening Independent*, February 12, 1963.

70. "Phils Fail to Get Boston Players," *Philadelphia Inquirer*, February 10, 1915.
71. Nasium, Philadelphia Inquirer, March 7, 1915.
72. Thomas D. Richter, "Philadelphia Points," *Sporting Life*, February 27, 1915. Seiglie was referred to in the article as a "sure-enough" Cuban because he was the brother of Oscar Seiglie, secretary of the Cuban legation in Washington, DC The phrase indicates they were not affiliated with the many Cubans seeking independence for the island from the United States.
73. James C. Isaminger, "Moran Will Put Up Hard Fight to Keep Cuban Who Flew the Coop," *Evening Independent*, March 19, 1915.
74. Nasium, *Philadelphia Inquirer*, March 5, 1915.
75. "Row Threatened Over a Player," *Evening Independent*, March 5, 1915.
76. Jim Nasium, "Same Old Gavvy Hits 'Em a Mile," *Philadelphia Inquirer*, March 6, 1915.
77. Nasium, *Philadelphia Inquirer*, March 8, 1915.
78. Nasium, *Philadelphia Inquirer*, March 6, 1915.
79. Ibid.
80. Isaminger, *Evening Independent*, March 19, 1915.
81. Paul W. Eaton, "At the Capital," *Sporting Life*, March 27, 1915.
82. Thomas D. Richter, "Philadelphia Points," *Sporting Life*, March 27, 1915. There is no evidence the Seiglie issue was ever raised with the Commission.
83. A famous quotation from William Shakespeare's *Hamlet*. It has come to mean that one's vehement and frequent objections to something may create doubt about the sincerity of the denunciations.
84. "Nifty Twirling by Phils Hurlers," *Philadelphia Inquirer*, March 19, 1915.
85. Paul W. Eaton, "At the Capital," *Sporting Life*, May 8, 1915.
86. Paul W. Eaton, "At the Capital," *Sporting Life*, December 18, 1915.
87. It is unclear why more games were not played against the close-by Cubs. Phillies' business manager William Shettsline attempted to arrange additional contests but was unsuccessful for reasons that are not clear. "Phillies' Schedule is Announced; Mack's Men Here for Two Games," *Evening Independent*, March 4, 1915.
88. William G. Weart, "Phillies Have Reached Second Stage of the Preliminary Work," *Evening Independent*, March 8, 1915.
89. "Big Crowd at Coffee Pot Park to See Phillies and Cubs Open Season," *Evening Independent*, March 8, 1915. A large turnout was important for symbolic reasons. St. Petersburg had to demonstrate to the Phillies that the city would support the club sufficiently to make it financially attractive to return for training in future years. Better weather and financial inducements were the initial lures that brought the Phillies to St. Petersburg, but prospects for profits would determine whether the club stayed beyond 1915. Baker's commitment to train in the city was only for one year.
90. Even Phillies' president Baker, who was wintering in Bellaire, Florida, stopped playing golf long enough to attend the game. Nasium, *Philadelphia Inquirer*, March 9, 1915.
91. The Pennsylvania Society in St. Petersburg arranged for an excursion train to Tampa so a large number of fans could cheer on the Phillies. William G. Weart, "Phillies Will Have a Busy Week with Four Games Already Booked," *Evening Independent*, March 15, 1915.
92. An emery board or paper is used to roughen part of a baseball so that it will achieve an unnatural break when thrown. http://www.baseball-reference.com/bullpen/Emery_ball.
93. William G. Weart, "Cubs Use Emery Ball in Contest in Which They Down the Phillies," *Evening Independent*, March 17, 1915.
94. "Mighty Hurlers for the Phillies Hold Cubs Safe All the Contest," *Evening Independent*, March 24, 1915.
95. William G. Weart, "Philadelphia Teams Play a Tie in First Contest of City Series," *Evening Independent*, March 13, 1915.
96. Weart, *Evening Independent*, March 15, 1915.
97. "Phillies Win and Lose One," *Evening Independent*, March 29, 1915.
98. After leaving Florida, the Phillies played a series of exhibition games against various teams as they meandered north for an Opening Day contest against the Braves in Boston on April 14. The schedule included games against the Atlanta Crackers of the Southern Association, the Norfolk Tars of the Virginia League, the Washington Nationals, a four-game City Series against the Athletics in Philadelphia—each team winning two games—and three games against the Providence Grays of the International League to wind up pre-season. *Philadelphia Inquirer*, various dates, March 30–April 14, 1915.
99. Jim Nasium, "Gavvy Starts Early Breaking 'Em Up," *Philadelphia Inquirer*, March 10, 1915.
100. Scores of the six games the Phillies won were: 3–2, 8–1, 6–3, 4–1, 7–0, 4–0 in games played on March 9–11 and March 17–19, respectively. *Evening Independent*, various dates, March 10–20, 1915. The single game the Reds won—the final one in the series—was by a score of 3–2 on March 21. It was against a squad of Phillies' reservists. "Reds at Last Win One Game," *Evening Independent*, March 22, 1915.
101. It should be noted the day of the game was described as "cold and raw" by one reporter, which undoubtedly contributed to the paltry turnout. Jim Nasium, "On Two Hits Phils Scored 4 Runs and Beat Havana Reds," *Philadelphia Inquirer*, March 18, 1915.
102. The term "Yanigan" was commonly used in 1915 and dates back to the nineteenth century in baseball. It was applied exclusively during spring training to rookie and reservist players. Charles Dryden, "Baseball Term Which Applies to the Second Team in Practice," *Philadelphia North American*, April 10, 1904. "Yanigan" has long since fallen into disuse.
103. Curve balls were not permitted to be thrown in intra-squad games. This may have been intended to reduce the strain on pitchers' arms in meaningless games. "Phillies Play Despite Showers," *Evening Independent*, March 5, 1915.
104. Jim Nasium, "Mushy Grounds Keep Phil Belligerents from Mixing it Up," *Philadelphia Inquirer*, March 16, 1915. He notes both sides were "thirsting for gore" in playing the game. In a second article on games between "Yanigans" and "Regulars," Nasium commented that Jack Martin—who piloted the "Yanigans"—boasted to Moran that his squad "would open the eyes of the Phil leader as to what kind of a squad of reserve material he is harboring under cover here once they get wrapped up in the thick of a real fuss." Jim Nasium, "Martin's Yans to Meet Moran's Team," *Philadelphia Inquirer*, March 15, 1915.
105. "Phils Break from Coffee Pot Park," *Philadelphia Inquirer*, March 25, 1915.
106. Birmingham was the Southern Association champion. The "Yanigans" won the first game against the Barons, 9–2, while the teams tied in the second game, 5–5. Nasium, *Philadelphia Inquirer*, March 15, 1915.
107. William G. Weart, *Evening Independent*, March 15, 1915. St. Patrick's Day was still celebrated at Coffee Pot Park. Philadelphian Francis X. Murphy sent the Phillies a large green harp decoration—something he did every year as a good luck charm for the team—and Moran had it hung up at the ballpark on March 17. William G. Weart, "Phils in Tampa for a Game; Cubs May Come Here Next Week," *Evening Independent*, March 16, 1915.
108. It is uncertain if refreshments were sold at the ballpark as another source of revenue. The presence of refreshments is not mentioned in reports on Phillies' spring training games. There is no evidence scorecards were printed for games.
109. *Evening Independent*, March 4, 1915.
110. Fountain, *Under the March Sun*, 24.
111. William Weart, *Evening Independent*, March 4, 1915. The article notes players had to be in their beds by 11:30PM according to Moran's rules.
112. Jim Nasium, "Moran Lets Up on Sabbath," *Philadelphia Inquirer*, March 8, 1915. He identified those who attended church on Sundays as Eppa Rixey, Stan Baumgartner, and team trainer Mike Dee.
113. With the exceptions of limits on gambling and a strict curfew, Moran took a light hand in regulating his players' behavior when not in training. As long as their off-field pursuits did not interfere with their on-field performance, Moran permitted his players to do as they wish without supervision. Nasium, *Philadelphia Inquirer*, March 18, 1915.
114. Mormino, *Tampa Bay Times*, February 21, 2014. Prohibition was unpopular in the area, and the numerous inlets along the coast became havens for rumrunners transporting alcohol from Cuba. As long as one was discreet in one's drinking, obtaining alcohol was relatively easy and almost always unpunished. https://en.wikipedia.org/wiki/Pinellas_County,_Florida. Moran was a heavy drinker, and he earned the nickname "Whiskey Face" honestly. A biography of Moran, written as part of SABR's Baseball

Biography Project, acknowledges his heavy drinking and how it almost certainly contributed to his early death. See Daniel R. Levitt, "Pat Moran," http://sabr.org/bioproject/person/5375ed39. Alexander's struggles with alcoholism are chronicled by Jack Kavanagh, *Ol' Pete: The Grover Cleveland Alexander Story* (South Bend: Diamond Communications, Inc., 1996).

115. Fountain, *Under the March Sun*, 24.

116. http://www.stpeterinternationalbaseball.com/baseball_blvd.php.

117. After practice on March 10, for example, a "network" of fishing lines were seen in the bayou as numerous Phillies' players—still attired in their uniforms—went about the business of trying to reel in a big catch. Jim Nasium, "Curve Pitching No Terror to Phillies," *Philadelphia Inquirer*, March 11, 1915. In addition, Alexander "favored himself a duck hunter and used to bang away at Bay waterfowl from the prow of the Tampa-St. Petersburg boat." Bothwell, *St. Petersburg Times*, March 1, 1945.

118. "Grouper Bites Star Twirler," *Evening Independent*, March 8, 1915.

119. Scheduling a game at Fort Dade reflected the Phillies' and St. Petersburg's appreciation toward military forces guarding America's shores as World War I raged. There were no prospects for profit. As noted, the fort was isolated and opportunities for entertainment minimal. A baseball game featuring a major league team—even if reservists and rookies took the field—was a welcome respite from the monotony of garrison duty. Fort Dade, located on Egmont Key outside Tampa Bay, was built during the Spanish American War. The fort's community consisted of approximately 300 individuals. The fort was used as a training base during World War I and then deactivated in 1923. Brought back into service during World War II as a German U-boat lookout and bombing range, it was again deactivated after that war. The fort's ruins are today part of the Egmont Key State Park. http://info.flheritge.com/maritime-trail/forts/fort.cfm?name=Fort_Dade.

120. Mitchell's Beach Hotel was located at John's Pass Village. The dinner consisted of seven courses and included Russian Caviar, Stone Crabs, Corned Beef & Cabbage, Roast Philadelphia Capon, and Pineapple Cheese Champignon Salad. "Fine Outing for Phillies," *Evening Independent*, March 20, 1915.

121. "Bancroft Lays Claim to Fish," *Evening Independent*, March 22, 1915.

122. "Moran's Phillies Don Life Preservers," *Philadelphia Inquirer*, March 22, 1915. The author of this story noted that Mrs. Beals Becker, wife of a Phillies' player and the only woman aboard the Frank E, "stood the trip bravely."

123. Nasium, *Philadelphia Inquirer*, March 14, 1915.

124. "Star Pitcher Hurt," *Evening Independent*, March 15, 1915. The car in which Mayer was a passenger was driven by Miss Cleo Hall, who was unhurt in the accident.

125. The Shell Fence was created as a roadside attraction and curiosity by artist Owen Albright in the early 1900s. It was destroyed in a hurricane in 1921. http://www.narrowlarry.com/nlshellfence.tml.

126. Weart, *Evening Independent*, March 3, 1915.

127. William G. Weart, "Phillies Yanigans Arrive Here after a Hard Trip to Orlando," *Evening Independent*, March 12, 1915. Some "Regulars" were fooled by the ruse. George Whitted didn't check his watch and came downstairs for breakfast only to be informed upon arriving that he was an hour and a half early for the meal.

128. Ibid. St. Petersburg's streets were being paved at the time with blocks, part of the city's efforts to modernize its infrastructure.

129. Nasium, *Philadelphia Inquirer*, March 7, 1915.

130. Curbing was being installed along Beach Drive at the time, and although familiar with the area, the woman may have tripped over the curbing being unaware of its presence. What was meant by "pranking around" remains uncertain, and discretion precludes salacious speculation by this author. Lieb, *St. Petersburg Times*, December 22, 1965.

131. Lieb tells the story of this incident twice, once in his 1953 history of the Phillies, and again in more detail in a 1965 newspaper article describing the Phillies' experience in St. Petersburg in 1915. There is no mention of it in any period reporting on Phillies' spring training camp, and that may have been the result of a conspiracy of silence between the Phillies and the city to suppress what happened. The Phillies certainly didn't want their players portrayed as involved in lascivious behavior, and St. Petersburg would have been equally reluctant to allow word to get out that vigilante justice was still practiced in the city. Lieb, *Philadelphia Phillies*, 118, and Lieb, *St. Petersburg Times*, December 22, 1965.

132. Frederick G. Lieb, "Sunshine Al Lang Celebrates his 80th Birthday," *St. Petersburg Times*, November 16, 1950. Lieb notes Browns-related expenses incurred by MLBAC were considerably more than the businessmen anticipated.

133. Two vapor baths were installed in the hotel for Phillies' players to use after a day's training. William G. Weart, "Moran Keeps String of Phillies Practicing Steadily at Batting," *Evening Independent*, March 5, 1915.

134. Lieb, *St. Petersburg Times*, December 22, 1965.

135. Lieb, *Philadelphia Phillies*, 116. The story of Alexander nailing roast beef to the sole of his shoe almost certainly is apocryphal. Lieb tells another story in his history of the Athletics in which catcher Ossee Schrecongost received a "baseball steak," called such for its low-grade quality, so tough that he nailed it to the wall of the restaurant in which it was served. Lieb, *Connie Mack*, 85.

136. Meals were prepared by Mrs. O.K. Hall of the Fifth Avenue Hotel. Players had the option to walk to the hotel for lunch and then back to the ballfield for afternoon practice, but few did. Weart, *Evening Independent*, March 4, 1915.

137. Fortunately, the owner of the groves, William S. Downey, allowed Phillies' players to purloin his fruit for their consumption. As one newspaper report related, "Mr. Downey having generously placed his groves and the luscious fruit therein at the free disposal of the Phil players at any time they feel so inclined, and the evidence produced by those who have taken advantage of Mr. Downey's generosity leads to the suspicion that the said Mr. Downey's crop of oranges and grapefruit won't be worth much in the open market when the hungry Phil athletes get through with it." Nasium, *Philadelphia Inquirer*, March 7, 1915.

138. "Phils Raid Tampa, Chase Cubs and Grab Abundant Food Supplies," *Philadelphia Inquirer*, March 24, 1915.

139. Weart, *Evening Independent*, March 5, 1915.

140. "Phils Break From Coffee Pot Park, *Philadelphia Inquirer*, March 25, 1915.

141. William G. Weart, "Phillies Satisfied with Weather During Training Here," *Evening Independent*, March 18, 1915.

142. The Phillies' spring training stay in St. Petersburg lasted through pre-season in 1918. Then, the club resumed its wandering ways that included stops in North Carolina, Alabama, Mississippi, Texas, and various locations in Florida before settling in Clearwater in 1947, where it remains to this day. Lewis and Shenk, *Philadelphia Phillies History*, 155.

143. "Phillies Sign to Come Back," *Evening Independent*, April 12, 1915.

144. Lang undoubtedly had an ulterior motive in making the low-ball offer. If Baker had purchased the ballpark and grounds, the Phillies would have been obliged to conduct spring training in St. Petersburg each year, thereby alleviating—or even eliminating—the city's need to offer financial inducements for the club to return annually.

145. Lieb, *St. Petersburg Times*, November 16, 1950.

146. Ave and Krueger, *Tampa Bay Times*, March 22, 2008.

147. The St. Petersburg *Evening Independent* newspaper took great delight in pointing out that the Browns experienced awful weather in Houston during their 1915 spring training camp. It quoted an article that appeared in the *St. Louis Globe-Democrat* written by a reporter who covered the Browns pre-season training that year which concluded, "Last year Rickey's club had the best spring training weather ever enjoyed by a major league club; this year it had one of the worst." *Evening Independent*, April 12, 1915.

148. Mormino, *Tampa Bay Times*, February 21, 2014.

149. After the Phillies departed following 1918 spring training, other major league teams came to St. Petersburg for the pre-season, including the New York Yankees, St. Louis Cardinals, New York Mets, and Baltimore Orioles. The city hosted its last major league spring training camp in 2008, when the Tampa Bay Rays left and relocated to Port Charlotte, Florida. Stephanie Hays, "St. Petersburg Bids Farewell to Lovely Lady by Bay," *Tampa Bay Times*, March 28, 2008.

Black Baseball's "Funmakers"

Taking the Miami Ethiopian Clowns Seriously

Brian Carroll

Found almost exclusively in black newspapers, box scores for Miami Ethiopian Clowns games read like a cast list for a *Night at the Museum* sequel:

King Tut	Abbadaba
Tarzan	Ulysses Grant Greene
Wahoo	Goose Tatum
Highpockets West	Peanuts Nyassas
Haile Selassie, emperor of Ethiopia[1]	

Obscured by these vivid names and the vaudevillian antics that went with them is the fact that these entertainers also played first-rate baseball—as evidenced by the team's many Negro American League and semi-pro tournament titles—and did so for longer than any other Negro League team. Taking the Clowns throughout the country on a barnstorming schedule packed with as many as 200 games per year, their annual baseball journey began each year in Miami.

Perhaps it should not surprise that the state of Florida, home to Emmett Kelly, the Ringling Bros. and Barnum & Bailey Circus, and the Florida Clown College, can also claim the variously named Ethiopian Clowns, a club that continued and perhaps perfected a tradition of baseball buffoonery that has been traced to the 1880s and the very beginnings of professional black baseball.[2] Beginning in the late 1920s as the semi-professional Miami Giants, baseball's clown princes adapted and evolved along a timeline that stretched to the end of the Reagan Administration before disappearing into history's mists as murkily as they first appeared. While certainly the longest-lived of the black teams, the Miami-Cincinnati-Indianapolis Clowns arguably were also black ball's most successful business venture, a result primarily of the perseverance, business savvy, and adaptability of longtime Clowns owner Syd Pollock, a white Jew from Tarrytown, New York.

Because they survived so many existential threats, relocations, and changes in ownership, and due ultimately to their sheer longevity, this tireless band of baseball-playing "funmakers," as the black newspapers liked to call them, serves as a sort of bass line when relating the many riffs, zigs, and zags of black baseball history. Leagues came and went, but the Clowns remained, sometimes welcomed by those leagues, but more often not. Jackie Robinson burst through white baseball's color barrier, immediately siphoning off attendance at Negro Leagues games, but baseball's jesters just kept on clowning. The team's ownership changed hands several times, at least once in mid-season, but the barnstorming bus kept rolling, taking the club's unique blend of gags, showmanship, and diamond expertise from Dade County, Florida, to Denver, from Winston-Salem, North Carolina, where eighteen-year-old Clowns shortstop Hank Aaron spent spring training in 1952, to Wichita, Kansas, where it competed in the first of that city's many national semi-professional tournaments.[3]

The Clowns' comic traditions, which ultimately can be traced to African folk culture, were more directly borrowed from the team's immediate antecedents in Florida, the Cuban Giants, the country's first viable black baseball venture and, therefore the team that showed there was indeed money to be made in the sport even while the color line was being re-drawn. These baseballers were neither Cuban nor exceptionally large, and they may or may not have adopted Spanish-sounding "Cuban" gibberish to entertain white hotel patrons in St. Augustine, Jacksonville, and Palm Beach. What is known is that the Giants played "great ball, but, outside that they do more talking, yelling, howling and bluffing than all the teams in the league put together," according to a report in the *New York Sun* in 1888.[4] Baseball's first feel-good clown act was born.

The Giants owed their immediately profitable existence to the hotel building boom occurring along Florida's east coast, starting in St. Augustine and, as snowbirds will travel, stretching to Palm Beach and Miami. By day the Giants could entertain the wealthy white clientele at the new Hotel Ponce de Leon and the Hotel Alcazar in St. Augustine, and by night the ballplayers would serve those same guests as waiters in the hotels' restaurants. This black baseball-white hotelier business model fueled growth of the segregated sport well into the twentieth century.[5] As Florida's luxury hotels and resorts sprung up, black baseball teams followed.

By the mid-1920s, black baseball was on relatively firm footing, and though the Miami Giants' history is shadowy at best, several accounts credit Johnny Pierce, a numbers runner and bootlegger, and Hunter Campbell with the team's founding.[6] (A member of the 1934–36 Giants teams, John "Buck" O'Neil, remembered a teammate, coincidentally named Buck O'Neal, to have been a co-owner with Pierce, but that memory is not corroborated by any other source.[7]) Pierce's and Campbell's choice of "Giants" as team moniker is not surprising; black teams frequently adopted "Giants," and they did so throughout the history of the Negro Leagues, a practice that also saved owners advertising money. If fans saw "Giants" on an announcement or advertisement, according to Negro Leagues historian Larry Lester, they could assume it was a black team.[8]

Pierce's Giants frequently played Charles Henry's Zulu Cannibal Giants, another traveling "clowning" team that played its winter baseball in Miami. "Saturday [the Zulus] paraded up and down Second Avenue, a big avenue for blacks in Miami, and that Sunday we packed that little ball park there," Buck O'Neil remembered.[9] The parades were a form of promotion, to get the word out of an upcoming game, according to another Miami Giant, Leroy Cromartie. "We'd go all over town, riding on the car, blowing horns. That's the way we really got them in."[10] Based out of Louisville, Kentucky, the Zulus were known for wearing grass skirts and wigs, painting their faces in war paint, and performing war dances in

bare feet: an assortment of gimmicks that provides a lens through which to see why so many in the black community found these clowning teams at best problematic. Playing to the worst of black stereotypes, and distracting from these teams' otherwise impressive athletic achievements on the field, such "minstrel" acts prevented many black sportswriters from acknowledging these teams as full-fledged members of black baseball. The sportswriters blamed what they called "sideshows" for impeding the progress of the race. *Pittsburgh Courier* sports editor Wendell Smith wrote that he did not like the potential effect on the perceptions of whites regarding black baseball. Whites "like to believe" that the slapstick comedy and nonsensical approach "is typical and characteristic of all Negroes."[11] The *Chicago Defender* called such minstrelsy "a detriment to Negro league baseball."[12]

Nonetheless, Pierce and Campbell were apparently inspired by the Zulus to take their Giants along baseball's "minstrel circuit," as historian Donn Rogosin put it.[13] Campbell bought two Cadillacs with running boards to transport the team, and he contracted with Syd Pollock to book Giants' games in the Northeast, as Pollock was doing for the Zulus. Sometime in 1936, Pierce and Campbell re-cast the Giants as the Miami Ethiopian Clowns; newspaper reports first began featuring the new name in June of that year.[14] Perhaps the moniker was fashioned to quickly communicate both the color of the players and the comic entertainment with which they would intersperse games. "Clowns" makes sense; it references the shadow ball, pepper, and vaudeville sketches and routines the team would perfect and perform for more than fifty years. But why "Ethiopian"?

Pierce and Campbell seemed to have simply borrowed from the headlines of the black newspapers, including the big weeklies, the *Defender* and *Courier*. Benito Mussolini's Italy attacked Ethiopia in 1935, beginning a six-year war that the black press closely followed and routinely put on its front page, in sharp contrast to the mainstream press. In Harlem in March 1935, in the lead-up to war, for example, "everybody from elevator boys to jazz orchestra leaders was equally disturbed" by the possibility of armed conflict.[15] Throughout Italy's forced colonization, the black papers expressed sympathy for Ethiopia, which had a black leader (Haile Selassie).

The team's Ethiopia reference was seen by some as exploitation of black sympathy, which encouraged Negro league owners to

This undated publicity photo (circa 1944–49) of the Clowns includes Edward "King Tut" King and in the lower right inset, "baseball clown" Ed Hamman in full clownface. Hamman would eventually become sole owner of the Clowns.

oppose adding the Clowns to their ranks. Homestead Grays co-owner Cum Posey, for example, wrote in his weekly *Courier* column in 1942 that sportswriters would "always feel disgusted at Syd [Pollock] for… capitalizing on the rape of Ethiopia when that country was in distress."[16] The *Afro-American*'s E.B. Rea took a different view, calling the move to block the Clowns "as funny as the Clowns themselves." If so many were paying to see them joke and jest, how much more ardently would they turn out to see them play Negro American competition? Rea asked.[17] Importantly, however, the sports columnist took exception to the "buffoonery" for which the Clowns were known, describing it as unbecoming a team hoping to "crash white baseball."

Pollock did most of the booking of venues for the Clowns' barnstorming up and down the East Coast, which is why in 1937, with Pierce's health faltering, Pollock stepped in with much-needed capital to keep the team bus rolling. According to Pollock's son, Alan, his father paid Pierce's widow for his share, though in another of Alan Pollock's accounts, the transfer of ownership came as a result of his father funding the team's barnstorming season. Mohl describes Pierce as bitter over Pollock's takeover, meaning that the elder Pollock took an ownership stake before Pierce died in 1937.[18] Campbell, who was the team's business manager on the road, continued with the team until his death in December 1942.[19] In Pollock's and Campbell's care, the Ethiopian Clowns became a dependable box office hit in the late thirties, drawing crowds wherever they went, including Yankee Stadium and Comiskey Park, where they regularly outdrew major league clubs.[20]

Pollock's own career in black baseball began more than a decade earlier, in 1928, when he bought from Ramiro Ramirez the Havana Red Sox, a squad of mostly Cuban players that began each season in Miami. The Red Sox began barnstorming the next season with an eight-game set against an amateur team fielded by the Miami Athletic Club. After adding shadow ball and comic routines in 1930, the team became the Florida Cuban Giants, then for 1931 the Cuban House of David, and finally the Cuban Stars in 1932. The Cuban House of David name "borrowed" from a popular white barnstorming team, a Benton Harbor, Michigan-based band of bearded baseballers known as the House of David, which saw several copycat teams pop up throughout the country. To combat the name infringements, the pre-existing House of David team resorted to calling itself the House of David Originals.[21] "I originated the 'pepper game,' and now almost every traveling club in the country and eight or 10 university teams feature the game,"

Originals owner J.L. "Doc" Talley told a newspaper. Neither Cuban nor Jewish, Pollock's Cuban House of David players, likewise, grew their hair out to match their moniker, likely further irritating Doc Talley. According to Pollock's own promotional materials, these be-whiskered baseballers were "the strangest of baseball's aggregations and a weird and eccentric attraction."[22] St. Petersburg's black Florida Stars were frequent foes for the team, particularly on its annual treks north from Havana through Florida.[23]

Thus, when Pollock began steering the Clowns, he had already experimented with blends of baseball and comedy, and he had learned and even perfected how to promote the games in the pages of the black newspapers. Even a casual reading of these weeklies reveals how many of Pollock's advances, which today would be called press releases, made it into publication virtually unaltered: "Unmatched comedy, stellar big league baseball, plus all sorts of added attractions are on tap at Comiskey Park on July 4," read one such article, published as straight news in the *Chicago Defender*.[24] "Featuring the inimitable King Tut and his cohort, Spec Bebop, in the fun-laughing department, the 'Imps of the Diamond' are more popular today than ever before," the article states.[25] Trying to balance the values of entertainment with those of athletic competition, another of Pollock's advances, which ran in several newspapers, claimed that the team's "funmaking" in no way interfered with "their able playing, for with all their horse-play, they show more speed than a flock of gazelles, handle the ball with the dexterity of shellgame manipulators, and at any stage of a tilt, convulse the fans when infielders and outfielders alike recline on the ground while pitchers hurl their smoke ball past their batsmen."[26] By the early fifties, Pollock was sending out thirty thousand press releases a year.[27]

Dave Barnhill, who began with the Clowns before becoming a New York Cuban and, in 1949, a farmhand with the New York Giants, provided baseball historian John Holway with a vivid remembrance of game days with the funmakers: "We'd come to the park with [grease] paint on our faces like a clown. Even the bat boy had his face painted too. We wore clowning wigs and the big old clown uniforms with ruffled collars. My clowning name was Impo. We'd play 'shadow ball'…Then when we were supposed to get down to business, we pulled the clown suits off, and we had our regular baseball uniforms underneath. But we didn't change our faces. We played with the clown paint still on our faces."[28]

The fact that Barnhill, a player with Negro League bona fides such that he would be considered for a tryout with the Pittsburgh Pirates and eventually rise as high as Triple-A in the New York Giants organization, had to clown with a stage name of "Impo" demonstrates the sort of Faustian bargain black athletes and entertainers alike had to make in order to do what they loved most.[29] As Hall-of-Famer Hank Aaron put it, the Clowns "didn't have the luxury of concerning themselves with something like tradition."[30] Aaron joined the Clowns in 1952 as a brash eighteen-year-old from Mobile, Alabama; he refused to have anything to do with the clown acts, leaving that to the older players such as Reece "Goose" Tatum, the long-time on-field leader of and first baseman for the Clowns, and Buster Haywood.

This promotional card proclaims the clowns "1938 Colored World Champions" and advises those wishing to book the team to "Write Sid Pollock [sic], Booking Manager, N. Tarrytown — NY."

In the forties, many black newspapers simply refused to cover the Clowns, seeing them as an embarrassment to blacks everywhere.[31] The *Courier*'s Smith wrote in 1942 that "this aggregation travels around the country capitalizing on slap-stick comedy and the kind of non-sense which many white people like to believe is typical and characteristic of all Negroes." The pantomime acts belonged not on a baseball diamond, he wrote, but on "those Mississippi showboats."[32] Calling them a "fourth-rate Uncle Tom minstrel show," he objected again the next season, as well, this time to the club's "unnecessary monkeyshines."[33] Smith, Posey, and others believed that Pollock and other black baseball interlopers sought to exploit negative racial stereotypes in a trivialization of the black game, a view that in historical hindsight seems unfair. Pollock's contributions to black baseball were vast, even legendary. But he was not the only target. The *Courier* called Abe Saperstein, owner of the Chicago-based Harlem Globetrotters, a "bad influence," because by booking games for the Clowns he was "ridiculing Negro baseball, Negro players and the race in general."[34] Neither did the newspapers cover with any frequency similar "clown" acts, such as those of the Zulu Cannibal Giants, Louisville Black Spiders, Tennessee Rats, or Jax Zulos of New Orleans.[35]

For these reasons, in 1940 the Negro League owners agreed in a rare spirit of collaboration to prohibit member clubs from playing the Clowns. But many clubs simply ignored the ban, finding Pollock's drawing power too substantial to ignore. The Kansas City Monarchs and Chicago American Giants were among the first to schedule exhibition games. The next season,

owners again threatened to ban the Clowns over Pollock's use of "Ethiopian," an insult that Posey said "capitalized" on the downfall of the "only empire which really belonged to the Negro race."[36] For his part, Pollock said the name had been approved by Ethiopia's government before Italy's invasion.[37] Once again by June, Negro league teams were again doing business with the Clowns, who had added at least two new "reams" or acts: "the lightning two ball infield drill" and "a fishing act."[38] Even one of Pollock's most vocal critics, *Defender* sports editor Fay Young, conceded that, "whether some of us like the white chalk on the players' faces or not, the Clowns prove from the crowds they draw, that they have something the public wants."[39]

Unable to enforce yet another ban in 1942, a prohibition supported by "the sports editors of the various papers," the Negro American League agreed for the 1943 season to add the newly christened Cincinnati Clowns. The name change allowed the league and its owners to save face.[40] But as usual, the Clowns began their touring, traveling season at Dorsey Park in Miami.[41] In a league as topsy-turvy as the Negro American, the Clowns were a constant, playing in a dozen straight seasons and winning four out of five championships during the years 1950–54. Relocated to Indianapolis in 1946 after shuttling back and forth between Cincinnati and Indy for two seasons, the club weathered the post-integration storm, one that saw black fans switch allegiances to freshly desegregated squads such as the Dodgers, White Sox, and Cardinals. Founded in 1920 purposely to effect integration, the Negro Leagues discovered that achieving that goal made them increasingly irrelevant.[42]

For Smith, the Negro Leagues were by 1950, "on

the ropes and ready for the killing," a description that preceded "probably the worst [season] in the history of Negro baseball."[43] Larry Lester ends his history of the East-West Game in 1953, when it drew only 10,000 fans, even though the all-star game continued in some form until 1963.[44] He justifies his endpoint with the fact that the 1953 edition was the last to showcase a Negro leaguer on his way to the major leagues, Ernie Banks. Smith reported that big league scouts on hand to evaluate the fast-shrinking pool of talent that year were "underwhelmed" with what they saw.[45] Certainly by the mid-1950s the Negro American League was semi-professional at best. League games were diversions that relied ever more on sideshow entertainment and less on athletic achievement or competition. And this was of course perfect for the Clowns.

It is no mistake that Kansas City's home opener in 1953 versus the Clowns drew 18,205 fans—a good crowd by even major league standards—or that a Monarchs-Clowns doubleheader in June drew more than 21,000, one of the largest crowds to see any baseball game in Detroit that season.[46] The Monarchs had Ernie Banks, and the Clowns had professional baseball's first female, second baseman Toni Stone. Pollock wasn't finished pioneering. Though she was a solid player, the addition of Stone for a reported $12,000 was primarily a bid to sell tickets.[47] The former Minnesota high school star gave the Clowns "a road attraction unequalled in Negro baseball," according to the *Defender*, which at this critical stage of black baseball's viability did not question or criticize Pollock's latest gimmick.[48]

Over in Pittsburgh, failing to see any irony in his position, Smith criticized Pollock and Stone for breaking baseball's sex barrier. The champion of Jackie Robinson and Branch Rickey, the Boswell to Robinson's Johnson, Smith asserted that "a woman's place is in the home!" and not on a baseball diamond.[49] He wrote that "it is, indeed, unfortunate that Negro baseball has collapsed to the extent it must tie itself to a woman's apron strings in order to survive. ... Mr. Pollock is trying to convince us that she plays second base like Jackie Robinson." He wondered how bad black ball's hurlers had to be to enable "a doll" to hit .217—"not bad for a dame."[50] It meant that the pitchers had nothing on the ball "but the cover." More characteristic of coverage during this period, however, was that of the *Defender*, which heralded Indy's clown prince Ed Hamann for his "hilarious diamond entertainment," which included "in-throws, pepperball shennanigans [sic] and feats of new magic... guaranteed to make even the most case-hardened fan roar with glee."[51] The *Defender*'s coverage read just as one might think Pollock had wanted it to,

celebrating the entertainment values of the "Imps of the Diamond," a "baseball circus really worth seeing."[52] The newspapers were publishing Pollock's press releases without alteration.

In 1954, after losing Stone to the Monarchs, Pollock added two more female players—second baseman Connie Morgan and pitcher Mamie "Peanut" Johnson—in order to deliver "unmatched comedy."[53] All that remained for black baseball, it seemed, was barnstorming, which the Clowns did well into the late eighties, or long after Pollock's retirement after the 1964 season, through at least three more ownership changes, and despite reverse-integrating in 1968.[54] Thus, in important ways, the Clowns' history is black baseball's history: a product of segregation, a (mostly) black institution often exploited by astute white businessmen, an expression and celebration of black culture and identity, but also a vehicle for stereotype, misunderstanding, and at times degradation. Through it all, the Clowns proved innovative, resourceful, and resilient, much like the sport that so desperately needed them. And though they were required to "shine" in order to entertain and perhaps to reassure white audiences, many also dazzled with their play, showing skill that laughter cannot and should not obscure. ■

Notes

1. See, for example, the box score in "Crack Negro Teams Here," *Milwaukee Journal*, June 22, 1941, sect. III, 5.
2. "Black baseball established itself as a viable economic entity when the Cuban Giants were born" in the 1880s, according to Jerry Malloy, "The Birth of the Cuban Giants: The Origins of Black Professional Baseball," *Nine: A Journal of Baseball History and Social Policy Perspectives* (Spring 2004): 233.
3. Hank Aaron, *I Had A Hammer: The Hank Aaron Story* (New York: HarperCollins, 1991), 28. For much more on the Kansas state championship baseball tournament, see Brian Carroll, "'Praising my people': Newspaper sports coverage and the integration of baseball in Wichita, Kansas," in *Kansas History: A Journal of the Central Plains* 33, no. 4 (Winter 2010–11): 240–55.
4. Quoted in *Sporting Life*, September 5, 1888.
5. See Malloy's pioneering research on the Giants in "The Birth of the Cuban Giants." See also Brian Carroll, *When to Stop the Cheering? The Black Press, the Black Community, and the Integration of Professional Baseball* (New York: Routledge, 2007).
6. See, for example, Raymond A. Mohl, "Clowning Around: The Miami Ethiopian Clowns and Cultural Conflict in Black Baseball," *Tequesta LXII* (2002): 46; Neil Lanctot, *Negro League Baseball: The Rise and Ruin of a Black Institution* (Philadelphia: University of Penn Press, 2007), 108; and Alan J. Pollock, *Barnstorming to Heaven: Syd Pollock and His Great Black Teams*, James A. Riley, ed. (Tuscaloosa, Ala.: University of Alabama Press, 2006): 27, 49–50, 60.
7. John Holway, *Black Diamonds: Life in the Negro Leagues from the Men Who Lived It* (Westport, Conn.: Meckler Books, 1989), 94. In his recounting, O'Neil got his nickname, Buck, from O'Neal, who came to the team from Waycross, Georgia. According to Alan J. Pollock, O'Neal was with the Miami Giants until 1935, when he moved to New York City and became a groundskeeper at Yankee Stadium.

8. Personal interview, January 9, 2004, Chapel Hill, North Carolina. Incorporating "Giants" in a team name was homage to the Cuban Giants and, later, to the New York Giants. Long-time New York manager John McGraw very publicly supported integration and on occasion attempted to finagle a black player onto his roster.
9. Holway, *Black Diamonds*, 94. Second Avenue is in Overtown, which was called Colored Town during the Jim Crow era, home to Dorsey Park where the Miami Giants and Miami Clowns played.
10. Cesar Brioso, "Memories of the Game," (Fort Lauderdale) *Sun-Sentinel*, October 15, 2000, available: http://articles.sun-sentinel.com/2000-10-15/sports/00101502028_1_black-baseball-players-giants-player-land-developer. Cromartie's son, Warren Cromartie, played for the Montreal Expos and Tokyo Giants.
11. "Smitty's Sports-Spurts," *Pittsburgh Courier*, May 16, 1942, 17. Cromartie was speaking of the second iteration of the Miami Giants owned by Monk Silva, who bought the team's uniforms from Pierce. The Clowns typically played Silva's Giants at Miami's Dorsey Park to open and close their seasons, and Monk agreed to store the Clowns' bus during the winters (Pollock, *Barnstorming to Heaven*, 116, 137).
12. "Bar League Ball Clubs From Playing Clowns," *Chicago Defender*, January 3, 1942, 20.
13. Donn Rogosin, *Invisible Men: Life in Baseball's Negro Leagues* (Lincoln, Neb.: Bison Books, 2007), 146.
14. See "Ethiopian Clowns Play Here," *Montreal Gazette* CLXV, no. 152, June 26, 1936, 14.
15. "War Fears in Italo-Ethiopia Rift," *Literary Digest*, March 9, 1935, 14.
16. "Posey's Points," *Pittsburgh Courier*, April 4, 1942, 16.
17. E. B. Rea, "Down My Street," *The Afro-American*, January 10, 1942, 21.
18. Mohl, "Clowning Around," 63, citing a 1998 telephone interview with Alan J. Pollock, Syd Pollock's son.
19. "Hunter Campbell, "Clowns Ball Club Owner, Is Dead," *Chicago Defender*, December 19, 1942, 20.
20. "Black Yanks to Play Clowns," *The New York Times*, July 7, 1945, 8.
21. "House of David Originals to Trot Out Here Sunday Against Two Spokane Baseball Teams," *Spokane Daily Chronicle*, June 18, 1935, 16.
22. "Colored Cuban Club of House of David Coming to Victoria," *Victoria Daily Advocate*, March 2, 1931, 3.
23. "Negro Baseball Team to Tackle Cuban Tossers," *St. Petersburg Times*, March 29, 1931, 13.
24. "Clowns To Bring Lot Of Comedy," *Chicago Defender*, June 26, 1954, 12.
25. King Tut's given name was Edward King. Spec Bebop's was Ralph Bell. King played for the Clowns from 1938 to 1950.
26. In Mohl, "Clowning Around," 52.
27. Ibid., 51.
28. Holway, *Black Diamonds*, 139–40.
29. "Negro Ball Players Might Get Try-Outs," *Chicago Defender*, August 1, 1942, 25.
30. Aaron, *I Had A Hammer*, 29.
31. "Bar League Ball Clubs From Playing Clowns," *Chicago Defender*, January 3, 1942, 20.
32. "Smitty's Sports Spurts," *Pittsburgh Courier*, May 16, 1942, 17.
33. "Smitty's Sports Spurts," *Pittsburgh Courier*, January 23, 1943, 16.
34. "July 27 Set As Date Of East-West Game," *Pittsburgh Courier*, June 28, 1941, 16.
35. The Jax Zulos wore grass skirts and featured pitcher Bolo Power ("Zulos Play Houston Twin Bill June 25," *Pittsburgh Courier*, June 24, 1944, 12). The Rats were one of the earliest black clubs to pair minstrelsy with baseball ("90 Years Ago – Play Rats," *Lyon County* (Iowa) *Recorder*, August 4, 1999, 2).
36. "Posey's Points," *Pittsburgh Courier*, July 5, 1941, 16.
37. Lanctot, *Negro League Baseball*, 109. Because the government had been ousted, such a claim would have been impossible to verify.
38. "Crack Negro Teams Here," *Milwaukee Journal*, June 22, 1941, sect. III, 5. For the fishing sketch, King Tut and Spec Bebop would sit on the infield grass as in a boat, casting their bats like rods, and waiting for a bite. Tut would pretend to hook a marlin or tarpon, quaking and shaking with the ebb and flow of the big fish. Dragged underwater, Tut and Bebop would "swim" ashore (Pollock, *Barnstorming to Heaven*, 10).
39. Lanctot, *Negro League Baseball*, 109–10.
40. "12 League Clubs to Bar Clowns and 'Cuban' Teams," *Afro-American*, January 3, 1942, 21.
41. "Baseball Bits," *Afro-American*, March 27, 1943, 23. In a memorable spring season opener, Pollock brought Olympic gold medalist Jesse Owens, "the world's fastest human," to Dorsey Park in April 1940 (Elliott J. Pieze, "Miami," *Afro-American*, April 13, 1940, 23). Little evidence of Dorsey Park's central role in black Miami's cultural life of the thirties remains, though there is a part of what was the grandstand behind home plate. *Sun-Sentinel* writer Cesar Brosario called Dorsey Park a "focal point of Miami's African-American community" of the thirties and forties ("Memories of the Game").
42. Founders of the Negro National League believed that a product on the field equal or superior to major league baseball would force integration. One of those founders, Chicago's Rube Foster, also believed that integration would occur by adding an entire all-black team, and he had every intention of being the owner and manager of that all-black major league entry.
43. Wendell Smith, "The Sports Beat," *Pittsburgh Courier*, December 16, 1950, 24.
44. Larry Lester, *Black Baseball's National Showcase: The East-West All-Star Game, 1933–1953* (Lincoln: University of Nebraska Press, 2001).
45. Wendell Smith, "All-Star Tilt Fails To Impress Scouts From Big Leagues," *Pittsburgh Courier*, August 22, 1953, 14.
46. "21,399 See Kaycees Win Twin Bill," *Chicago Defender*, July 2, 1953, 27.
47. In Kansas City that Sunday in mid-May, Stone struck out and grounded out in three innings of play (Russ Cowans, "Richardson Gives 8 Hits To Loses [sic]," *Chicago Defender*, May 28, 1953, 30). For the season, Stone hit .243 in 74 at-bats and 50 games. Seventeen of her eighteen hits were singles, she knocked in only three runs, and she stole one base ("Monarchs Win Crown In NAL," *Chicago Defender*, September 24, 1953, 28). Monarch manager Buck O'Neil wrote in his autobiography that Kansas City's signing of Stone the next season was "not because she was the best second baseman around but because she could give us a boost at the gate." (*I Was Right On Time*, 194). Stone was in 1954 the highest-paid Monarch, but it is unlikely she was in fact paid $12,000. Alan J. Pollock guesses she made $300 per month (*Barnstorming to Heaven*, 243).
48. "Clowns Blazing in Second Half," *Chicago Defender*, July 23, 1953, 26.
49. Wendell Smith, "The Sports Beat," *Pittsburgh Courier*, June 20, 1953, 14.
50. Ibid.
51. "Clowns Using Giant, Comic To Win Fans," *Chicago Defender*, December 13, 1952, 13. See also "Clowns Blazing in Second Half," *Chicago Defender*, July 23, 1953, 26. For more on this era of the Clowns' history, see Bill Heward (with Dimitri V. Gat), *Some Are Called Clowns: A Season with the Last of the Great Barnstorming Baseball Teams* (New York: Crowell, 1974). The book is a memoir, however, and not a documented history.
52. "Clowns To Bring Lot Of Comedy," *Chicago Defender*, June 26, 1954, 12.
53. Ibid.
54. Pollock sold controlling interest in the team in January 1965 to long-time road manager Ed Hamann for $3,885, according to Pollock's son, Alan (*Barnstorming to Heaven*, 380). By the eighties, the team was entirely white.

Blurring the Color Line

How Cuban Baseball Players Led to the Racial Integration of Major League Baseball

Stephen R. Keeney

Rafael Almeida and Armando Marsans, who played for the Cincinnati Reds 36 years before Jackie Robinson came along, should be credited with crashing the color barrier.

—Felipe Alou[1]

On April 15, 1947, the story goes, Jackie Robinson of the Brooklyn Dodgers became the first black American to play baseball in the major leagues.[2] This is often the first image that comes to mind when people think about the color line in baseball. The moment is so important to baseball's popular psyche that fifty years later, Commissioner Bud Selig retired Robinson's jersey number, 42, throughout Major League Baseball.[3]

Jackie Robinson broke baseball's color barrier in the same way Thomas Edison invented the lightbulb. Both did something that nobody else had ever achieved. But both also benefitted from the trials, the failures, and, certainly in Robinson's case, the suffering of pioneers before them. Like the light bulb, Robinson's place on the Brooklyn Dodgers' roster was "the kind of innovation that comes together over decades, in pieces."[4] Inventors across the globe had been inventing incandescent light for 80 years before Edison's breakthrough made it available to modern masses.[5] Each new discovery and innovation built upon those before it. The same is true of baseball's color barrier. Black players began playing with white players as early as the nineteenth century. But at the sport's pinnacle, the major leagues, it was Cuban players who gradually blurred baseball's color line before Jackie Robinson could cross it.[6] Cuban players entered the league with gradually darker complexions, laying the groundwork for the idea that a black American could play alongside whites in baseball's top echelon. Jackie Robinson playing in the major leagues was not the beginning of integration in baseball, but another step in the evolution of racial integration that began decades earlier with the introduction of baseball to Cuba and the introduction of Cuban players to the United States.

BASEBALL IN CUBA

Baseball first came to Cuba in the 1860s. Some credit Nemesio Guillo, who returned to Cuba in 1864 after studying and learning baseball in the United States, with bringing the first ball and bat to Cuba.[7] Most scholars, however, say that it was a combination of many Cubans returning from American universities, United States Navy sailors and Army soldiers, and sheer proximity to the United States.[8]

The first official game between two all-Cuban teams took place in 1874 and saw the Habana (Havana) Reds beat their soon-to-be archrival Matanzas by a score of 51–9.[9] In 1868 Cuba had begun its first of three wars spanning thirty years, which ultimately led to independence from Spain in 1898.[10] In 1878, when the first war came to an end, the Pact of Zanjón declared independence for any slaves who fought in the war on either side, and on October 7, 1886, a Spanish royal decree officially abolished slavery in Cuba.[11]

During the wars of independence, the ideas of interracial cooperation and acceptance became battle standards for all who believed in freedom for Cuba. José Martí, one of the founding fathers of Cuba, wrote in the newspaper *Patria* ("fatherland," or "homeland"), "Men are more than white, more than mulatto,[12] more than negro. On the battlefields of Cuba white and black have died and their souls risen together to heaven."[13] He also wrote about how dividing men by race was "a sin against humanity."[14] This rings true in Cuban culture as well; Cuba as an independent nation has never had legal slavery, and Cuban baseball has always included whites, blacks, and mulattos playing side by side.

As baseball was growing in the United States during the mid-to-late-1800s, Cuba began to revolt against its colonizer, Spain. The struggle lasted for decades, and involved three separate wars. During this time, Cubans showed both Spain and the United States that the island wanted to be free from Spanish rule, and align itself with the growing United States. In a united act of cultural defiance, Cubans turned away from bullfighting, the Spanish spectator sport, and began making baseball, the top American spectator sport, the national pastime of Cuba.[15] The United States, looking for a pseudo-colony of its own, began to reach out to the Cuban people. As part of this cultural colonization process, by the end of the nineteenth century major league teams began playing baseball in Cuba against local teams.[16] These tours brought major league baseball and Cuban baseball face to face for the first time, and the two influenced each other.

DRAWING THE COLOR LINE

Organized baseball in the United States was segregated before it was professional. During the 1860s, when baseball was really taking hold as the national game, whites and blacks sometimes played each other.[17] But in December 1867, after the Pythians of Philadelphia, a black club, applied for membership in the National Association of Base Ball Players ("NABBP"), the first national organization overseeing the game, they were denied.[18] Not only was the Pythians' application denied, but the NABBP's Nominating Committee unanimously recommended "against the admission of any club which may be composed of one or more persons of color."[19] The stated goal was to "keep out of the Convention…any subject having a political bearing."[20] Being that this decision was made shortly after the Civil War and before the 14th and 15th Amendments were ratified, the issue of racial exclusion certainly had political bearing. Nonetheless, the NABBP and later major leagues maintained segregation in the game, officially or, more often, unofficially, for the next 80 years.

There had been a brief glimmer of hope that baseball's color line might not last into the new century. At least 54 black players played on racially integrated teams between 1883 and 1898.[21] In 1884 two black brothers, Moses and Welday Walker, played for Toledo of the American Association, a league which rivaled the National League in the 1880s and differentiated itself by "openly seeking the patronage of ethnics and workingmen."[22]

But white players saw potential for economic loss within their own ranks. In the days before professionalism, teams would often offer players easy jobs with high pay, usually working for a rich friend of the club, to induce the players to join the team. For example, an 1868 job advertisement for a first baseman read "The National Club of Washington are looking for a first baseman about here…Terms—First-rate position in the Treasury Department; must work in the Department until three o'clock, and then practice base ball until dark."[23] Once the best leagues in the country were professional, each roster spot given to a black player was potentially a spot lost by a white player.

When white players perceived a threat to their economic opportunities, from what *Sporting Life* referred to as the "mania for engaging [hiring] colored players,"[24] they acted out of both racial prejudice and economic fear. On September 11, 1887, the St. Louis Browns were scheduled to play the Cuban Giants, an all-black barnstorming team that rarely had more than a couple Cubans on the roster at any given time.[25] But the day before the game, while eating dinner at the Continental Hotel in Philadelphia, St. Louis's President, Chris von Der Ahe, received a letter signed by the majority of the players on the team. The letter stated that the players "do not agree to play against Negroes to-morrow,"[26] but they would "cheerfully play against white people at any time."[27] This "established the precedent that the white players must not play with colored men."[28] At the game's highest levels, the precedent was enforced by unofficial, unwritten agreement among the owners to not sign black players.

EARLY CUBAN PLAYERS IN AMERICA

Esteban Bellán is believed to be the first Cuban-born player to ever play professional baseball. He began playing in the National Association for the Troy Haymakers around 1870, right around the same time the Cincinnati Reds became the first openly all-professional baseball team.[29] Troy became a founding member of the National Association of Professional Base Ball Players, which had split from the all-amateur National Association of Base Ball Players to become the first professional baseball organization.[30] In 1875, a few of the best teams left the professional association to form the National League, which began play in 1876 and is part of Major League Baseball today.[31]

But Cubans did not start coming to the major leagues regularly until many years later, once major league teams decided that playing exhibition games in Cuba would help build their brands abroad while also giving them a warm climate in which to prepare for the upcoming season. It was in Cuba, during a 1908 tour, that the Cincinnati Reds first encountered the men who would become the first Latino players in modern major league history, despite being suspected by many as having "Negro blood."[32] In a game against a Cuban team, the Reds encountered three outstanding local talents: Rafael Almeida, Armando Marsans, and José Méndez. Marsans scored the game's only run, and in fact had already turned down one offer to play professionally in the United States the year before.[33] Méndez, a pitcher, shut out the Reds.[34] In fact, in that 1908 season, from his first pitch against Cincinnati, to a series against a team from Key West, and ending with a game against Habana, Méndez racked up forty-five straight scoreless innings.[35]

Méndez's pitching was the standout performance of the day, and all three players had the talent to play with any major league team. But one big difference made Almeida and Marsans more signable than Méndez. Almeida and Marsans descended from European families, which meant that their skin color was very light, and indeed almost white.[36] They were "of 'swarthy' complexion, which meant definitely white, but darkish in a Spanish or Italian sort of way."[37] Méndez, however, was of mostly African heritage, and he was black. Even his Cuban teammates nicknamed him "Congo."[38] His nickname changed to "Black Diamond" once he became a national hero in Cuba because of his talents on the field.[39] Quite simply, Méndez was too dark-skinned to play in the major leagues.

But for the two players from that 1908 team who happened to be close enough to white, they were able to rise through the ranks of professional baseball. Both players made their way to the New Britain team in the Connecticut League, from which Cincinnati signed them.[40] In May 1911, before the Reds had officially purchased the rights to Marsans and Almeida, team ownership underwent a massive public relations campaign to try to convince the fans that these two players "had earned their opportunity to compete against white ball players."[41] The goal of the marketing campaign was to convince the public of the "whiteness" of the two players.[42] This "whiteness campaign" tried to convince the general public that both players were "born of the best, and whitest families in Cuba."[43] Club President Gary Herrmann even took it upon himself to write a friend in Cuba to confirm that Marsans had no African ancestry.[44]

On July 4, 1911, Almeida and Marsans both debuted with the Cincinnati Reds, becoming the first Cuban players in the major leagues.[45] Both players went 1-for-2 in substitution efforts against the Cubs in Chicago.[46] The only mention of Marsans and Almeida in their first game was two sentences in the *Cincinnati Enquirer* which stated that both "appeared to be very fast on the bases and equipped with strong throwing arms."[47]

In Cuba, both players were "mulatto," of mixed Spanish and African-Cuban blood. American society classified both players as "colored." Unlike Cuba, where your skin color could fall anywhere on a long spectrum of racial combinations, in the United States of the late nineteenth and early twentieth centuries you could only be "white" or "colored." To many, both players were "colored" and nothing more. Both Reds fans and opposing fans constantly taunted and harassed Almeida and Marsans for their color.[48]

While Almeida and Marsans were being scouted by and playing for the Reds, the pitcher from that 1908 game was making his own impact in the baseball world. José de la Caridad Méndez was born in Cardenas, Cuba, in the late 1880s.[49] He began pitching when he was 16 years old, and in 1908, when the Cincinnati Reds played in Cuba, Méndez pitched an impressive complete game one-hit shutout in the previously mentioned 1–0 win over the Reds.[50] But while Almeida and Marsans were playing professional baseball at the highest level in the world, the legendary arm of Méndez was barnstorming with Negro League teams and devastating major league hitters from outside their ranks.[51]

With the color line already having been drawn in the major leagues, the closest Méndez would ever get

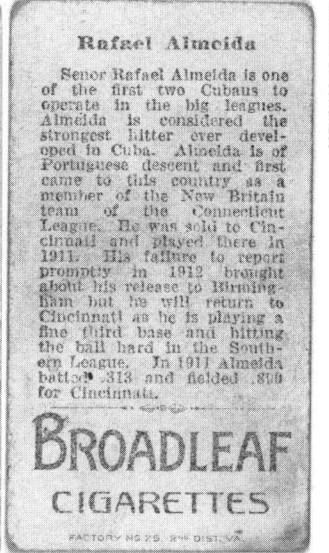

Rafael Almeida and Armando Marsans as depicted on their 1912 American Tobacco Company baseball cards while members of the Cincinnati team.

was playing for the Cuban Stars and in the Negro Leagues, starting in 1909.[52] After the world champion Philadelphia Athletics had been defeated by Méndez in two consecutive starts, the A's veteran catcher Ira Thomas said that in his and his teammates' opinions Méndez "ranks with the best in the game."[53] But despite being one of the best pitchers of his time, Méndez was not given the same opportunities as his former teammates because he was black.

THE COLOR LINE GETS BLURRY[54]

Since Almeida and Marsans were close to white, they were the ones the Reds decided to sign. There were likely no underlying political or social motives to signing the players. Owner Garry Herrmann and manager Clark Griffith simply wanted "cheap talent and a chance to draw on the growing Latin community" to increase profits.[55] Much like Branch Rickey would do with Jackie Robinson decades later, Griffith and Herrmann merely exploited a market inefficiency by recruiting players other teams ignored out of racial prejudice.[56]

Even though black players were excluded from the top leagues, people in baseball knew just how good some black and Cuban teams were. During an exhibition series in Cuba, New York Giants manager John McGraw said that he would pay $50,000 each for Méndez and his catcher "Strike" Gonzalez if they were white.[57] Legendary Cuban broadcaster Rafael "Felo" Ramírez—member of the Caribbean Baseball Hall of Fame and 2001 recipient of the National Baseball Hall of Fame's Ford C. Frick Award—spoke of a joke that went around Cuba that, "if they painted Méndez with white paint he would finally be good enough to be a superstar in the United States."[58] A 1914 poster promoting a game between the Cuban Stars and Marshall, a professional team from Cleveland, tried to entice fans to attend by saying that "Méndez, considered by experts as the best pitcher in the world, will probably pitch."[59] While Méndez's skill is more important to us now, in the early 1900s race was the only important issue.[60] By exemplifying, and often even creating, stories of whiteness about the early Latino players, the leagues and the owners were able to maintain their overarching goal of black exclusion, while also capitalizing on the availability of cheap nonwhite talent.[61] Despite his talent, team owners simply refused to sign Méndez because he was black.

The mere presence of two "swarthy" Cubans in the major leagues was enough to alarm some observers. An undated article from the Negro League Museum asked, "Is Baseball To Lower Color Line?"[62] The article headline claimed that the signing of Marsans and Almeida by the Reds was a "Step Towards Letting in the Negro."[63]

> …it has always been understood that no Negro should play in the major leagues…Griffith has signed two Cubans who may or may not be part Negro. These particular Cubans may be of Spanish descent and they may be of African…the peculiar social conditions of the island making it mighty hard to determine the exact standings of most of the natives regarding color.[64]

Articles like this showed that "some within baseball circles perceived the Cubans as occupying an in-between space along the color line as neither black nor white."[65] By creating and occupying a space between black and white, Cuban players found their way onto major league rosters which were no longer just white.

TREATMENT OF CUBAN PLAYERS

After the introduction of Almeida and Marsans in 1911, and the success of Marsans in the league, more Cuban and other Latino players followed. "Latin American players came to the United States with growing regularity, and with each wave their impact on the major leagues enlarged."[66] The first true Latin American star was Cuban Adolfo Luque (1914-1935), who led all pitchers with a record of 27–8 and an ERA of 1.93 in 1923 with the Cincinnati Reds.[67] Between 1900 and 1950, 43 Cuban players made their debuts in the major leagues.[68] Most of them entered the major leagues by signing with the Cincinnati Reds or the Washington Nationals.[69] Clark Griffith was largely responsible for signing Cuban players, which he began with the Reds and continued with the Nationals.

Even though the color line was being blurred by Cuban players in terms of roster spots, American society and baseball culture continued to enforce racial divisions by how they treated players. Cuban players faced aggressive pitching, taunting by the fans, and worst of all, taunting from their own teammates. One of the most troubling aspects for many Latin American baseball players in the decades to come was that they had expected to find the "American dream" where "success came by virtue of merit," but instead they found mostly racism that mirrored the larger American society.[70]

In a 1940 Collier's article, sportswriter Bob Considine wrote about baseball's racism toward the Cuban players in an article entitled "Ivory from Cuba."[71] He called Cuba a "gold mine of baseball players" and wrote about how Cuban players often did not receive "just salaries."[72] He also told us that Cuban players were "handicapped by a rather widespread inability on the part of the American ballplayers to differentiate between Cuban and Negro athletes."[73]

Racism among baseball players often included throwing at batters on purpose. Considine admits that such actions were sometimes strategy and not racism. For example, Cuban Roberto Estalella was known to crowd the plate, so sometimes pitchers were merely backing him off as they would a white batter. However, Considine goes into further detail about the general treatment of Cuban players:

> They get beanballs thrown at their heads by closed-shop (and closed-brained) rivals. They face pitchers who willingly throw away their arms bearing down on them in an effort to escape the "ignominy" of yielding a hit to them. They get a measure of grass-singeing abuse from the "jockeys" on the enemy bench. From their own team they get rock bottom pay, and from their own teammates they get a wintry ostracism. Those who want to befriend them are halted by the differences in languages.[74]

Thus, Cubans playing baseball in the United States often suffered from racial, cultural, and linguistic isolation.

Fortunately, there were also players and people around baseball who saw the absurdity in the game's racism. It was easy for most people to "deal with" the Cuban presence at first because most of the Cuban players came by way of only two teams, the Reds and the Nationals. With articles like Considine's and the success of Cubans in the major leagues, the number of Cubans continued to grow. This forced baseball culture to begin to "deal with" the changes, eventually leading to understanding and acceptance in the game.

BLACK PLAYERS REACT

Despite the progress made by Cuban players, most black players were in no rush to try to cross the color line themselves. The treatment of the "almost-white" Cubans was bad enough to make most black players fear how bad their lives in the major leagues could be.[75] The black players on non-major league and Negro League rosters found a way to "deal with" the gradual inclusion of the Cuban players and the continued exclusion of black American players. While Cuban players were blurring the color line, black American players were blurring the nationality line.

American society recognized Latinos as something outside of the sharp racial divisions of black and white

Adolfo "Dolph" Luque was the first true Latin American star and spent 20 seasons in the big leagues. In 1923 he led all pitchers with a record of 27–8 and an ERA of 1.93 with the Cincinnati Reds.

that had existed for so long in the United States. For white Americans, the biggest distinction between Cubans and black Americans was language. Armando Vásquez, a dark-skinned Cuban playing in the Negro Leagues in the 1940s, recalled how he would conveniently "forget" any English he had picked up.[76,77] He would go to restaurants that did not serve blacks and begin speaking Spanish, and the restaurants would often serve him.[78] Despite his black skin color, by speaking Spanish Vásquez become something else. Once he opened his mouth, he was no longer just black—he was a foreigner.[79]

This distinction was enough to get many Cuban players better treatment in segregated parts of the country. Other Negro Leaguers began to notice. Many teams made sure to have at least one Latino on their roster so that he could order for the whole team in whites-only restaurants, while the other players pretended to not speak English. That way, they could all be served.[80] Black players pretended they were Cuban by intentionally speaking broken English with a Spanish accent, or actually speaking Spanish if they knew enough of it.[81] This practice spread to the larger black community. Black poet and statesman James Weldon Johnson, in his autobiography *Along This Way*, describes several instances where speaking Spanish and masquerading as a Latino helped him and his family get better treatment on trains and other segregated facilities.[82,83] So not only did Cuban baseball players help blur baseball's color line, but they also provided black Americans a pathway, absurd though it was, to better treatment in certain parts of the country.

*   *   *

In the years following Bob Considine's article, the idea of racial acceptance in baseball became more of a reality. Exactly five years to the day before Jackie Robinson's major league debut, Hiram "Hi" Bithorn became the first Puerto Rican to play major league baseball.[84] The color line had blurred enough for Bithorn, who was light-skinned but still "dark" by major league standards, to be able to play at baseball's highest level.[85] In 1947, Robinson's entrance onto the major league stage paved the way for more black Americans to play at the highest levels, but it in no way ended the racism in baseball.

Just like any culture, baseball has been steadily changing—and integration increasing—since the game's inception. To use the old baseball phrase, Jackie Robinson's signing with the Dodgers did not just come out of left field. It was partially the work of Cuban players, who suffered extreme resistance and racism, that made it possible for players like Jackie Robinson to not just play the game at its highest levels, but to become heroes to generations of people of all races. ■

Notes

1. Felipe Alou and Herm Weiskopf, *Felipe Alou: My Life and Baseball* (Waco, TX: Word Books, 1967). Quoted in Nick C. Wilson, *Early Latino Ballplayers in the United States: Major, Minor, and Negro Leagues, 1901–1949* (Jefferson, NC: McFarland and Company, 2005), 25. Alou played 17 years and managed 14 years in the major leagues and was the manager of the Dominican Republic team for the 2009 World Baseball Classic.

2. See Endnote 32 for the definition of "major leagues" as used in this paper. More recent research suggests that the first black American to play in the major leagues, as herein defined, was actually William Edward White, who played one game as a substitute for the National League's Providence Grays on June 21, 1879. White's father was a white slave-owner, and White's mother was one of his slaves. While White was legally black, he could pass for white, and his death certificate lists him as "white." See John R. Husman, "June 21, 1879: The Cameo of William Edward White," SABR.org, http://www.sabr.org/gamesproj/game/june-21-1879-cameo-william-edward-white, last accessed May 31, 2016, and Peter Morris and Stefan Fatsis, "Baseball's Secret Pioneer: William Edward White," Slate.com, http://www.slate.com/articles/sports/sports_nut/2014/02/william_edward_white_baseball_s_first_black_player_lived_his_life_as_a_white.single.html, last accessed May 31, 2016.

3. Players who were already wearing the number were allowed to keep it until their retirement.

4. Steven Johnson, *How We Got to Now: Six Innovations that Made the Modern World* (Riverhead Books: New York, 2014): 209.

5. Ibid, 206.

6. See Endnote 32 for the definition of "major leagues" as used in this paper.

7. Luis Hernández, cited in Eric A. Wagner, "Sport in Revolutionary Societies: Cuba and Nicaragua," *Sport and Society in Latin America: Diffusion, Dependency, and the Rise of Mass Culture*, ed. Joseph L. Arbena, (Westport, CT: Greenwood Press, 1988), 118.

8. Samuel O. Regalado, *Viva Baseball!: Latin Major Leaguers and Their Special Hunger* (Urbana, IL: University of Illinois Press, 1998), 10; Thomas Carter, "Cuba: Community, Fans, and Ballplayers," George Gmelch, ed. *Baseball without Borders: The International Pastime* (Lincoln: University of Nebraska, 2006), 147–59.

9. Some sources (see Regalado, 10) put this game's date as 1868.

10. For more on the culture and history of baseball in Cuba, see Roberto González Echevarría, *The Pride of Havana: A History of Cuban Baseball* (Oxford University Press, 2001).

11. J. A. Sierra, "End of Slavery in Cuba," History of Cuba. http://www.historyofcuba.com/history/race/EndSlave.htm.

12. Mulatto is a Latin American term generally used to describe people descended from a mixture of colonial Spanish and either native or black blood.

13. José Martí, "My Race," *Patria*, April 16, 1892.

14. Ibid.

15. Louis A Pérez, "Between Baseball and Bullfighting: The Quest for Nationality in Cuba, 1868–1898," *The Journal of American History* 81 (1994): 494, 506.

16. Stephen A. Riess, *Touching Base: Professional Baseball and American Culture in the Progressive Era* (Chicago: University of Illinois Press, 1999), 193–94.

17. Dean A. Sullivan, ed., *Early Innings: A Documentary History of Baseball, 1825–1908* (Lincoln: University of Nebraska Press, 1995): 68.

18. Ibid.

19. Ibid, 68–69.

20. Ibid, 68.

21. Benjamin Rader, *Baseball: A History of America's Game* (Urbana and Chicago, IL.: University of Illinois Press, 1992): 51.

22. Ibid, 51.

23. Charley Rosen, *The Emerald Diamond: How the Irish Transformed America's Greatest Pastime* (Harper Collins: New York, 2012): 22–23.

24. Rader, 51.

25. The rest of the players were black Americans. Many Negro League teams used the word Cuban to play on the differences in treatment received between the black American players and the Latin American players. Some teams in the Negro Leagues had Native Americans on their rosters.

26. "A Color Line in Baseball," *The New York Times*, September 12, 1887.

27. Ibid.

28. Ibid.

29. There seems to be some disagreement among the sources as to when Bellán started playing professionally. See Wilson, 3 (1871); Brian McKenna, "Steve Bellán," SABR.org, http://sabr.org/bioproj/person/78dbf37d, last accessed June 1, 2016 (1868); and, "Steve Bellán," Baseball-Reference.com, http://www.baseball-reference.com/players/b/bellast01.shtml, last accessed June 1, 2016 (1871).

30. Benjamin Rader, *Baseball: A History of America's Game* (Urbana and Chicago, IL.: University of Illinois Press, 1992). 37.

31. According to Major League Baseball, the National League was the first officially recognized professional baseball league. David Pietrusza, *Major Leagues: The Formation, Sometimes Absorption and Mostly Inevitable Demise of 18 Professional Baseball Organizations, 1871 to Present* (Jefferson, N.C.: McFarland & Company, 1991).

32. Throughout this paper, when I refer to the major leagues, I am referring to the National League, the American League, the Western League (fore-runner to today's American League), and the current MLB organization. As far as determining the first Cuban major leaguers, this interpretation is supported by the sources. See "Baseball Notes," *The New York Times*, June 30, 1911 (Marsans and Almeida are "the first Cuban players to be signed by a major league club."). See also, Regalado at 3–4, and Wilson at 23–26, both referring to the introduction of Marsans and Almeida as

the beginning of Cuban baseball in the major leagues. For reference to public perception of ancestry, see Eric Enders, "Armando Marsans," SABR.org, http://sabr.org/bioproj/person/f2c0b939, last accessed June 2, 2016.

33. Wilson, 23.

34. Wilson, 7–9.

35. Wilson, 7–9.

36. Marsans was of Spanish ancestry while Almeida was reported by papers at the time as "a scion of Portuguese royalty." Wilson, 23–24.

37. Erardi, F1.

38. Wilson, 8.

39. Wilson, 8.

40. "Baseball Notes," *The New York Times*, June 30, 1911.

41. Wilson, 23.

42. Wilson, 23. The Reds also tried to play up their political allegiance to the United States, often embellishing or creating stories about how the players fought with the Cuban rebels against Spanish rule. It was hoped that this allegiance would take the edge off of the color issue.

43. Wilson, 24.

44. John Erardi, "Coming Home: Reds Open Stadium and a Native Son's Aboard the Titanic," *Cincinnati Enquirer*, April 8, 2012, F1.

45. Eric Enders, "Armando Marsans," SABR.org, http://sabr.org/bioproj/person/f2c0b939, last accessed June 2, 2016.

46. "National League Box Scores," *Cincinnati Enquirer*, July 5, 1911.

47. Jack Ryder, "The Morning Game," *Cincinnati Enquirer*, July 5, 1911. This may have in fact been part of the "whiteness campaign" because it did not promote them too much but it also was complimentary. However, I have found no direct evidence of this.

48. Wilson, 23–25. For more on Almeida and Marsans, see Wilson, 23–37.

49. Various sources listed his birthdate as January 2, 1885 or March 19, 1887. See "José Méndez," Baseball-Reference.com, http://www.baseball-reference.com/nonmlbpa/mendejo99.shtml, last accessed June 2, 2016 (lists birthdate as January 2, 1885); "José Méndez," BaseballHall.org, http://baseballhall.org/hof/mendez-jose, last accessed June 2, 2016 (lists birth year as 1885); John B. Holway, "Cuba's Black Diamond," SABR.org, http://research.sabr.org/journals/cubas-black-diamond, last accessed June 2, 2016 (lists birth year as 1887); "José Méndez," (assigned but not completed biography page) SABR.org, http://wwwdev.sabr.org/node/27084 (lists birthdate as March 19, 1887); and Wilson, 7 (lists birthdate as March 17, 1887).

50. Wilson, 7–9.

51. Barnstorming is when teams would travel to many other cities to play local opposition for long stretches of time, somewhat similar to the Harlem Globetrotters. The term also describes the way many American teams would play in Cuba, when they toured the country playing against local teams.

52. Wilson, 7, and "José Mendez," Negro Leagues Baseball Museum, nlbm.com, at http://coe.k-state.edu/annex/nlbemuseum/history/players/mendez.html, last accessed June 2, 2016.

53. Wilson, 7.

54. Cuban baseball players played a major role in blurring the color line in baseball. However, it would be failing the goal of due credit to not mention two other distinct groups of players who helped make racial integration in baseball possible. The first is the Negro Leaguers who suffered abuse across the country with barnstorming teams, whose names often included the word "Cuban" in an attempt to improve the treatment of the players. The second is Native American ballplayers, who suffered a cultural prejudice similar to that suffered by Cubans, but were

somewhat redeemed by their lighter skin and apparent willingness to "act" like white Americans. For more on the Negro Leagues, see Lanctot, note 4, and Leslie A. Heaphy, *The Negro Leagues: 1869–1960* (Jefferson, NC: McFarland & Co. 2003). For more on the Native American experience of integration into baseball, see Jeffrey Powers-Beck, "'Chief' The American Indian Integration of Baseball, 1897–1945," *The American Indian Quarterly*, v. 25, 508–38 (Fall 2001).

55. Wilson, 23.

56. J.C. Bradbury, *The Baseball Economist: The Real Game Exposed* (Plume: New York, 2008): 129.

57. Wilson, 8.

58. Wilson, 9. See also, "Caribbean Baseball Hall of Fame," Baseball-Reference.com, http://www.baseball-reference.com/bullpen/Caribbean_Baseball_Hall_of_Fame, last accessed June 2, 2016, and "2001 Ford C. Frick Award Winner Felo Ramírez," BaseballHall.org, http://baseballhall.org/discover/awards/ford-c-frick/felo-ramirez, last accessed June 2, 2016.

59. Wilson, 7, 9.

60. Wilson, 23–37.

61. Burgos, 141.

62. Reproduced in Wilson, 29.

63. Ibid.

64. Wilson, 29.

65. Adrian Burgos, Jr., "Book Reviews: Wilson, Nick C. Early Latino Ballplayers in the United States," *Journal of Sport History*, v. 32 (2005): 266–67.

66. Regalado, 3.

67. Cesar Lopez, "Adolfo Luque," Cubanball, http://www.cubanball.com/Images/Majors/MajorsHL/LuqueA/luquea.html and "Dolf Luque," Baseball-Reference.com, http://www.baseball-reference.com/players/l/luquedo01.shtml.

68. Regalado, 7.

69. Regalado, 3–4.

70. Regalado, 3.

71. Bob Considine, "Ivory from Cuba," *Collier's*, August 3, 1940: 24, 19. For full article see pages 19–24.

72. Ibid.

73. Ibid.

74. Ibid.

75. Neil Lanctot, *Negro League Baseball: The Rise and Ruin of a Black Institution* (Philadelphia, PA: University of Pennsylvania Press, 2004), 213.

76. "Armando Vazquez," Baseball-Reference.com, at http://www.baseball-reference.com/register/player.cgi?id=vazque000arm.

77. Adrian Burgos, "Making Cuban Stars: Alejandro Pompez and Latinos in Black Baseball," *Playing America's Game: Baseball, Latinos, and the Color Line* (Berkeley: University of California Press, 2007), 112–37.

78. Ibid.

79. Ibid.

80. Ibid.

81. Ibid, 137.

82. Jason A Pierce, "James Weldon Johnson, 1871–1938," Rare Books and Special Collections, University of South Carolina Libraries, http://www.sc.edu/library/spcoll/amlit/johnson/johnson.html.

83. Burgos, 137–8.

84. Jane Allen Quevedo, "Hi Bithorn," SABR.org, http://sabr.org/bioproj/person/0ebf1b32, last accessed June 1, 2016.

85. Ibid.

NAPBL Gathering in Miami Gave Birth to the Caribbean Series

Lou Hernández

The 46th National Association of Professional Baseball Leagues winter meeting took place in Miami during the first days of December 1947. The convention was held at the McAllister Hotel, located on the corner of East Flagler Street and Biscayne Boulevard in the heart of downtown. Upon its completion a quarter century earlier, the ten-story "ultra-modern high-rise" boasted 300 rooms, all with private baths.

Many of those rooms offered scenic views of Biscayne Bay, just a few hundred feet to the east. Guests in these pricier rooms could have witnessed from their balconies the assassination attempt of President-Elect Franklin Roosevelt in early 1933 after he delivered a speech at Bayfront Park, directly across the street from the McAllister. Only a few years before the NAPBL gathering, the hotel served as ritzy housing for wartime enlisted men in the US Navy. By this time, the McAllister had been expanded to 550 rooms with two additional wings.

The once-grand hotel would be razed in 1988, making room for a steel skyscraper, but that was still four decades away at the time more than 1,500 attendees—1,200 registered baseball delegates and 300 diamond officials and players—descended on Miami for the NABPL gathering. The sleepy southern town did not disappoint its Chamber of Commerce, with clear skies and balmy temperatures in the 70s throughout the representatives' days-long stay. "News stories filed with Western Union by the approximately 100 writers attending the sessions totaled a half million words," according to one estimate. "Besides press service, a non-profit service was established to record programs direct from the scene for rebroadcast."[1]

So what was the hot news that winter that generated so much copy? Baseball, on all its broad circuit levels, was booming, following its second prosperous season after World War II. But the growth was being achieved perhaps too rapidly, at least at the non-major league level. George Trautman, the president of the National Association, urged caution in an opening statement to the convention. "As of now the association with 54 leagues and 388 teams is a growing concern," said the minor league czar. "Our main job is not to seek additional leagues but to strengthen all of our existing leagues."[2]

One minor league in particular was seeking to better its station among its many peers. "The coast league is asking the right to be called the Pacific Coast Major League," alerted one communiqué, "[while] still remaining part of the minor league organization. However, it would be under the direct jurisdiction of Commissioner Happy Chandler and the major league executive council."[3] The PCL's petition to be recognized as a third major league, or "super minor circuit," did not receive the required voting support from its constituents for the self-aggrandizing proposal to pass. (Falling short of the required three-quarters majority, 32 of the 54 leagues voted in favor of the PCL's desire.)

A measure all leagues did come to an agreement on was the adopting of a uniform baseball throughout the minor leagues, beginning in 1949. Currently, the lower-circuit balls were said to be more lively than the balls used in the majors and therefore did not gauge a prospect's talent accurately.

The Philadelphia Phillies backed a (failed) amendment to eliminate the "bonus baby rule" less than a year

PHOTO BY W.A. FISHBAUGH. STATE ARCHIVES OF FLORIDA, FLORIDA MEMORY.

The famed McAllister Hotel in Miami, shown here in a photo dated 1927, was the site of the 1947 NAPBL winter meeting.

since its inception. "The Phillies had paid $55,000 for [pitcher] Curt Simmons," explained one source, "who cannot be farmed out unless every other club is offered a chance at his contract for $10,000."[4]

If the Internet had existed 70 years ago, without question, the biggest trending topic from the entire conference would have occurred on December 3. It would have involved the apparent pending resolution of suspended Brooklyn Dodgers manager Leo Durocher. Dodgers president Branch Rickey was holding talks with Commissioner Happy Chandler, who had suspended Durocher the preceding April for association with unsavory types detrimental to baseball. New York writer Roscoe McGowen captured the prevailing news sentiment with his filed story that day: "From Miami, Fla., where practically all of major league baseball are assembled to attend the minor league meetings, the sole topic of conversation yesterday was Rickey and Durocher, and there was considerable sentiment in favor of the return of the manager."[5] In only a few days, after the conclusion of the convention, Durocher would be reinstated by Chandler and allowed to take the reins of the NL champion Dodgers for the 1948 campaign.

Durocher would be overseeing a team that had been the first to champion integration in the sport in the previous season. The Dodgers had decided to train in Panama and Cuba to shield their pioneer black player, Jackie Robinson, in 1947. But with a new scheduling eye on more traditional spring training locales for 1948, the team and player must have been greatly heartened by another newspaper account from the Sunshine State: "An interesting development was information pointing unmistakably to a sharp revision of racial feelings against the Dodgers' Jackie Robinson in many sections of the Deep South and Southwest. No Florida town has offered to pull out the welcome mat for the Flock if Robinson appears in the lineup. Not only have the Dodgers been invited to play exhibitions in Georgia, Texas and Oklahoma, but each invitation has been accompanied by a special request that the Negro star appear in the lineup."[6]

Among the baseball executives and players in Miami were New York City's other two current baseball pilots, Bucky Harris of the New York Yankees and Mel Ott of the New York Giants. Both failed in their open attempts to land new players for their teams. A deal to secure Early Wynn and/or Walt Masterson from the Washington Nationals fell through on the Yankees skipper. Mel Ott struck out in trying to land Johnny Van der Meer from the Cincinnati Reds. Ott also turned down an offer from the Phillies for any one

Baseball Commissioner Happy Chandler, one of the many attendees to the 1947 conclave in Miami.

of their four starting pitchers in exchange for rookie hurler Clint Hartung.

Another manager with a New York affiliation came into town from the unusual southern direction. "Lefty Gomez, former southpaw ace of the Yankees who managed their Binghamton farm club last summer," identified one report, "flew in from Cuba, where he is managing Cienfuegos, a name he has difficulty in spelling. However, he had the translation for it, 'one hundred fires—and believe me, when we lose they build half of them right under my seat.'"[7]

Cienfuegos was one of the four teams of the Cuban Winter League that had joined Organized Baseball earlier in the calendar year as an "unclassified affiliate" of the National Association. That initiation—spurred from the fallout of the player war between OB and the Mexican League's Jorge Pasquel in 1946—turned out to be a historic one for international winter baseball, as this press release from the Magic City stated: "Prospects of a Pan-American World's Series among the champions of Panama, Puerto Rico, Venezuela and Cuba—details of which remained to be worked out—brightened as a result of conferences between representatives of those countries and the National Association here."[8]

The Sporting News went so far as to hail the agreement in its December 10, 1947, issue's editorial page:

At the minor leagues' convention in Miami last week, representatives of leagues in Venezuela, the Republic of Panama, and Puerto Rico expressed their intention of joining Cuba under the protective wing of the National Association, with the privileges which this will bring. Among these privileges are the right to use designated players from American minor leagues during the winter season, and a non-raiding agreement with other countries.

Much credit is due Trautman, the National Association, and Commissioner A.B. Chandler, for taking the initial steps toward closer relations between the game in this country and our Latin American neighbors.

Eventually, perhaps, the majors might even establish farm clubs in Latin American leagues and uncover future big-time prospects among native talent.[9]

Four months later in Havana, on April 12, 1948, an accord was created between officials from Cuba, Panama, and Puerto Rico, to establish La Confederación de Baseball Profesional del Caribe, with an initiative for a fourth country, Venezuela, to join, which the country shortly thereafter accepted. The Caribbean Professional Baseball Federation, comprising the Latin American Winter Leagues, created the original plans for the Caribbean Series, to take place at the close of the following winter season.

The new Latin American baseball championship tournament was realized with the inauguration of the first Serie del Caribe on February 20, 1949. Held at Gran Stadium del Cerro de la Habana, the double-round-robin competition showcased championship teams from four Caribbean basin winter league nations. The opening ceremonies featured players from all the teams filing out toward the center field flagpole to raise their own country's colors. Walter Mulbry, representing Commissioner Chandler's office, hoisted the flag of the Confederación del Caribe to punctuate the history-making occasion. George Trautman threw the ceremonial first pitch.

Pitcher Pat Scantlebury recorded the first win in Caribbean Series history, a 13–9 victory over Puerto Rico's Mayagüez Indios, in the first of two games played on that date. The Canal Zone native, pitching the distance for the Spur Cola Colonites, benefited from strong run support in throwing the 16-hit triumph. (The contest, apparently running long, was purposely shortened to eight innings, so as not to interfere with the start time of the second game of the evening.) In the nightcap, Dalmiro Finol of Cervecería Caracas, slugged the initial Caribbean Series home run. The Venezuelan's blast accounted for the only run for his Andean team, which was embarrassed 16–1 by the Almendares Scorpions of Cuba. Conrado "Connie" Marrero cruised to the four-hit win.

Marrero's Almendares club went on to win the first tournament with an undefeated 6–0 record. Scorpions left fielder Al Gionfriddo became the first person to

The Phillies hoped in vain to have the "bonus baby" rule lifted so they could offer pitcher Curt Simmons (pictured here) to other teams for more than the required $10,000.

play in a World Series and Caribbean Series and hit for the highest average in the competition: .533 (8 for 15). Outfield mate Monte Irvin led all hitters with 11 RBIs. Marrero's pitching cohort, Agapito Mayor, was named first MVP of the Series. The left-handed Mayor won three games, including two in relief.

George Trautman proclaimed the tournament a success although not one of the six day's cards produced a sellout, and the overall attendance remained lower than expected. Part of his closing statement read:

The first Caribbean series will be remembered for many years to come as the realization of the dream of baseball leaders of Cuba, Panama, Puerto Rico, and Venezuela. The 1949 series has proven the possibility of using the game's good neighbor policy to tighten friendship ties.

Cuba can consider itself proud of the work it has done in this series. The new Havana Stadium is one of the best baseball parks in the world. The four contenders of the first Caribbean series have been true contenders and have been guided by excellent sportsmanship.[10]

Teams from Cuba won seven out of the first twelve Caribbean Classics played. (Each country alternated hosting the games.) Talented squads from Puerto Rico took home the championship trophy four times, including 1955, with its native club featuring 23-year-old Willie Mays. Panama City's Carta Vieja Yankees captured the Caribbean crown in 1950. Following the 1960 competition, the tournament was interrupted. Cuban dictator Fidel Castro abolished all professional sports on the island and expropriated hundreds of millions of dollars in US and Cuban citizens' property. Included in the totalitarian usurpation was Gran Stadium, which was the first million-dollar baseball stadium erected in Latin America and had been built by Cuban

NATIONAL BASEBALL HALL OF FAME LIBRARY, COOPERSTOWN, NY

The fate of Leo Durocher was a hot topic in Miami and he was reinstated a few days after the end of the meeting.

businessmen Miguelito Suárez Jr. and Bobby Maduro. The stadium, renamed "Latinoamericano," is still considered the main baseball venue in Cuba today.

After a ten-year absence, the Caribbean Series was revived in February of 1970. Original members Puerto Rico and Venezuela were joined by a new national associate from the Dominican Republic. Played in Caracas, the Magallanes Navegantes, the home nation's team, delighted the faithful by capturing Venezuela's first Caribbean Series championship with a 7–1 record.

In 1971, Mexico's Naranjeros of Hermosillo joined the other national squads as a fourth representative, returning the tournament to its original 24-game, double-round-robin format. Five championship series later, in 1976, Hermosillo brought back the first Caribbean Series title to Mexico, posting a 5–1 record. Superstar slugger Héctor Espino was selected the tournament's MVP.

In 1990 and 1991, the Series was ceded to Miami. It was played in the Orange Bowl in the former year and Bobby Maduro Stadium the next. Neither showcases financially warranted playing another in the US.

The Latin American baseball championship tournament progressed as an annual event into the twenty-first century. The exception was 1981, when the Caribbean Series did not materialize due to an owners and players' dispute over the distribution of gate proceeds and meal money.

The 56th edition of the Caribbean Series, held on the isle of Margarita in Venezuela, opened the way for the reintegration of a Cuban national team. In 2014, with US State Department pre-approval, Cuba's Villa Clara Naranjas appeared in the reformatted five-team competition, where there are two rounds of play and the team with the best record is not guaranteed the championship hardware.

The 2016 Caribbean Series was held at Estadio Quisqueya, the Dominican winter home of the Licey Tigers—the team that has won the most Caribbean

Series championships with ten. Juan Marichal threw out the ceremonial first pitch. The former great pitcher was bestowed with an honorary recognition by the tournament. "When you think about all that he has done for baseball and the Dominican Republic, we wanted to dedicate this great event to Mr. Marichal," Caribbean Confederation commissioner Juan Francisco Puello Herrera said on the eve of the event. "He has brought so much pride to the country on so many levels. Every host country has the option to dedicate the tournament, and Marichal was an excellent choice to represent the Dominican Republic."[11]

Mexican representative Venados de Mazatlán (the Mazatlán Deer) won the 2016 Series in the most dramatic fashion. In the championship game versus Venezuela's Aragua Tigers, February 7, Mazatlán's DH Jorge Vásquez smacked a leadoff, walk-off home run in the bottom of the ninth inning to lift the team to a thrilling 5-4 championship victory. The win gave the Venados a perfect 6–0 mark in the seven-day competition and conferred the fourth Caribbean Series crown in six years to a Mexican squad. ∎

Sources

Buddy Nevins. "The End Of An Era." *Sun Sentinel*, January 6, 1988.

Monte Cely. Serie del Caribe 2016 in Santo Domingo. Society for American Baseball Research.

"The McAlister Was City's First High-Rise." Miami Archives

The Caribbean Series. Baseball-Reference.com.

Notes

1. "1,200 Register For The Convention." *The Sporting News*, December 10, 1947, 5.
2. "Minors Are Urged Not to Expand, But to Bolster Existing Leagues." *The New York Times*, December 2, 1947, 41.
3. AP. "Baseball Moguls Opening Annual Meeting in Miami." *The Post-Standard*, December 1, 1947, 10.
4. Ibid.
5. Roscoe McGowen. "Rickey Talks With Chandler, Naming of Dodger Pilot Near." *The New York Times*, December 4, 1947, 48.
6. John Drebinger. "International League Provisionally Approves Coast's Quest of Major League Status." *The New York Times*, December 2, 1947, 41.
7. Roscoe McGowen. "Rickey Talks With Chandler, Naming of Dodger Pilot Near." *The New York Times*, December 4, 1947, 48.
8. Edgar G. Brands. "Latin American Nations Flock to O.B. Banner." *The Sporting News*, December 10, 1947, 7. The idea for the Caribbean Series was originated by Venezuelan promoters Oscar "El Negro" Prieto and Pablo Morales, according to contemporary reports circulated by Wikipedia and Baseball-Reference.com. The author was unable to find any specific, dated information to corroborate this. Both Internet sources mentioned appear to have confused the NAPBL meeting in Miami in 1947 with the Caribbean Professional Baseball Federation's establishment in Havana, four months later.
9. "Majors Can Aid Latin American Unity." *The Sporting News*, December 10, 1947, 12.
10. Pedro Galiana. " '50 Caribbean Series to Puerto Rico; Bigger Split Arranged For Players." *The Sporting News*, March 9, 1949, 28.
11. Jesse Sánchez. "Caribbean Series begins Monday with balanced field." MLB.com, January 29, 2016.

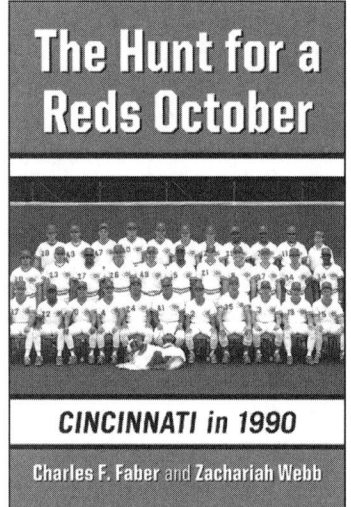
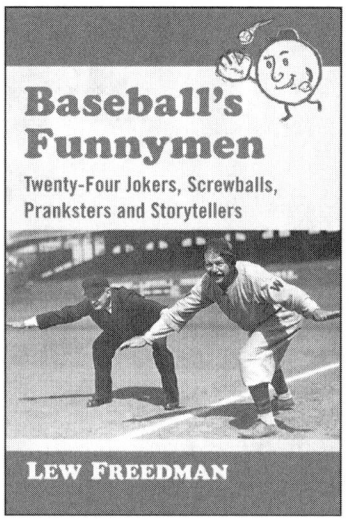
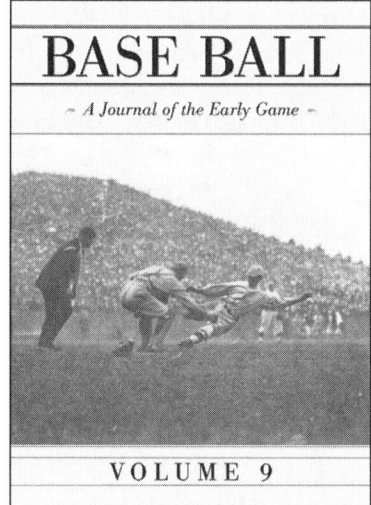

The Long Forgotten Florida International League

Steve Smith

The Florida International League (FIL) existed but a brief eight and one-half years, folding in the middle of its ninth season. During those years countless exciting games were played by some of baseball's most recognizable cast of characters. The league served as the catalyst for Havana's entry into Organized Baseball. *The Sporting News* (TSN) once said the FIL is a league "where bizarre incidents come with startling frequency."[1]

THE BIRTH OF THE FLORIDA INTERNATIONAL LEAGUE

The onset of World War II saw the slow demise of many minor league teams as well as entire leagues due to wartime restrictions, focus on the war effort, and the shortage of players. At the end of the 1945 season, there were only twelve minor leagues in existence.[2] The end of the war saw the revival of minor league baseball. Forty-three minor leagues opened for business in 1946, including the FIL.[3] Shortly after the war's end, two managers from the defunct Florida East Coast League— former major leaguers Max Rosenfeld and Herb Thomas—began steps to organize a new league.[4] In addition, Cuban-born Merito Acosta, a former outfielder for the Washington Nationals and the Philadelphia Athletics, lobbied for a team from Havana to enter Organized Baseball. However, at this time Cuba was not under the jurisdiction of the National Association, the umbrella organization for minor-league baseball.

The FIL's first season included five Florida teams— Miami, Miami Beach, West Palm Beach, Tampa, and Lakeland—and Havana. Havana was the key to the league. With over one million people, its population was bigger than the other five cities combined.[5] But its presence would also cause disagreement and dissension, thanks to the built-in rivalries with Miami and Tampa and their large Cuban populations. The league would initially operate as a Class C league.

The FIL was deemed qualified by the National Association on December 6, 1945.[6] The league had previously been denied admission by President W. G. Branham and the executive committee because of a general policy of not admitting any Cuban or Mexican city. In reversing its position, the committee issued a statement saying that:

> Havana be given permission to enter the National Association for the purpose of playing professional baseball in Havana, Cuba, under the rules and regulations of the National Association on strict probation, from month to month, until they have satisfied the membership of the National Association that they are operating and working under said rules.[7]

Only three of the teams had major league connections: Havana with the Washington Nationals, the Miami Beach Flamingos with the Boston Braves, and the Miami Sun Sox with the St. Louis Browns.[8] The other three teams operated as independents. The league would expand to eight teams in 1947 with the addition of St. Petersburg and Ft. Lauderdale. In 1949, the league became Class B.

The league hired six umpires for the 1946 season with two being Cuban.[9] The teams had a monthly salary limit of $2,200 (which was largely ignored by everyone). Furthermore, each team could only have three veterans (players with three or more years of experience) and four limited players (less than three years of experience). The balance of the roster would be players new to professional baseball.[10] These requirements were to cause trouble for Havana.

Havana was important to the league because of its potential for profits. Not only was it the largest city in the league, it had the largest stadium. La Tropical Stadium had a seating capacity of 18,000, but could hold crowds up to 30,000.[11] Installed in the stadium for the 1946 season was a 420,000-watt lighting plant for the first night games in Cuban history. All of the Cubans' games were to be played under the lights.[12]

From the league's inception, Havana was given special consideration. Due to the added costs to travel to Havana, the league constitution contained special financial provisions for the Cubans. Article VII (a) provided that the gate receipts of all games would be retained by the home team. Article VII (b) however provided that, "In all games between Havana and the other five clubs of the league, Havana agrees to pay other visiting clubs 25 per cent of the gate receipts, or a guarantee of all expenses for 17 men to and from Havana and 10 per cent of the gate receipts whichever amount is greater."

The FIL became the first league to use air transportation on a regular basis. The league office entered into an agreement with Pan American Airways for charter service to Havana from Miami and Tampa.[13] Clark Griffith, however, wasn't taking any chances. His Washington team was scheduled to play several exhibition games in Havana in 1946 and he announced that his players would make the trip in groups on several small planes.[14]

April 17 was opening day for the FIL. The Miami Beach Flamingos opened the season at Havana before a crowd of 17,000, which was billed as Havana's largest crowd ever for a night game.[15] Bill Klem, a winter resident of Miami Beach, was the honorary umpire for the first game.[16] Herbert A. Frink, mayor of Miami Beach, raised the American flag and Francisco Batista, mayor of Marianao, raised the Cuban flag.[17] Rafael Rivas threw the first pitch to Norm Olsen of the Flamingos to the delight of the Cuban fans. Havana got off to a 5–0 lead after five innings before giving up three runs in the sixth. The Cubans held on to win 5–4 with Rivas striking out two of the final three batters.

On April 24, Havana played its first game in the United States winning 12–4 at Miami Beach. The mayor of Miami Beach had extended an invitation to Cuban president Ramon Grau San Martin to attend the game. He declined. The game however was attended by Fulgencio Batista, the former president and future dictator of Cuba.[18]

THE HAVANA PROBLEM
The league was a success from the beginning. Havana drew over 200,000 for the season, which not only was the second largest for any Class C team but also greater than any Class A or B team.[19]

From the beginning, Havana dominated the league. Playing with all Cuban players, many of whom were veterans of the Cuban winter leagues, the Cubans won the 1946 regular season championship with a 76–41 record, while winning their first 19 games of the season. However, Havana was upset in the first round of the playoffs by West Palm Beach and the playoff championship was won by Tampa, who was named league champion.

Havana fans were incensed. *TSN* described the situation:

The 1946 season was a stormy one and resulted in something new being written into baseball history. The league started playing a 140 game split season. Havana got so far in front that the directors, in a hot session, voted to replace the split season playoff with the Shaughnessy playoff. In their argument, they forgot to designate the means of picking a champion and Havana, first half winner, was beaten in the Shaughnessy.[20]

The season was not without more controversy. Because of the 19-game winning streak, an investigation was initiated and it was determined that Havana had too many veteran players on its roster. The team was required to forfeit 17 games, but still finished the season with the best record.[21]

The following season, three of Havana's players—Rafael Rivas, Limonar Martinez, and Mario Diaz—were signed by the Brooklyn Dodgers and assigned to Triple-A Montreal.[22] The players complained they were receiving less money in Montreal than in Havana. An investigation determined that Havana had paid the players under the table. The Havana team was fined $500 and the players returned to Havana.[23]

Havana had the league's best record for the next four seasons although they lost in the playoffs in 1949 and 1950. That would be the end of the reign for Havana. *TSN* shed light on the "Havana problem":

For four years the Class B Florida International League has been discussing the dominance of the Havana Cubans but indications now are something may be done about it. The Cubans only offense is winning the pennant for the first four years of the league and threatening to make it five in a row.[24]

The article reported that the league president had formed a committee to explore the problem. One solution that was not on the table was expulsion from the league. The league constitution stated that only unanimous consent of the owners could provide that result. Even though most owners were in favor of kicking the Cubans out, owner Tom Spicola of Tampa publicly stated that he would not vote for it.[25]

TSN reported:

Many of the Florida International League clubs would like to get rid of Havana in the league but since they are unable to oust the club, they plan to dig up some Cuban players to more or less fight fire with fire. The latter are not subject to military draft and the clubs which face loss of talent regard the Cubans as a backstop for these losses.[26]

TSN had previously reported that some of the FIL clubs winked at the monthly salary limits in an effort to build better teams to catch Havana.[27] Long time FIL player Bitsy Mott said, "I played for Tampa in 1946, 1947, and 1948. Because of all the under the table money that was coming in we were able to attract some real good ballplayers."[28]

In the winter of 1950–51, Havana business manager Joe Cambria broke up the Cubans. *TSN* reported:

Cambria did such a good job that Havana currently occupies fourth place after spending the early part of the 1951 season in the second division. Havana, once the Class B loop's biggest attendance city, has suffered proportionately at the gate and the blame for this is being leveled at Cambria.[29]

The Cubans fell to mediocre records for the next three years. League attendance fell as well going from 900,000 in 1949 to 277,000 in 1953.[30] Former major leaguer and FIL player Roger McKee confirmed the "Havana problem":

In those years I think the FIL was possibly the best "B" league in the country. I also think the Havana teams could have been in triple "A" leagues and had winning records. Some of their pitchers would pitch in the FIL one week and the next week be in Washington winning in the major leagues.[31]

A PITCHER'S LEAGUE

The FIL was a pitcher's league from its inception. Native Cuban Conrado "Connie" Marrero may have been the best. Marrero pitched three years in the FIL (1947–49) compiling a record of 70-25 with ERAs of 1.66, 1.67, and 1.53. In 1950, at the age of 39, Marrero went to the Washington Nationals directly from the FIL and became a staple of the Nationals pitching staff from 1950 to 1954, making the All-Star team in 1951. Other Havana pitchers who went directly from Havana to the majors were Miguel "Mike" Fornieles, Camilo Pascual, Sandalio "Sandy" Consuegra, Raul Sanchez, and Julio Moreno.

Chet Covington, a major leaguer with the Phillies in 1944, played all or parts of eight seasons in the FIL with four different teams. He compiled a 79–38 record in the FIL with a season best 28-8 in 1946.[32]

Charlie Cuellar, who had a mid-season cup of coffee with the White Sox in 1950, pitched seven years in the FIL compiling a record of 78-47 with four teams including a controversial no-hitter in 1947.[33] (Allegedly, the final batter purposely struck out to preserve the no-no.)[34]

Maybe the greatest individual season was put up by Billy Harris. He compiled a 25–6 record with an ERA of 0.83 in 294 innings with Miami in 1952. Harris went on to have two cups of coffee with the Dodgers, pitching one game in each of the 1957 and 1959 seasons.

Roger McKee stated, "I thought the pitching in the league was outstanding, especially with the Havana and Miami teams."[35] Theories for the dominance of pitching included perpetually rain soaked fields (summer is the rainy season in Florida), low altitude, and large ballparks.

INTEGRATION

Paul Waner was named manager of the Miami Sun Sox in 1946, when he publicly declared that he wanted the bias against Negroes erased forever. Only he was talking about fans not players. "I don't care if I have to build 'em and pay for 'em myself, but I'm going to have special stands built here for them. They are Americans and baseball is an American game. It'll be a tough fight, but I'll see it through."[36] Waner had apparently gotten upset when he learned that Negroes had never been allowed in some minor league parks in Florida. The separate treatment of Negro fans was set forth in the league constitution which set the admission price for white male adults at \$.62 for all Florida teams while the admission price for "ladies, children, and colored people" could be set by each club.[37]

The league was not integrated until 1952. *TSN* reported in February 1952 that teams planned to use black players for the upcoming season. Joe Cambria of Havana planned to use 36-year-old Silvio Garcia, a longtime winter leagues player and formerly of the Cuban Stars in the Negro Leagues. Havana also planned to use Angel Scull, a speedster who ultimately went to spring training with the Nationals but never played a game in the majors. Miami Beach drafted second baseman George Handy, a former Negro Leagues player, from St. Hyacinthe of the Provincial League and signed veteran Negro Leagues pitcher Dave Barnhill. Tampa acquired former Negro Leaguer Claro Duany. *TSN* also reported that if these teams used Negro players then Miami Sun Sox owner Harry Taber would ask the Brooklyn Dodgers "to provide them with a Negro or two." Portending the future, *TSN* stated "Addition of

Connie Marrero

Mike Fornieles

Camilio Pascual

Sandy Consuegra

Paul Waner was the first ex-major leaguer to join the league, being hired in 1946 as manager of the Miami Sun Sox. Waner was fired at the end of the season because he didn't "get out and hustle" and he didn't develop players to sell to higher leagues.[43] Jimmie Foxx was named manager of St. Petersburg for 1947. He lasted only a couple of months on the job. Former major leaguers Tony Cuccinello, Travis Jackson, Wes Ferrell, and Ben Chapman managed Tampa in 1947, 1949, and 1951. Joe Medwick managed Miami Beach in 1949 and Tampa in 1952.

The fiery Pepper Martin took the helm of Miami 1949–51 before moving to Miami Beach in 1952, Fort Lauderdale in 1953, and back to Miami Beach in 1954. In 1949, he attacked an umpire and was suspended for the remainder of the season.[44] In 1950, he left the team when fans booed him but returned the following night.[45] In 1951, he attacked a fan in Lakeland and was fined $25 by the league.[46]

Oscar Rodriguez, a career minor leaguer, managed the Cubans to five pennants in five years and was succeeded by former major leaguers Dolph Luque in 1951, Mike Guerra in 1952, and Armando Marsans in 1953.

In addition to the aforementioned Covington and McKee, many former major-league players were attracted to the league. Former Tiger Ned Harris played three years for West Palm Beach. Former Dodger, Phillie, and Boston Brave Stan Andrews played five years in the FIL for three different teams. Chile Gomez, Luis Suarez, Jose Zardon, Gil Torres, Jorge Comellas, Izzy Leon, Bobby Estalella, and Sandy Ullrich were among the ex-major leaguers to suit up for Havana.

Negros to the rosters of any (FIL) teams would pose only minor problems concerning housing and eating. Under local customs they would not be permitted to stay at the same hotels with their teams."[38] It would be 1961 before St. Louis Cardinal players protested this custom, finally receiving integrated facilities in 1962.[39]

In April 1952, *TSN* reported:

The color line in the Florida International League, southernmost of all loops in Organized Ball, has been quietly lifted, according to a survey conducted by the *St. Petersburg Times*…Of the eight clubs queried on their attitude toward Negroes playing in the circuit, seven said they had no objection while Lakeland replied "No comment."[40]

THE ALLURE OF FLORIDA

Bill Beck of the *St. Petersburg Times* once called the FIL, "a home for ballplayers who played baseball elsewhere and came here to rest."[41] For many reasons, most notably its location, the league attracted a number of former major leaguers. *TSN* noted, "Players of the loop stop at hotels much better than those used in many higher leagues. They occupy rooms for $3 during the summer season which in the winter months cost free-spending tourists five times that amount."[42]

THE DEATH OF THE FLORIDA INTERNATIONAL LEAGUE

The 1952 season provided the final thrills for the FIL in a fantastic pennant race that saw Miami edge Miami Beach by one game. The difference was a game in early August when Miami Beach beat Miami 5–2. However, Miami protested the game alleging that Miami Beach used an ineligible player, infielder Knobby Rosa, who had been suspended for insubordination. The protest centered on Rosa's return from the suspended list. The league rules stated that for a player to be eligible, the league office must be informed prior to game time. The league president ruled that a wire sent to the league office did not arrive until 47 minutes after the game had begun, thus the game was forfeited to Miami. Miami Beach argued that the wire was sent in good faith, however it was to no avail and an exciting pennant race was decided in the league office rather than on the field.[47]

By 1953 the league had been reduced to six teams as minor-league attendance began to decline. The 1953 season was the first in which at least one FIL team failed to draw 100,000 fans. Havana drew only 23,000 for the season.

The FIL opened the 1954 season without Havana, which had been granted a Triple-A franchise largely because of its success in the FIL. Miami and Tampa folded on May 5 leaving only four teams. The league ceased operations on July 27, 1954, and the Florida International League passed into the annals of history. ■

Notes

1. Jimmy Burns, "Beach Flaps Wings on a Loss by a Forfeit," *The Sporting News*, August 27, 1952.
2. Lloyd Johnson and Miles Wolff, Eds., *Encyclopedia of Minor League Baseball, Third Edition* (Durham, NC: Baseball America).
3. Lloyd Johnson and Miles Wolff, Eds., *Encyclopedia of Minor League Baseball, Third Edition* (Durham, NC: Baseball America).
4. The Florida International League is often considered to be a loose revival of the defunct Florida East Coast League which had ceased operations in 1942. The Florida East Coast League contained four Miami area teams (Miami, Miami Beach, West Palm Beach and Fort Lauderdale) and four Orlando area teams (Orlando, Deland, Fort Pierce, and Cocoa).
5. The population of Havana was over one million people in 1950. According to the 1950 census the population of the other league cities was: Miami 249,276, Tampa 124,681, Miami Beach 46,282, West Palm Beach 43,162, Lakeland 30,851.
6. *The Sporting News*, December 13, 1945, 7.
7. Ibid.
8. John Phillips, *A Short History of the Florida International League* (Kathleen, GA: John Phillips, 2003), 2.
9. Unpublished paper, Howard Garson, date unknown.
10. *Constitution and By-Laws*, Florida International League, 1946, Article X.
11. Pedro Galiana, "Havana Will Install Lights for Debut in Organized Ball," *The Sporting News*, February 7, 1946, 6.
12. Ibid.
13. "Consider Flights to Havana," *The Sporting News*, March 28, 1946.
14. *The Sporting News*, February 28, 1946, 15.
15. John Phillips, *A Short History of the Florida International League*, (Kathleen, GA: John Phillips, 2003), 3.
16. Unpublished paper, Howard Garson, date unknown. Klem also umpired the opening game in Tampa.
17. John Phillips, *A Short History of the Florida International League* (Kathleen, GA: John Phillips, 2003), 3.
18. Unpublished paper, Howard Garson, date unknown.
19. Lloyd Johnson and Miles Wolff, Eds., *Encyclopedia of Minor League Baseball, Third Edition* (Durham, NC: Baseball America). We do not have attendance totals for all minor leagues, but based on those we do know, Salt Lake City, in the class C Pioneer League, drew 205,861 fans—about 3,000 more than Havana.
20. Jimmy Burns, "Florida Int. Host to Convention, Has Troubles and Growing Pains," *The Sporting News*, December 6, 1950.
21. The penalty removed 17 wins from the team's record but did not add 17 losses, or Havana would have finished second.
22. Martinez may have played too few games to be identified in the Baseball Guide but he was mentioned in 1946 news accounts. In 1947 he was with Havana.
23. "Allen Opens Investigation of Cuban Club," *St. Petersburg Times*, August 4, 1947.
24. Jimmy Burns, "Fla. Int. Prepares to Act on Havana," *The Sporting News*, August 2, 1950.
25. Ibid.
26. Jimmy Burns, "Miami Beach Flamingos in New Hands," *The Sporting News*, January 17, 1951.
27. The Sporting News, August 2, 1950.
28. Wes Singletary, *Florida's First Big League Baseball Players* (Charleston, SC: History Press, 2006), 102.
29. "Cubans' Success with Nats Bring Protests in Havana," *The Sporting News*, July 18, 1951.
30. Lloyd Johnson and Miles Wolff, Eds., *Encyclopedia of Minor League Baseball, Third Edition* (Durham NC: Baseball America).
31. Personal correspondence to the author from Roger McKee, September 25, 2007. McKee is sometimes referred to by his birth name, Rogers, though he ceased including the "s."
32. Baseball-Reference.com.
33. Baseball-Reference.com.
34. Wes Singletary, *Florida's First Big League Baseball Players* (Charleston, SC: History Press, 2006), 102.
35. Personal correspondence to the author from Roger McKee, September 25, 2007.
36. "Paul Waner to Fight Race Discrimination in the South," *The Sporting News*, March 21, 1946.
37. *Constitution and By-Laws*, Florida International League, 1946, Article VIII.
38. Jimmy Burns, "Three Fla. Int. Clubs May Use Negro Players, *The Sporting News*, February 6, 1952.
39. Bill Lucey, "When Hope Didn't Spring Eternal for Black Baseball Players in Florida," The National Pastime Museum, March 1, 2015.
40. Charlie Johnson, "Florida International Loop Okays Use of Negro Players," *The Sporting News*, April 2, 1952.
41. Bill Beck, "Time for Sports," *St. Petersburg Times*, April 18, 1953.
42. *The Sporting News*, December 6, 1950.
43. "Miami Sun Sox Fire Waner, *Spartanburg Herald-Journal*, October 18, 1946.
44. "Replacement Sought for Pepper Martin," *Prescott Evening Courier*, November 15, 1951.
45. Ibid.
46. Ibid.
47. Jimmy Burns, "Beach Flaps Wings on a Loss by a Forfeit," *The Sporting News*, August 27, 1952.

The Short but Exciting Life of the Havana Sugar Kings

John R. Harris and John J. Burbridge Jr.

The Havana Sugar Kings played in the International League between 1954 and 1960. It was a short existence, but a memorable one. The Sugar Kings began with hopes of a major league franchise, experienced a shooting during a home game and a political revolution, won the International League's Governor's Cup and the Junior World Series, and ended their stay in Havana with a one-way trip to Jersey City.

ORIGINS OF CUBAN BASEBALL

Baseball is Cuba's national pastime. Many would attribute its origins as such to a game played on Sunday, December 27, 1874, between Matanzas and the visiting Habana Baseball Club at Palma del Junco in Matanzas with the Habana team winning 51–9.[1] The Matanzas team was composed of the crew from an American ship forced to dock in the Matanzas harbor. However, if this was the first game, how did the Habana Baseball Club originate?

While attending college at Spring Hill University in Mobile, Alabama, Nemesio Guilló, his brother Ernesto, and Enrique Porto were introduced to baseball. They returned to Cuba in 1864 desiring to bring the game to Cuba and started the Habana Baseball Club in 1868.[2]

THE GOLDEN AGE

The period between the Spanish American War and the early 1930s has been called the Golden Age for both Cuba and Cuban baseball.[3] As Cuba advanced both culturally and economically, baseball flourished at four different levels. First there was the professional game with the winter Cuban League dominating the scene. The second level was semipro baseball with teams sponsored by companies and open to all including Negro players. The third was probably the most intriguing, sugarmill baseball. Obviously, this was tied to the sugar industry with teams representing the various mills throughout the island. Finally, there was amateur baseball played by clubs many of which were in Havana. These were the descendants of the Habana Baseball Club.

Several notable Cuban players did join major league teams during this era. The most significant of these players was Adolfo Luque who pitched for the Cincinnati Reds from 1918 until 1929, and other teams in a career that spanned 1914–35. Luque's record would include 194 major league wins.[4]

Another player of note was Mike Gonzalez who played for several major league teams between 1912 and 1932 and became a coach with the St. Louis Cardinals in 1934. Gonzalez was named manager of the Cardinals in 1938 when Frankie Frisch was fired. Gonzalez thus became the first Cuban manager in the major leagues.[5]

THE HAVANA CUBANS

While American players, mainly from the Negro Leagues, played in Cuba, it wasn't until 1946 that a Cuban team had a presence in what Americans would call Organized Baseball. From 1946 until 1953 the Havana Cubans were in the Florida International League. Joe Cambria, a popular figure in Cuban baseball and a Washington Nationals scout who had signed Cuban players for the major leagues, organized this team and was able to affiliate them with the Washington Nationals. From 1946 to 1950, the Cubans were very successful, finishing first in the standings in each of the years and winning the league championship twice.[6] However, from 1951 until 1953, the Cubans struggled on the field and change was forthcoming.

ROBERTO (BOBBY) MADURO

On May 4, 1953, Bobby Maduro became the majority owner of the Cubans. Maduro had high aspirations. During the 1950s major league baseball franchises were relocating as evident by the Boston Braves moving to Milwaukee, the St. Louis Browns to Baltimore, and the Dodgers and Giants going to the West Coast. Bobby Maduro envisioned the possibility of a major league franchise in Havana.

In moving forward with such aspirations, Maduro obtained the rights for the Springfield, Massachusetts, franchise in the IL and got approval to move them to Havana at the end of the 1953 season. The new name of the team was the Havana Sugar Kings. With an IL

Bobby Maduro

franchise, Havana now had a team one level below the major leagues. Maduro was the owner of the Sugar Kings during their entire stay in Havana.

THE HAVANA SUGAR KINGS

With the change in ownership, the association with the Washington Nationals. also ended. The Sugar Kings became affiliated with the Cincinnati Redlegs which was appropriate given that the most prominent Cuban player in the major leagues, Luque, played with them. Maduro's dream was to have the Sugar Kings become the epicenter of Latino baseball with players from throughout Latin America.[7] In 1954 approximately 50% of the Sugar Kings roster was composed of Latino players with the remainder being Americans such as Clint Hartung and Johnny Lipon.[8]

The Sugar Kings, managed by Reggie Otero, finished fifth in that inaugural year but finished third in 1955 and made the playoffs. Unfortunately, the team lost to second-place Toronto in the first round. 1956 through 1958 were disappointing as the team finished in sixth, sixth, and eighth place in those respective years. In 1956 Otero was replaced as manager by Napoleon (Nap) Reyes.

The team also struggled at the gate. In 1954, 295,453 fans attended their home games, averaging approximately 4,000 per game. Given their successful playoff run in 1955, the total attendance increased to 313,232. Attendance declined from 1956 to 1958, with 1957 being the low point with an average attendance of slightly more than 1,000.[9]

Possibly, Cuban baseball fans were not used to baseball during the summer given that the traditional Cuban League games were in the winter. In addition, the caliber of play may have been below what the Cuban fans were used to. While the players were high-level minor leaguers, the Cuban League playing during the winter months attracted major league players. Finally, although the Sugar Kings attracted many Latino players, the Cincinnati farm team was still subject to decision-making concerning player personnel at the major league level.

REVOLUTION

After seven years of insurrection, the Batista government collapsed on January 1, 1959. Fidel Castro, a key leader of the insurgents, quickly became Prime Minis-

ter on February 16, 1959.[10] Despite continued American investment and some optimism for an economic relationship between the two countries, distrust and political maneuverings pushed the two governments apart.[11] The Havana Sugar Kings were now at the nexus between two governments. They quickly became the anointed team of a new Cuban nationalism fronted by a leader who loved the sport.

Bobby Maduro met with Castro in April 1959 and was guaranteed the team a permanent home in Havana and given permission for plans for an eventual major league franchise.[12] The Castro government also organized an injection of up to $70,000 to the franchise to bolster its sagging revenues.[13] Some of that money came from the Cuban Sugar Stabilization Institute.[14]

IMPROVING TEAM

While Cuba was in the midst of political turmoil, the 1959 Sugar Kings were showing the results of a rebuilding process on the field. Younger Cuban players were replacing older favorites and Preston Gómez had been hired to manage. Of the Cuban players, future major leaguers Tony González, Leo Cárdenas, and Cookie Rojas stood out, as did Venezuelan Elio Chacón, and Americans Jesse Gonder, Larry Novak, and Ted Wieand. Given this improvement and the new political atmosphere, attendance increased in 1959.

However, 1959 also saw growing unease by certain American players and International League team owners. American players were still well received and no particular hostility was displayed but the presence of armed revolutionaries, often at the field, was somewhat ominous.[15] However, from a Cuban perspective, journalist Fausto Miranda noted "how different from the baseball with fans being frisked at the gates, or the

Mike Cuellar—Miguel Ángel Cuellar Santana—went on to pitch 15 seasons in the major leagues, including a Cy Young award in 1969 with the Baltimore Orioles.

afternoon when the students were clubbed on this very field"[16] as had occurred recently under the Batista regime.

26TH OF JULY

Incidents at midseason reinforced these perspectives concerning the atmosphere surrounding the games. With the Rochester Red Wings in town for a weekend series, Cubans were preparing to celebrate the anniversary of the attack on the Moncada barracks, which took place on July 26, 1953, and marked the beginning of Castro's insurrection. To begin the weekend, a two-inning exhibition game was planned prior to the Friday night game. With obvious political symbolism, a team of revolutionary leaders called "The Bearded Ones" (Los Barbudos), which included Camilo Cienfuegos at shortstop and Castro on the mound, played a team composed of military police. While the game was sheer entertainment and is recalled as a high point of the weekend's activities, it demonstrates the strength of theatricality and baseball in Cuban political life.

The next night's contest heightened concern about the Havana franchise. With the game running late, the stroke of midnight heralded the beginning of the 26th of July anniversary with riotous cheers and celebratory gunfire erupting from in and around the stadium. Rochester player/coach Frank Verdi was stuck by a falling bullet on the padding-lined hat he was smart

NATIONAL BASEBALL HALL OF FAME LIBRARY, COOPERSTOWN, NY

Elio Chacón Rodríguez was from Venezuela and was initially signed by Cincinnati in 1956 as a free agent, but did not make the majors until 1960. While with the Mets in 1962 he was famously involved in an outfield collision with outfielder Richie Ashburn who was shouting "I got it!" in English. Reportedly Ashburn switched to yelling "Yo la tengo!" instead and was promptly run over by Frank Thomas who had missed the discussion about the switch to Spanish.

enough to be wearing and Havana shortstop Leo Cárdenas was grazed on the shoulder.[17] Neither was seriously hurt but the Rochester manager, Cot Deal, who had been ejected earlier in the game, pulled his team from the field and returned to the States the following day. The series was cancelled, the Sunday doubleheader forfeited, and an effort by Maduro was needed to keep the franchise in Cuba.[18]

SUCCESS

The Sugar Kings had a particularly strong defense—including a pitching staff bolstered by former major leaguers Wieand and Walt Craddock, younger Cubans Mike Cuellar and Raúl Sánchez, and Puerto Rican reliever Luis Arroyo—and finished 1959 at 80–73, nine games behind Buffalo but comfortably in third place. As a result, they were in the playoffs, during which they first defeated second-place Columbus in four games, then fourth-place Richmond in six games, winning the International League championship. The Richmond series exemplifies the defensive nature of the squad as Havana scored only 10 runs over six games. The Cuban newspaper, *Revolución*, had a picture of Castro in the victor's dressing room with winning battery mates Sánchez and Enrique (Hank) Izquierdo.[19]

The Junior World Series against the Millers, the Red Sox affiliate and American Association champs, was scheduled to be three games in Minneapolis and four games in Havana, but with one rainout and an early chill in the forecast, it was decided to move the remaining games to Havana with the series tied at one game apiece.[20]

CHAMPIONSHIP

On October 2 both teams arrived in Havana to a rousing welcome but only one team had the expectation of a nation. That nation would not be disappointed. Games Three and Four were extra inning affairs both won by Havana. Game Three featured a home run by 20-year old Carl Yastrzemski of the Millers. Each game had a party-like atmosphere and the new government took every opportunity to share the spotlight. Castro threw out the ceremonial first pitch of Game Three. Several heads of state and dignitaries such as Che Guevera watched Game Four from designated box seats and Castro, blurring lines more than could be expected, sat in the dugout during the Sugar Kings' Game Six loss. While no violence was reported, members of the Millers, including manager Gene Mauch, reported intimidation and generalized unease at the environment.[21] Minnesota battled back to tie the series at three games heading into October 6 finale.

Game Seven, postponed one day due to rain, saw an overflow crowd of 35,000 including members of the inner circle of the new government. The final game was a gem with the Sugar Kings tying the score at two in the eighth inning and winning it in the bottom of the ninth in classic small-ball fashion: lead-off walk, sacrifice bunt, fly out, intentional walk, and bouncing grounder up the middle to score pitcher Sánchez with a head-first slide. Film footage of the winning score attests to what would be imagined: jubilation with fans, soldiers and players filling the field, and celebrating in front of the presidential box seats for hours. This was a moment of great success for an internationally diverse team paying temporary dividends to a government wanting to rally its people. The overall attendance of this seven game series was 103,808 but only 3,548 attended the two Minneapolis home games.[22]

1960 AND THE MOVE TO JERSEY CITY

As 1959 progressed, relations between Cuba and the United States deteriorated and by early 1960, the effects were being felt in the world of baseball. Jackie Robinson refused to attend an event for black athletes in Cuba,[23] American players were returning early from their Cuban winter league teams,[24] and the refusal of several Baltimore players to go to Cuba caused the cancellation of a preseason match in Havana between the Reds and Orioles.[25] The International League granted long-time president Frank Shaughnessy power to remove the Sugar Kings from Havana at his sole discretion.[26]

The continued efforts of Maduro prevented an immediate reassignment so the Sugar Kings began 1961 in Havana. However, Maduro could not address external factors such as the Cuban government nationalizing parts of the sugar and other industries and the United States reducing the sugar quota, the amount of sugar purchased by the United States at a fixed price.[27] As a result of this and other actions, the United States Secretary of State, Christian Herter, pressured MLB Commissioner Ford Frick who in turn pressured Shaughnessy to take action. The decision was then made to revoke the Havana franchise citing the "emergency" in Cuba and concern over the "safety and welfare" of personnel. Hasty meetings were arranged with representatives of the Reds and Sugar Kings but on an early July road trip through Miami the team was notified that they would be relocating to Jersey City, New Jersey. Bobby Maduro called the decision "completely outrageous" and bemoaned its calamitous effects on his personal finances and on the relations between the baseball communities of the two countries.[28]

Before the Miami series, Shaughnessy had contacted Jersey City Parks Commissioner Bernard Berry to discuss the lease of Roosevelt Stadium.[29] Officials in Jersey City, seemingly enthralled with the idea of another chance at professional baseball, offered easy access and favorable terms to the stadium, and on July 8, the transfer of the franchise was announced. The first game was to be July 15, after the Miami series ended. Players were given a chance to go back to Cuba to bring their families.

Manager Tony Castaño, who had replaced Gómez at the beginning of the season, resigned from the team in protest and the Cuban government made clear their displeasure, but eleven Cuban players under contract made the decision to stay with Jersey City.[30] For Cookie Rojas the choice was simple. "It wasn't a hard decision for me, I wanted to play professional baseball, they didn't allow professional baseball in Cuba, so I had to stay."[31] He went home to Cuba to collect his pregnant wife and young child and moved to New Jersey, as of yet never to return to Cuba.

The team was hastily named the Jerseys and early on July 15 arrived in Jersey City. The motorcade that took them to their first game at Roosevelt Stadium was greeted by cheers in "areas where Puerto Rican, Cuban, and Negro families predominate." The first car of the motorcade held new and former manager Nap Reyes and the current Miss Jersey City.[32]

Reyes, a veteran of years playing in both countries, including a stint with the Jersey City Giants in 1942–43, was not fazed by being denounced by Castro for accepting the job, even when extra security was put in place for the team and police dispatched to the dugout.[33]

The Jerseys began their existence in fourth place but ended the year in fifth and out of the playoffs. The season ended with high expectations for 1961 but also clear concern over the poor attendance in what was increasingly a "Yankees-on-TV" town.[34]

1961

Despite free parking at Roosevelt Stadium, pledges of support from local officials and an appearance by actress Yvonne DeCarlo on opening day, attendance in the 1961 season was more disappointing than the previous year.[35] In mid-May, with the Jerseys vying for first place, a Saturday game only drew 1,529, "including a few drunks who congregated in the rear of the Jersey dugout."[36]

Nap Reyes, as he watched his team "march-funeral-style back to the dressing room" after losing a Labor Day doubleheader, summed up the sad end to the Sugar

Kings in Jersey City with, "I've seen happier men dangling from the end of a rope."[37]

On October 3 the decision that had long been rumored took place and the Jerseys were moved to Jacksonville and renamed the Suns. Bobby Maduro retained ownership and the team was now affiliated with the Cleveland Indians.[38] While Maduro continued with Jacksonville, the revolution and the Jersey City experience left him in severe financial straits.[39] After the 1965 season, he left the Suns and the last vestige of the Sugar Kings was gone.

CONCLUSION

Despite a major league stadium and support from the city, relocating to Jersey City was a bad and hasty move forced upon the franchise and Bobby Maduro. The support of the community was never there. While Toronto and Buffalo would regularly get crowds of 10,000 fans, the Jerseys barely got 1,000. Adding to attendance woes were the high operating costs in Jersey City, eventual loss of radio and TV revenue, and, not least, Maduro's "growing, personal financial crisis."[40] If the Sugar Kings were allowed to stay in Cuba, would this have been a mechanism for better relations between the United States and Cuba? Probably not, but the question is worth asking.

Though the Sugar Kings had a sad ending, their years in Havana are quite uplifting. The drama created by a team that underperformed for five seasons and then won the Junior World Series during a year in which a revolution was occurring is an amazing story. The Sugar Kings were a team of destiny intertwined with something larger than themselves. Were they the best minor league baseball team in 1959? Probably not, but external developments created a much bigger stage on which they performed and triumphed.

It is ironic that a team embodying a shared aspect of distinct cultures became the object destroyed by those cultures. The Sugar Kings were a team that straddled eras, an experiment with one shining moment but unfortunately never given the chance to fulfill its potential. The individual who should be best remembered is the idealistic Maduro, who lost a great deal but stayed loyal to his beloved sport and team even after moving to Jersey City. The legacy of the Sugar Kings are also its players, especially Cuellar, González, Rojas, and Cárdenas, who took the drama embraced in 1959 and carried it through long and successful major league careers. ∎

Notes

1. Mark Rucker and Peter C. Bjarkman, *SMOKE: The Romance and Lore of Cuban Baseball* (Kingston, New York: Total Sports Illustrated. 1999).
2. Robert González Echevarría, *The Pride of Havana A History of Cuban Baseball* (Oxford, Oxford University Press 1999), 90.
3. Ibid, 112–88.
4. http://www.baseball-reference.com/players/l/luquedo01.shtml.
5. Joseph Gerard, SABR Bioproject Biography of Mike Gonalez, http://sabr.org/bioproj/person/75c3d9b1.
6. http://www.baseball-reference.com/bullpen/Florida_International_League.
7. Rory Costello, SABR Bioproject Biography of Bobby Maduro, http://sabr.org/bioproj/person/c34ce106.
8. http://baseball-reference.com/register/team.cgi?id=dcl9fdbc.
9. http://www.milb.com/documents/2010/08/06/13100514/1/Cuba.pdf.
10. http://history.com/this-day-in-history/castro-sworn-in.
11. http://www.coldwarstudies.com/2010/12/13/cold-war-havana-prelude-to-american-sanctions.
12. "Havana Team to Stay," *The New York Times*, April 24, 1959, 33.
13. Robert González Echevarria, *Cuban Fiestas* (New Haven, Yale University Press 2010), 205.
14. "Havana Baseball $20,000 Sweeter," United Press International, April 29, 1959 as quoted in Rory Costello, SABR Bioproject Biography of Bobby Maduro, http://sabr.org/bioproj/person/c34ce106.
15. Robert González Echevarría, *Cuban Fiestas* (New Haven, Yale University Press 2010), 204.
16. Fausto Miranda, Revolución, October 2, 1959 as quoted in Robert González Echevarria, *The Pride of Havana A History of Cuban Baseball* (Oxford, Oxford University Press 1999), 341.
17. Robert González Echevarría, *Cuban Fiestas* (New Haven, Yale University Press 2010), 202.
18. Ibid.
19. Ibid, 203.
20. "Cold Halts Junior Series," *The New York Times*, September 30, 1959, 45.
21. http://www.stewthornley.net/millers_havana.html.
22. Ibid.
23. Robert González Echevarría, *Cuban Fiestas* (New Haven, Yale University Press 2010), 209.
24. Ibid.
25. Robert González Echevarría, *The Pride of Havana A History of Cuban Baseball* (Oxford, Oxford University Press 1999), 345 and Milton H. Jamail, *Full Count: Inside Cuban Baseball* (Carbondale, Southern Illinois University Press 2000, 122.
26. Ibid (Echevarría).
27. Ibid.
28. Rory Costello, SABR Bioproject Biography of Bobby Maduro, http://sabr.org/bioproj/person/c34ce106.
29. "Meeting is Planned," *The New York Times*, July 8, 1960, 24.
30. Joseph O. Haff, "Ex-Sugar Kings Get a Noisy Welcome in New Home," *The New York Times*, July 16, 11.
31. *The Jersey Journal* (Jersey City, NJ), April 16, 1999, 7.
32. Joseph O. Haff, "Ex-Sugar Kings Get a Noisy Welcome in New Home," *The New York Times*, July 16, 1960, 11.
33. Ibid.
34. Howard M. Tuckner, "Jersey City Facing Loss of Ball Team," *The New York Times*, July 9, 1961, 51.
35. "Night Game With Buffalo to Start at 8," *Jersey Journal*, April 18, 1961, 3.
36. *Jersey Journal*, May 13, 1961, 27.
37. *Jersey Journal*, September 5, 1961, 5.
38. "Franchise Shifted, Jerseys a Memory," *Jersey Journal*, October 4, 1961
39. Rory Costello, SABR Bioproject Biography of Bobby Maduro, http://sabr.org/bioproj/person/c34ce106.
40. Devine, Tommy, "Ultimatum by IL Directors Puts on Heat," *Miami News*, June 7, 1961, 5B, as quoted in Rory Costello, SABR Bioproject Biography of Bobby Maduro, http://sabr.org/bioproj/person/c34ce106.

Satchel Paige

Twilight with the Marlins

Alan Cohen

At the end of the 1956 season, writer Oscar Fraley observed that Satchel Paige was "a rounders robot who reportedly inspired Abner Doubleday to invent baseball."[1] That was after Paige had—at age 50—gone 11–4 with two shutouts, 13 saves, and a 1.86 ERA for the Miami Marlins of the International League.[2] Paige spent three seasons with the Marlins, which were both successful and controversial.

The story of how, quite by accident, the International League wound up in Miami was recounted by Bill Veeck some years ago. In 1955, Syracuse had drawn 85,191 fans, by far the least of any Triple-A team. Their owner wanted out. One night, at a restaurant in Columbus, Ohio, the owner heard Sid Salomon say, "If I could buy a club, I wouldn't hesitate to move it to Miami." Soon thereafter, Salomon had himself a ball club, and hired his close friend Veeck to run the organization.[3]

Veeck, as the Marlins' Executive Vice-President, signed Satchel Paige to pitch for the team. Satchel had first pitched for Veeck with the Indians in 1948, and had also pitched for him with the St. Louis Browns

Satchel Paige, shown here in Miami uniform, was brought to the team by executive vice president Bill Veeck, for whom he had pitched in the major leagues with Cleveland and St. Louis.

from 1951 through 1953. When the Browns moved on to Baltimore in 1954, both Veeck and Paige had joined the ranks of the unemployed. For two years, Paige pitched in exhibitions and did a stint with the Kansas City Monarchs, but was out of Organized Baseball.

The hiatus ended on Opening Day 1956, as 8,806 fans came to Miami Stadium to see the new team in town complete with the usual Veeck trimmings. Paige was supposed to arrive at the mound via helicopter prior to the first pitch, but things got a bit disorganized. He arrived in a cloud of dust after the first inning, when the helicopter landed on the infield dirt near second base, and Paige assumed a seat in a rocking chair by his team's dugout.[4] The experience resulted in Paige concluding, "Veeck better think up something new, cause I ain't gonna ride in no more of them things."[5] Although he did not appear in the first game, it was not long until he did see action and start contributing to his team's success.

His first appearance was on April 22, the sixth game of the season, and he needed a wakeup call. He came in to relieve in the seventh inning of the second game of a doubleheader. The first game had gone 18 innings and more than seven hours had elapsed, leaving very few of the announced crowd of 3,486 around to see Paige. His wild pitch advanced runners to second and third, but then he bore down and got the game's final batter Mel Nelson to hit a comebacker for the final out.[6] The 3–2 win broke a string of four losses for the Marlins.

After three successful relief appearances, including two saves, he had his first start of the season on April 29. Against the Montreal Royals, in front of a crowd of 5,536, the largest since Opening Day, he pitched a seven-inning complete game shutout in the second game of a doubleheader for his first win of the season, allowing only four singles. He threw only 83 pitches, but was not allowed to use his hesitation pitch.[7] Subsequently, league President Frank Shaughnessy ruled that Paige could throw the pitch in the International League. The complete game was the first of the season by a Marlins pitcher.

He was pitching mostly out of the bullpen and sometimes in bad luck. On May 26, he entered the game in the seventh inning after three Miami hurlers had not been able to solve the bats in the Richmond lineup. As noted by Shelley Rolfe in the *Richmond Times-Dispatch*, "They laughed when Ol' Satch shuffled to the mound but after a while the (Richmond) Vees and the crowd discovered Paige was no laughing matter. It wasn't that the Vees failed to threaten Satch, it was just that Paige knew what to do every time they did, and he did it in his own good time."[8] The game went into the 13th inning. Paige struck out eight batters in his seven innings of work, but Richmond pushed across a run in the bottom of the 13th for the win, bringing Paige's record to 1–2 with three saves.

A big crowd of 6,895 came to the Miami ballpark on Memorial Day and got a double-dose of Satchel. In the first game, he entered the game with two outs in the fifth inning and allowed neither a hit nor a run over the balance of the seven-inning game for his second win. In the second game, he recorded the final out for his fourth save of the season.

Signed on initially to help the attendance figures, Paige was quickly becoming the pre-eminent reliever in the league. On June 24, in the second game of a doubleheader against Toronto he played the stopper role. The Maple Leafs had started the series in Miami by defeating the Marlins 13–1 and 12–0, and Miami starter Frank Snyder had yielded three runs in the first inning. Paige came into the game with two outs and went the rest of the way. The Marlins came from behind to win, Paige's record stood at 5–2 with seven saves, and the Marlins were four games above .500. His ERA stood at 1.50, and he even had contributed with a single in three at-bats on June 24.[9]

Veeck was always quick with a promotion to spur attendance, and on July 11, old age was on the program as the ageless Satchel (four days past his 50th birthday), was matched up against Connie Marrero, the 45-year-old former Washington hurler, now pitching with Havana. Close to 6,000 spectators looked on as Paige pitched the first six innings, striking out eight, and Miami won, 1–0, for Satchel's sixth win of the season.

Top-flight entertainment in the form of Clay Poe's Greater Miami Goodwill party brought a record 11,836 through the turnstiles three days later. The Vagabonds, Dagmar, Micki Marlo, and Pat Manville took center stage during the 45-minute extravaganza.

Satchel was thriving in the warm weather of Miami and pitched his best ball on Sunday afternoons, capturing six of his first eight wins on Sundays. After being sidelined by a bad cold in the early part of July,

he made sure that on subsequent trips to the northern stretches of the International League, he would be prepared. He would wear four sweatshirts and a rubber shirt beneath his uniform. "I'm never going to be cold again when I pitch in Buffalo, Toronto, or Montreal."[10]

The Marlins were in first place for a brief moment on July 29, after Satchel hurled six scoreless innings in relief as his team won 5–4 in 13 innings against Montreal, but hit a tough stretch in August.

On August 7, the Marlins moved their show to the Orange Bowl and packed in an all-time minor league record 57,713 fans to witness Paige's fourth start of the season. Paige not only was the pitching star that night, but his long double to deep left-center field scored three runs as Miami defeated Columbus 6–2. Proceeds from the contest, which featured four bands in an entertainment extravaganza, went to charity.[11] Satchel struck out five batters and scattered seven hits in 7⅔ innings of work for his ninth win of the season. Having lost five straight, Miami was in danger of dropping out of contention before Paige stopped the losing streak.

Paige's finest performance came on the evening of August 13 when he defeated Rochester, yielding but one hit for his tenth win of the season. He struck out three batters and walked none in his seven-inning masterpiece. The only hit of the game was a fourth-inning single off the bat of Tommy Burgess. In his first 31 games, Paige was 10–3 with 10 saves and had a 1.50 ERA. In 90 innings, he had struck out 64 and walked only 20.

His longest outing of the season came on August 19 against Buffalo. He started but was not very effective, yielding three runs over the first six innings. But he was able to put his team up 5-3 with a two-run double in the bottom of the sixth. After the sixth inning, there was a two hour and eleven minute rain delay, but Satch remained in the game, lasting 8⅔ innings as the Marlins won 5–4.[12]

Satchel led his team in appearances with 37 as they finished third in the league with an 80–71 record. In games in which Paige appeared, the Marlins were 27–10. The third-place finish earned the Marlins a place in the playoffs against Rochester. Down two games to none, the Marlins staged a come-from-behind rally to win the third game of the playoffs. Paige set the side down in order in the eighth inning and was credited with the win. Miami lost the series to Rochester in five games.

When 1957 rolled around, Satch showed up for spring training in Stuart, Florida, ready to go. On arrival, he said, "I've already contacted my Indian friend who makes my special snake oil. And I hear Stuart is a

Paige would spend three seasons with Miami.

fine place for spring training…good fishing, I mean."[13] It was still 1957 and still very much the Jim Crow South. When he showed up, he was informed that the Marlins were a bit short-handed in the pitching department and he might need to be used as a starter on Opening Day. His response was vintage Paige. "I'll be ready to pitch if I don't have any miseries between now and then. So don't you go running me and getting my feet tired."[14]

One year in Miami was enough for Veeck and he arranged the sale of the team to Miami media mogul George Storer prior to the 1957 season. Showmanship was still on the agenda for the April 17 opener against Toronto, courtesy of impresario Ernie Seiler. Entertainment was provided by, among others, Preacher Rollo and his Dixieland Saints, and during the National Anthem, bombs burst in air as fireworks illuminated the sky beyond the left-field fence. And then the teams took to the field and engaged in a marathon that lasted well into the night before being halted at 12:50AM by curfew. After 16 innings and four hours and 49 minutes, the score was tied 3–3.[15]

Paige did not pitch in the opener, but he had developed a new pitch for his noted arsenal. He called it the Hum Bug Pitch. "It hums and makes the batters buggy. It has nothing to do with my dipsy-doodle pitch, my hesitation pitch, or any of the others."[16]

A well-rested Paige pitched for the first time on April 28 in the second game of a Sunday doubleheader. He went the entire seven innings, scattering six hits and striking out nine as Miami defeated Buffalo and Luke

Easter, 7–1. The Marlins were in first place and would stay there through the first two weeks of May. Then the wheels fell off. The team's bats went to sleep and each of the pitchers suffered. By June 18, Satch's record stood at 3–3. In his three losses, he had allowed only eight runs in 22 innings, losing by scores of 2–0, 3–0, and 3–2. The team had fallen to seventh place and was 10 games below .500.

By the time Satch's 51st birthday rolled around, the team had risen to sixth place and they were playing in Columbus. It was the fifth inning on July 7 and the Marlins were clinging to a one run lead. Starting pitcher Earl Hunsinger was tired and reliever Dick Bunker had been ineffective. In strolled Paige and he went the rest of the way to record his fifth win of the season.

The team could not establish anything in the way of momentum and during the last week of August, the bats went into the deep freeze again, and once more Satch was the victim of shutout pitching. On August 29, he was on the short end as the Marlins lost to Columbus 3-0. He went all seven innings in the first game of a doubleheader only to be shut out for the fourth time in his eight losses. His record stood at 8–8 with six saves.

On Labor Day, games were scheduled for both morning and afternoon and Paige took to the mound in the opener. In the bottom of the fifth, Miami scored three runs but nobody was really noticing. By then 15 Havana batters had come up, and 15 Havana batters had been retired. Satchel had a perfecto going and he kept it going until the eighth inning when with two outs, Elio Chacón singled for the first Havana hit. Paige went the whole nine innings, giving up three hits while striking out eight for the 3–0 win, his ninth of the season.

The Marlins went into the last week of the season challenging for a playoff spot. They won 10 of their last 14 games, including two wins by Paige to edge out Rochester for a playoff berth. In the playoffs, the Marlins won the first round, defeating Toronto in six games, but fell to Buffalo in five games for the league championship. Against Buffalo, Paige pitched seven innings in the opener, losing 2–0, and in the finale, he lost 7–1.

Nevertheless, it was another good season for Paige who went 10–8 during the regular season with a 2.42 ERA in 119 innings.

Early in the 1958 season, Paige was on the wrong side of the law when he was arrested and convicted for speeding and having an improper driver's license. Satch found the judge, Charles H. Snowden, to be a fan. The Judge deferred the 20-day jail sentence until after the season, and put forth some criteria that could lessen the sentence. Paige would receive one day off for each win, be credited for one day off for each run scored, and be credited for one day off for each time he struck out Luke Easter.[17]

That season, the Marlins got off to a bad start, losing 18 of their first 27 games before putting together a seven-game winning streak. Paige tossed a three-hitter against Columbus to win the final game of the run.

However, Satch was losing more than he was winning in the early going. Through June 8, he was only 3–4 with two saves and the way he was going, it looked as though he would be the guest of the City of Miami at season's end. The team was not doing well either. At the close of business on June 11, they were in seventh place, nine games behind the league leaders, and Paige found himself on the disabled list. He missed 14 of his team's games but came back to win his fourth decision of the season, defeating Montreal 4–1.

As June turned into July, the Marlins made their way toward the first division and Paige saw more action. He made seven appearances between June 29 and July 13, going 4–1 with one save as the Marlins climbed over .500. On July 10, he entered a game with two on and one out in the eighth inning. He recorded the final five outs to save a 5–2 win over Havana.

As good as Satchel was on the field, his off-the-field behavior was irking management. He missed flights and was unreliable in terms of showing up for work. On July 27, he had shut out Toronto 3–0, in a nine inning complete game. But less than ten days later, things took a turn for the worse as Paige feuded with management, mostly over money. The pitcher was suspended indefinitely on August 5. At the time, his record was 9–7 with three saves and an ERA of 3.09.[18] Indefinitely was 12 days. He came back to defeat Buffalo 6–1 for his 10th win, but the Marlins were left fighting for the last playoff spot going into the last two weeks of the season.

Sometimes, one's reputation can cause problems and such was the case late in the season when the Marlins were flying back to Miami from Havana at the end of August. Satchel showed up 15 minutes before takeoff only to find out that his seat had been sold to someone else, the airline thinking he would be a no-show. He went back on a later flight.[19]

On September 1, Miami played the first of a four game set against Columbus. They needed to sweep Columbus and Havana in their last seven games to move past Columbus in the standings for the final playoff spot. Paige started for Miami against Columbus and allowed only two runs, but his teammates were unable to score and there would be no more starts for Satchel Paige. He pitched a scoreless inning

in relief in his team's finale on September 6 to end the season with a 10–10 record and a 3.04 ERA.

He didn't quite get the credit he needed to stay out of jail for the preseason traffic violation, but the judge was in a forgiving mood and gave Satch credit for effort.[20]

At season's end, Paige hung up his spikes, and it was made official when he was released by the Marlins in April 1959. Although there would be barnstorming and brief appearances, often as publicity stunts, over the next several years, including a five-game stint with Portland of the Pacific Coast League in 1961 and his last major-league appearance with Kansas City in 1965, it was over. As Satchel said, "I'm not runnin' out of baseball. It's just that mabba baseball is runnin' out of Satchel."[21] ∎

Sources

In addition to the sources shown in the endnotes, the author used Baseball-Reference.com and the following:

Fraley, Oscar. "Ageless Satchel Paige Called 'Most Wondrous Performer,'" *Panama City Herald*, August 15, 1956:10

Paige, Satchel with David Lipman. *Maybe I'll Pitch Forever* (New York, Grove Press, 1961)

Notes

1. Oscar Fraley, Panama City News, November 14, 1956, 8.
2. Saves were not an official statistic at the time. Total based on author's calculations.
3. Bill Veeck with Ed Linn, *Veeck as in Wreck* (Chicago, University of Chicago Press, 1962):311.
4. Jimmy Burns, "8,806 at Marlins' Game See Fireworks and Delivery of Satchmo by Helicopter," *The Sporting News*, April 25, 1956:27.
5. Oscar Ruhl. "88-year battery—Satch and McCullough," *The Sporting News*, December 19, 1956:15.
6. George Beahon, "Wings Top Miami, 10–6, In 18 Innings, Then Lose," *Rochester Democrat and Chronicle*, April 23, 1956:18. (*The Sporting News* recorded a passed ball rather than wild pitch.)
7. "Ol' Satch Hurls Miami to 3–0 Shutout Victory," *Boston Traveler*, April 30, 1956:24.
8. Shelley Rolfe, *Richmond Times-Dispatch*, May 27, 1956:B1.
9. Burns, "Satch Aging, He has 1.50 ERA and He's Still Hittin'," *The Sporting News*, July 4, 1956:30.
10. Burns, "Satch Miami's Sunday Ace—Enjoys Afternoon Work," *The Sporting News*, August 8, 1956:28.
11. Burns, "Marlins Set 57,713 Gate High at Orange Bowl Show," *The Sporting News*, August 15, 1956:17.
12. *Richmond Times-Dispatch*, August 20, 1956:19.
13. Burns, "Satchel Checks on Snake Oil, He's all Set for Spring Drills," *The Sporting News*, March 13, 1957:36.
14. Burns, "Miami Marlins All Smiles—Satchel Paige Shows Up," *The Sporting News*, April 3, 1957:31.
15. Burns, "Seiler Whips Up 'Spectacular' at Marlin Opener," *The Sporting News*, April 24, 1957:27.
16. *The Sporting News*, April 24, 1957:27.
17. "Satch Can Pitch Himself out of Jam," *Fort Pierce News-Tribune*, April 24, 1958: 1.
18. Burns, "Paige Suspended by Miami to Climax a Hectic Interlude," *The Sporting News*, August 13, 1958:36.
19. Burns, *The Sporting News*, September 3, 1958:32.
20. *The Sporting News*, January 7, 1959:27.
21. "Legendary Satch Turns to Movies," *Fort Pierce News-Tribune*, September 30, 1958:5.

Woody Smith

The Original Mr. Marlin

Sam Zygner

When you ask a Miami Marlins fan today, "Who is Mr. Marlin?" without hesitation you will get the response, "Jeff Conine," who starred with the team for eight seasons. However, old-timers, who harken back to the days when minor league baseball ruled Miami, will give you a different answer: Woody Smith, a sure-handed third baseman with movie-matinee-idol good looks. Forest Elwood Smith was born on February 25, 1927, in University City, Missouri, to Roscoe Phillip Smith and his bride, the former Beulah V. Tessereau, who both hailed from the Farmington/Fredericktown area of southern Missouri. "Forry", his given nickname, was the middle of three children; his older brother Roscoe Phillip Jr., known as "Pete," was three years older and younger brother Jerry came along 17 years after Forest. They were all born and raised in University City, an inner ring suburb of St. Louis County.[1]

Young Forry stayed active driving a truck and making deliveries for the family's dry cleaning business, running a paper route, attending church, and playing baseball whenever he could find the spare time. Jerry remembers his older siblings fondly, and how they seemed more like parents to him than brothers. "We were middle-class and both of the boys were in school and working jobs to help out." He added, "I think they were both highly active in church and we had some people in our church that were professional athletes, or had been." Mound City has always been a hotbed for baseball and the boys naturally gravitated to the sandlots to compete in pick-up games throughout the city.[2]

After finishing high school at University City High, Forest figured there were limited opportunities for him staying in the area, so he focused on two choices for his future: pursue a career in baseball or join the military like his older brother had. During World War II, Pete served in the Army in France.

Reggie (Forest's son), remembers family stories about fate stepping in and how it changed the course of his father's life. "He wanted to go into the Army, but dad was not allowed to go into the service because of a kidney infection."[3] Ultimately, he chose to play

baseball. Jerry said of his brother, "Forry was pretty independent. He was driven and goal-oriented. Baseball didn't find him; he found it."[4] With that, he began a journey that defined him the rest of his life.

Forest launched headlong into his new vocation and lifelong passion. He was originally signed as a pitcher by scout Jim McLaughlin to his first professional contract in 1946 with the St. Louis Browns organization.[5] The wiry nineteen-year old was assigned to the Wausau Lumberjacks of the Class-D Wisconsin State League.[6] Although his beginnings were inauspicious with a 4–3 record and a less than stellar 6.44 ERA, the Browns saw potential in the youngster. He made a dramatic improvement his sophomore season with the Ada Herefords of the Class-D Sooner State League, dominating the opposition, leading the league in wins (23–7), and ERA (2.00). He also batted .286 in 140 at-bats.[7]

The 1948 season proved to be one of both frustration and great joy. Not only was Smith reassigned four times that year, bouncing between Aberdeen, Hannibal, Muskogee, and Springfield, having worked 265 innings the year before in Ada, he came down with a sore arm and spent considerable time off the field with a bum wing.[8] Nevertheless, away from the playing field he presented another type of diamond to the joy of his life, his bride-to-be, June A. Oswald. They exchanged nuptials on September 24 in St. Louis, the beginning of 56 years together.[9] In 1949, rested and ready to return to full-time play, Smith was designated for assignment to the Gloversville-Johnstown Glovers of the Class-C Canadian-American League. There Forest met new player/manager and regular third baseman James Cullinane, who would have a profound effect on his career. His new skipper immediately assessed Forest's hitting and fielding abilities and saw that his career path was better suited at the far corner of the infield versus toiling on the mound. Cullinane, known for his fielding prowess, would set a Can-Am League record that same year by collecting 308 assists.[10] Smith continued to take the mound for the Glovers while Cullinane took him under his wing and tutored him in the finer points of hitting and fielding. Smith struggled (10–7, 4.99, 128 IP) on the mound, yet despite his inconsistencies on the hill, under the tutelage of his mentor he began to learn the intricacies of playing third base during off time, while playing outfield and first base part-time between pitching assignments. He impressed Cullinane by batting a glossy .324 and collecting 29 RBIs in 216 at-bats.[11]

By 1950, Cullinane was in the midst of his last season of professional baseball and yielded his playing time to Smith who took over as the Glovers' regular third sacker. Not only was his performance at his new position extraordinary, Forest was effective with the bat, hitting .288 with 13 home runs in 137 games.

From 1951 to 1955 Smith continued to climb up the minor-league ranks. He was acquired by the independent Class-B West Palm Beach Indians of the Florida International League in the spring of 1951, and his performance caught the eyes of several major-league organizations. Serving as the club's everyday third baseman, he bashed an impressive .320 and finished the year only 12 points behind league-leading hitter, Ted Cieslak.[12]

It was with the Indians that his new nickname "Woody" appeared in the press. In interviews with family members it is unclear how he acquired his nickname, but his brother Jerry surmised it most likely derived from his middle name of Elwood, or in connection with his first name.

He once again found himself changing organizations, having been acquired by the New York Yankees prior to the 1952 campaign. He was assigned to the Beaumont Roughnecks of the Double-A Texas League where he turned heads with his flashy glove work all the while batting .281 in 117 games. He earned a promotion to the

Infield anchors of the 1956–57 Marlins: Smith, Micelotta, Tompkins (left to right).

MIAMI NEWS COLLECTION, HISTORYMIAMI

Kansas City Blues of the Triple-A American Association in 1953 and led all third basemen in the league in double plays turned with 31, and tied for the league lead in assists with 288.[13] In 1954, the Yankees were high on 23-year old prospect Kal Segrist Jr., so there was little playing time for Smith. Yankees brass decided to assign Woody to their other Triple-A affiliate in Richmond, Virginia, and after a very brief stay he was optioned to the Philadelphia Phillies Triple-A affiliate, the Syracuse Chiefs of the International League, where he regained his everyday position.

Smith returned to the Yankees in 1955, this time with the Denver Bears of the American Association. Finding little playing time again, he was sold to the Charleston Senators. Although Smith excelled with the glove and bat, the Senators struggled to a league worst 50–104 record. Woody would soon find himself packing his bags again, and in December of 1955 was sold to the Havana Sugar Kings of the International League. However, his stay would be brief. The newly minted Miami Marlins, a Philadelphia Phillies affiliate owned by Sid Salomon Jr. and headed up by baseball maverick Bill Veeck, were looking to make a splash in the minor-league market. Veeck had already made a blockbuster move when he signed the ageless wonder Leroy "Satchel" Paige not only as a gate attraction, but as an effective swingman on the mound. With the goal of winning a pennant in their inaugural season Veeck sought to improve his team by any means. One of the team's glaring weaknesses was at third base where 38-year old Sid Gordon, a 13-year major league veteran famous from his days with the Boston/Milwaukee Braves, New York Giants, and Pittsburgh Pirates, held down the job at the hot corner. Although Gordon was adequate with the bat, he had slowed down to the point of having very little range at his position. On July 26, 1956, Veeck, who had his eye on Smith since the beginning of the season, pulled the trigger and purchased the slick gloveman from the Sugar Kings for $15,000. According to Greg Mulleavy, manager of the Montreal Royals, Smith "didn't like Havana and told me at the all-star game in Toronto that he wasn't going back there next year."[14] In an interview with Luther Evans of the *Miami Herald*, Smith enthusiastically said, "...golly would I like to play for this club." Woody found a new home and would settle into his position for the next four and half seasons.[15]

Smith debuted on the night of July 26, 1956, in front of 5,658 rabid fans at Miami Stadium, and it was a night to remember. When his name was announced for the first time the crowd answered with thunderous applause. The evening was an auspicious beginning as he accepted four chances at third without an error and collected four singles and a base on balls in five plate appearances, helping the Marlins defeat the Toronto Maple Leafs 4–3.[16,17]

Woody's presence solidified the infield, teaming up with shortstop Mickey Micelotta, second baseman Benny Tompkins, and first baseman Ed Bouchee. This combination would stay intact through the end of 1957, with the exception of Bouchee who was replaced by Francisco "Pancho" Herrera in 1957.

Spurred by Smith's arrival, Miami surged into first place temporarily on July 29, when they split a twin bill with Montreal, while the Toronto Maple Leafs dropped a nail-biter to Havana, 2–1. On the day Smith went three for five in the first game helping Paige earn the victory, and three for four in the second tilt, including two doubles. One double seemed to be Smith's first home run for the Marlins, but it was overruled by the umpiring crew. This drew the consternation of Marlins manager Don Osborn, who felt the ball had deflected off the light tower in left-center field, not the fence, making it a homer.[18] The Leafs escaped the inning unscathed and won a game they would have lost with a different call.

Smith's season continued to be eventful. He played in one of the most famous games in minor-league history, the Orange Bowl Game on Tuesday August 7, 1956. The Marlins squared off against the Columbus Jets and played inside the world-famous football stadium. The field was especially configured to accommodate baseball. Veeck, with the intention of breaking the minor league record for attendance, arranged to use the Orange Bowl and surrounded the event with special promotions, pomp, and circumstance including performances by singers Cab Calloway, Margaret Whiting, and the Russ Morgan Band, among others. He called on Satchel Paige to take the mound in front of 57,713 fans.[19] For his part, Smith had one base knock in three at-bats and drove in one run on a sacrifice fly in the 6–2 Marlins win.[20]

Although Miami (80-71) ultimately faded to a third place finish in 1956 and were eliminated in the first round of the Shaughnessy playoffs by the Rochester Red Wings, Smith's year was a successful one as he finished with 19 home runs, 83 RBIs, and a .267 batting average.

Over the next four seasons the "Fish" as a team failed to put together another winning campaign, yet Smith held down his usual position with aplomb, batting .277 with 14 home runs and 73 RBIs in 1957, .291 batting average, 13 home runs, and 79 RBIs in 1958, and .274 batting average, 16 home runs, and 78

Woody Smith receiving his 1959 Rawlings Silver Glove Award and shaking hands with team owner George B. Storer.

RBIs in 1959, before slumping in 1960 to a mere .213 batting average with only 49 RBIs, though with 11 home runs.[21] Smith was named team's most valuable player from 1957–59 and was widely regarded as the team's most popular player. In 1958, he was awarded a Rawlings Silver Glove for his defensive prowess, one of the awards he was most proud of during his career.[22] The trophy was given each year to nine members (one at each position) comprising every team and its players in the National Association based on their official final fielding average.[23] That same season he broke the International League record for consecutive games without an error at third base, 86 straight, smashing the old record of 56 set by Irvine Jeffries of the 1937 Montreal Royals.[24]

Although the inaugural season in Miami, under the guidance of Veeck, had been a successful one, interest in the club soon waned. By 1960 the third owner of the Marlins, Bill MacDonald was taking heavy financial losses that were attributed to a less than satisfactory stadium lease agreement and sagging attendance. On September 11, 1960, Miami played their last game against the Richmond Virginians on the road. In the abbreviated game that was ultimately called after five innings due to a torrential downpour, Woody homered in his last at-bat as a Marlin in what proved to be the game winner.[25] Just as he had come in with a bang, he left in the same way.

For all his outstanding efforts, one of the great mysteries to fans and teammates was why the Philadelphia Phillies never called Woody up to the big leagues. In a 2010 interview, Tommy Qualters reminisced about his teammate and how he was mishandled by the Phillies, "Yeah, Woody Smith, I'll tell you a little story about him. He was probably the best defensive third baseman you could ever see. He was unbelievable." He added, "So he had come to spring training...We just needed a body and there was no chance he was going to make the team. And it was just obvious. I don't know what the hell they were thinking. They just didn't treat him right. They just didn't show any interest in him at all and he just packed his stuff and went home. Well, Roy Hamey was the General Manager and he black-balled Woody."[26]

The Baltimore Orioles took over the Miami affiliate prior to the 1959 season, and ended their working agreement at the close of the 1960. In 1961 Miami did not host a minor league team, and so Smith was signed by the Minnesota Twins and assigned to their Triple-A affiliate in Syracuse, New York. It was the 35-year old veteran's last season as a regular player before he closed out his career with the Rochester Red Wings, appearing in 10 games in 1962.

In 1969, Smith made a triumphant return to the city where he was so esteemed. Miami, now a member of the Class-A Florida State League, was being run by general manager Bill Durney Jr., under the tutelage of his father Bill Durney. The elder Durney worked for the club in various capacities dating back to the original Marlins in 1956, Bill Jr., had learned the ropes starting out as a ballboy, then pitched batting practice, and eventually was promoted to a front office position. The youthful GM had been mostly compliant with the Baltimore Orioles when it came to who was assigned to the club as its manager, but when he saw the opportunity to bring Smith back to Miami, he was insistent with the parent club's vice president Harry Dalton that Woody was their man for the manager's vacancy. Durney Jr. exclaimed, "Since Woody was certainly the acquisition we wanted, and it came down to the very end when they hired him, because we were really pushing for him. And I think they had someone else in mind."[27]

With Smith at the helm the Miami Marlins/Orioles reeled off the most dominating stretch in Florida State League history.[28] From 1969–72, the club won four straight division titles and four straight league championships, compiling a combined record of 335–201.[29] Going back to 1919, no other FSL city has won more than two consecutive league titles.[30] Under Woody's watchful eye, players like Don Baylor, Rich Coggins, Jim Fuller, Kiko Garcia, John Montague, Mike Reinbach, and Tom Walker, just to name a few, climbed the ladder to the big leagues.

During the fall of 1972, after four years of unprecedented success, Smith got a phone call from Baltimore Orioles Director of Player Development, Don Pries at his home in St. Louis to set up a meeting at the airport. June, his wife remembered, "So, Woody was all excited...he just thought oh gosh he's getting a promotion...And so he went to meet Don and after about an hour or two he came back, he walked in, and I said, 'What happened?' He said, 'I got fired.' According to June, the reasons given by Pries were that they did not have any place for him to move up or down since managers Cal Ripken Sr. and Joe Altobelli were at the higher levels and they hated to ask him to come back for a fifth season. It was a shock to Smith who had done everything the Orioles had asked of him.

Woody remained resilient despite his disappointment. "He was never bitter, or that upset over being let go that year," declared June. "He was at the very first when he was let go after four years after he won four pennants. People would think he would be terribly upset, but he went right on."[31]

And move on Woody did, managing the Key West Conchs during the 1973 season. He gained some measure of satisfaction by beating his old team on opening day in the Keys, 7–6. He and his team traveled the next night to Miami's home opener in Miami Stadium to what the *Miami Herald* described as being like "Woody Smith Night." The 1972 championship banner was raised and Smith was honored by the North Shore Kiwanis Club with a plaque for outstanding achievements. He was met with wild applause from the 4,177 fans that turned out to honor their hero. It must have felt odd to the many in attendance to see Smith sporting a big KW on the front of his ballcap.[32]

After the close of the 1973 season, Woody was hired by the Cleveland Indians and moved on to manage at San Antonio of the Texas League for two years (1974–75), Waterloo of the Midwest League (1977–78), and Chattanooga of the Southern League (1979–81). In his first year in San Antonio, Woody managed Dennis Eckersley, who went on to a Hall of Fame career.[33] He also served as the Midwest Scouting Director for the Tribe from 1981 through 1987, and also worked in the same capacity with the California Angels from 1988–90 before retiring that same year.

Sadly, later in life Smith struggled with dementia. Although physically he was still a strong man, his mind deteriorated to the point that many of his baseball memories would no longer come to him. Finally, On February 4, 2005, Forest Elwood "Woody" Smith succumbed to natural causes leaving behind his wife June and sons Woody Jr. and Reggie, and daughter Gale.

Woody's greatest legacy was not only that he was a great player and manager, but also a person who left a positive impact on his friends, family, teammates, and players who had the opportunity to share the playing field with him. Lenny Scott, a pitcher who played under Smith from 1970–72, described his skipper:

> Oh, he's the manager's man…He knew how to talk to you. You know he didn't talk at you…He knew how to bring things to the table. He had a lot of hardship. You know Woody would be out on the field practicing while we was out there practicing taking ground balls, and he would talk about the opportunities. And doing whatever you got to do, and take the opportunities and take advantage of it, right. But, he never got that opportunity and I could never understand it. He was a very delightful man. Very knowledgeable about the game and he was a very knowledgeable guy.[34]

June remembered Woody always saying, "I was their manager, their teacher, and a father to those 25 kids. They would bring me all of their troubles into my office and I would talk to them." Then he said, "I had to go on to the field and instruct every one of them. I mean you had to know everything."[35]

Earl Hunsinger, pitcher and teammate of Woody's on the 1957 Miami club, put it best: "Woody was not only the favorite of the players but of the fans too. Woody was very outgoing, hustled all of the time, and never slacked up. He was a third baseman and I'll never forget, you know after each groundout you used to throw the ball around the infield. The third baseman always throws it back to the pitcher. And Woody, when he threw the ball back to you, always had something good to say. He was quite a gentleman."[36]

Acknowledgments

My sincere appreciation to the Smith family; Jerry, Reggie, Gale, and June for sharing their experience. Thank you to HistoryMiami for providing photographs. I am grateful to Bill Durney Jr., Earl Hunsinger, Tom Qualters, and Lenny Scott for imparting their thoughts on Woody Smith. And last, but not least, I am indebted to my wife Barbra who supports me in all my writing endeavors and who always inspires me.

Notes

1. Ancestry.com and Jerry Smith, phone interview, January 6, 2016.
2. Jerry Smith, phone interview, January 6, 2016.
3. Reggie Smith, phone interview, December 4, 2015 and March 2, 2016.
4. Jerry Smith, phone interview, January 6, 2016.
5. Information located by son Reggie Smith in family records.
6. Baseball-Reference.com.
7. Peter G. Pierce, *Baseball in the Cross Timbers* (Oklahoma Heritage Association, Oklahoma City, OK 2009) 205, 341.
8. Baseball-Reference.com. Reggie Smith passed on personal information given to him by his father who told him that the 1948 season was disappointing because of his struggles with an arm injury.
9. Ancestry.com.
10. John L. Halpin, "Steve Salata Top Fielding Catcher In Cam-Am," *Oneonta Star*, January 20, 1950, 10.
11. *Sporting News Baseball Guide and Record Book*, 1950, 286–89.
12. Baseball-Reference.com.
13. Ibid.
14. Jimmy Burns," Marlins Deaf to First-Year Pennant Warning by Betzel," *The Sporting News*, August 8, 1956, 28.
15. Luther Evans, "Marlins Buy New Infielder: Smith," *Miami Herald*, July 26, 1956, 1-D.
16. *The Sporting News*, August 8, 1956, 27.
17. Luther Evans, "Marlins Chill Leafs on Walk in 9th," *Miami Herald*, July 27, 1956, 1-D.
18. Eddie Storin," Marlins Split, But Grab Lead," *Miami Herald*, July 30, 1956, 1-D.
19. Norris Anderson, "Marlins Claim Record 51,713 See 6–2 Victory," *Miami News*, August 8, 1956. The official record was noted by *The Sporting News* as 57,713, which was acknowledged as the minor league record that the Denver Bears broke in 1980.
20. *The Sporting News*, August 15, 1956, 30.
21. Baseball-Reference.com.
22. Clifford Kachline, "Rookie In Class D Crashes All-Star Minor Glove Team," *The Sporting News*, December 10, 1958, 14.
23. *The Sporting News*, October 1, 1958, 51.
24. Norris Anderson, "Smith's I.L. Fielding Record Verified," *Miami News*, July 18, 1958.
25. "It's All Over Now for Marlins," *Miami News*, September 12, 1960.
26. Tom Qualters, phone interview, March 5, 2010.
27. Bill Durney Jr., phone interview, July 19, 2014.
28. The franchise was referred to as the Marlins in 1969 and 1970, and the Orioles in 1971 and 1972.
29. Baseball-Reference.com.
30. Milb.com. Florida State League Champions. The cities that have won back-to-back championships are DeLand 1951–52, St. Petersburg 1966–67, Lakeland 1976–77, and Tampa 2010–11.
31. June Smith, phone interview, September 22, 2014.
32. Luther Evans, "7–2 Home Opening Win," *Miami Herald*, April 19, 1973, 1-C.
33. Baseball-Reference.com.
34. Leonard Scott, phone interview, August 25, 2015.
35. June Smith, phone interview, September 22, 2014.
36. Earl Hunsinger, phone interview, March 15, 2010.

Spring Training, Safe at Home!, and Baseball-on-Screen in Florida

Rob Edelman

Occasionally, baseball films spotlight sequences or storylines that are Florida-centric. Not surprisingly, they primarily are linked to spring training—and some even have real-world connections. *Slide, Kelly, Slide* (1927), for example, features the New York Yankees working out in Delano—and highlights guest appearances by Mike Donlin, Bob Meusel, Irish Meusel, and Tony Lazzeri. *Big Leaguer* (1953), starring Edward G. Robinson as ballplayer-turned-talent evaluator John B. "Hans" Lobert, is set in a New York Giants tryout camp in Melbourne. In *Fear Strikes Out* (1957), Boston Red Sox rookie Jimmy Piersall (Anthony Perkins) heads for spring training in Sarasota.

Others are fictional. *Kill the Umpire* (1950) stars William Bendix as an ex-ballplayer, loudmouth, and die-hard fan who resides with his family in St. Petersburg, where he sneaks off to Grapefruit League contests between the New York and St. Louis nines. *Strategic Air Command* (1955) toplines James Stewart as a B-29 bomber pilot-turned St. Louis Cardinals all-star third sacker who trains in St. Petersburg; in the film's first shot, a car pulls up outside Al Lang Field, the designated "Winter Home (of the) St. Louis Cardinals." In *Major League* (1989), a menagerie of has-been and never-were ballplayers shows up for Cleveland Indians' spring training (albeit in Arizona, rather than Florida). But there is a Sunshine State connection: The snooty ex-showgirl who has just taken over team ownership schemes to move the Tribe to Florida. The city of Miami has promised her a new stadium, a Boca Raton mansion, and a Palm Beach Polo and Country Club membership. So how can she refuse?

In *Fever Pitch* (2005), the following dialogue is spoken between Ben (Jimmy Fallon), a Boston Red Sox fanatic, and Lindsey (Drew Barrymore), his new girlfriend:

Ben: "...every year during Easter vacation...uh, me and my friends, we go down to Florida."

Lindsey: "You and your buddies go down to Florida for spring break? At your age?"

Ben: "No, no, no, not spring break. Spring training with the Red Sox."

Lindsey: "Oh, you get to train with the Red Sox? Are you allowed to do that?"

Ben: "Well, we don't actually...We watch the games."

Lindsey: "Aren't those just practice games?"

Ben: "Yeah, yeah, but there's more to it than that. We scout the players. We...We say which players they should keep...which they should get rid of."

Lindsey: "And the Red Sox ask your opinion?"

Ben: "Well, not yet...."

Ben heads south and, later on, Lindsey tells him: "I saw you on ESPN." He responds: "Oh! We looked like morons, didn't we?" And his excuse: "Well, it's very hot, you know, it's Florida."

Of all baseball films with Sunshine State/spring training connections, however, the one that most typifies the Grapefruit League world is not one of the first-division sports yarns. Far from it. For indeed, the best that can be said about *Safe at Home!* is that it is an innocuous kiddie film—and despite its spotlight on the New York Yankees, one need not wrap oneself up in pinstripe pride to savor it. The film (which was released in 1962) is a must-see if only because it stars the M&M boys themselves, Mickey Mantle and Roger Maris. The previous season, of course, Maris had whacked 61 dingers to top Babe Ruth's single-season record, while Mantle chimed in with 54 round-trippers. Unlike *Slide, Kelly, Slide* and countless other films which feature real-life ballplayers in cameo appearances, these genuine American heroes not only shag flies and smash fastballs but also are called upon to act.

Safe at Home! is the saga of Hutch Lawton (Bryan Russell), a motherless, baseball-mad ten-year-old Little Leaguer who has moved to Palms, Florida, with his father, Ken (Don Collier), a struggling charter boat operator. Henry, a fellow Little Leaguer and patronizing banker's son, harasses Hutch because the elder Lawton is immersed in his work and unable to watch the team practice. Hutch responds by bragging that his dad not only is more baseball-savvy than any other parent but is best buddies with New York Yankees players—and specifically Mickey Mantle and Roger Maris. The youngster even claims that Ken Lawton is "Roger Maris's best friend in the whole South."

Hutch of course is dumbfounded upon being pressured to bring the ballplayers to a league dinner. What will he do? "I'm gonna go see 'em," he declares. "That's what I'm gonna do. I'm gonna ask 'em to help. They just gotta say yes." So the youngster sneaks off to Fort Lauderdale, then the Yankees' spring training home, by hiding in the back of a fish truck operated by a friend's father. Upon his arrival, he sneaks into the Mick's hotel room and Fort Lauderdale Stadium; showers in the same stall where the ballplayers clean up; falls asleep in the team's locker room while garbed in Maris's jersey and employing Mantle's as a blanket; and is confronted by Bill Turner (William Frawley), a quick-tempered yet sympathetic Yankees coach. As any young fan might, Hutch imagines himself a flychaser who is cheered on as he smacks base hits and makes circus catches. Plus, he endlessly sighs, "Mickey Mantle…Roger Maris…Gosh…Gee…." In the tradition of happy-ever-after Hollywood finales, Hutch realizes that fibbing is bad business, Ken learns that his son requires attention and understanding, and Hutch and his teammates get to visit Fort Lauderdale and spend quality time with Mantle, Maris, and their teammates.

Robert Creamer, writing in *Sports Illustrated*, observed that *Safe at Home!* "was designed for cheap, quick filming, a [spring training 1962] release date and a fast buck." The previous summer, as Mantle and Maris were smashing dingers, Tom Naud, the film's eventual producer and story co-author, conjured up the idea of starring them onscreen. He contacted Frank Scott, the ballplayers' agent, and a deal quickly was struck. In the original storyline, Mantle and Maris were to play deaf-and-dumb siblings—perhaps because they could not read lines believably—but the concept was nixed by Scott. What then emerged was the scenario that was used in the film and, by November 1961, all was in place for the spring shooting schedule.[1] *The New York Times* added that *Safe at Home!* was produced by Columbia Pictures "on a comparatively

After their on-field exploits of 1961, Mantle and Maris were sought by film producer Tom Naud for a Hollywood feature.

modest budget" of "about $1,000,000," with Mantle and Maris "dividing a guaranty of $50,000."[2]

On February 7, 1962, the *Times* reported that the duo was "heading for Fort Lauderdale…but not for baseball. For the next few weeks they will be here strictly as actors, appearing in the Columbia picture 'Safe At Home!' Scenes will be shot at the ball park and at the club's quarters in the Yankee Clipper Hotel."[3] A week later, it was announced that star hurler Whitey Ford and skipper Ralph Houk had been added to the cast. The paper also noted a bit of off-camera drama: "…during the filming of the preliminary shots at nearby Pompano Lake, there was quite a to-do when one of the camera men, Irving Lippman, lost, or thought he had lost, a valuable ring. Mantle sailed right in and spent some fifteen minutes trying to find it in the loose dirt. When the cameraman returned to his hotel, he found the ring on top of his dresser. He was all apologies but Mickey assured him he should 'think nothing of it. The exercise did me good.'"[4]

On February 15, the *Times* ran a feature on the production. "The Yankees went Hollywood today, and for more than four hours, Manager Ralph Houk's well-regulated training camp became a merry shambles," wrote John Drebinger. The scribe noted that the otherwise "obliging" Houk, certainly a novice at moviemaking protocol, gave the film's director, Walter Doniger, full control of the ball park. However, "by the time the field was well-cluttered with sound

Actor William Frawley, far left, is shown in this publicity still with various members of the cast and crew of Safe at Home, including Mantle and Maris.

trucks, cameras, ladders, wires and whatnot, Houk felt he had obliged enough." The manager also was ill-prepared for the presence of the make-up artist, who was to groom him for his on-camera emoting. "For the Major is still a rugged military man," noted Drebinger, "and the rouge and powder made him squirm. Especially when he found himself in the center of the astonished stares of the players." Adding to Houk's frustration was that his few lines with Bill Frawley had to be re-shot eight times.[5]

Ten days later, Drebinger penned another piece on the progress of the shooting. He observed that, according to Doniger and Tom Naud, Mantle and Maris "are not performing as actors but as themselves. Their lines are what they would say as ballplayers." Drebinger was quick to disagree, however, given that "the jargon of the dugout could be a trifle rough." But he added: "Mantle and Maris are doing well, so far. Mantle, in particular, seems to be enjoying himself. He laughs easily and takes everything in stride. Asked whether he preferred being an actor to a ballplayer he replied: 'Why, this life is a breeze. Shucks, in this business when you make a mistake you do it over and over and over until you do it right. Around the ball field when you misjudge a fly ball or let a third strike whiz by they don't give you another crack at it.'"[6]

Drebinger reported that Doniger "insists that Mantle, Maris and the other Yanks in the picture, including coach Johnny Neun and some twenty rookies who provide background, have been a most agreeable surprise. 'They've really amazed me,' he says, 'by their poise and

the relaxed manner in which they handle themselves, especially in the outdoor scenes with spectators gaping at them from all sides. Even professional actors sometimes feel a bit self-conscious working under such conditions. But ballplayers, I guess from the nature of their business, are so accustomed to playing before a crowd that it doesn't bother them in the least'." (Drebinger also noted that one of the junior ballplayers in the cast was none other than "freckle-faced David Mantle, Mickey's 6-year-old son.")[7]

In retrospect, it is no surprise that Mantle and particularly Maris do not give Oscar-caliber performances in *Safe at Home!* What matters is who they are: clean-cut all-American champions being marketed as models for young American boys. And they are not the sole Yankees spouting dialogue. Whitey Ford speaks a line: "Hey Rog, Mickey. Houk wants to see you right away." Ralph Houk has several interchanges: "Hey, Bill, can I see you for a minute....What's that youngster doing on the bench?...Keep on running. Run harder than that..." (For sure, the *Safe at Home!* screenplay was not penned by Ernest Hemingway.) And as the Yankees train, the names "Tom" and "Phil" are detectable. Could they be "Tresh" and "Linz"? When somebody cries "Pepi," he has to be citing Joe Pepitone.

Also of note in *Safe at Home!* is the presence of Frawley, a lifelong baseball fan whose Coach Bill is a variation of the crabby but endearing characters he played on *I Love Lucy* and *My Three Sons*, his hit TV series. In one scene, the coach and Mantle and Maris pass the hours away from spring practice by playing Scrabble in a hotel room—and M&M gently tease him on his ineptitude at spelling. "Who says so?" Bill growls. "Webster," is Mantle's answer. "What club's he with?" the coach responds. At one point, Bill dubs Mantle and Maris (who then were as celebrated as any big leaguer) a "bunch of mangy rookies."

Less than two months after its filming, *Safe at Home!* was released theatrically to coincide with the start of the 1962 season. Its premiere was no star-studded Hollywood event; the film opened on a double bill with Chubby Checker's *Don't Knock the Twist*, another Hollywood product attempting to cash in on the era's zeitgeist. Both were combined in their advertising copy, which was headlined: "2 GREAT HITS ON ONE GRAND SLAM TWISTIN' PROGRAM,"

SAFE AT HOME!
CREDITS

DIRECTOR: Walter Doniger.
PRODUCER: Tom Naud.
SCREENPLAY: Robert Dillion, based on a story by Naud and Steve Ritch.
MUSIC: Van Alexander.
A NAUD-HAMILBURG PRODUCTION.
CAST: Mickey Mantle (Himself); Roger Maris (Himself); William Frawley (Bill Turner); Patricia Barry (Johanna Price); Don Collier (Ken Lawton); Eugene Iglesias (Mr. Torres); Flip Mark (Henry); Bryan Russell (Hutch Lawton); Scott Lane (Mike Torres); Charles G. Martin (Henry's Father); Ralph Houk (Himself); Whitey Ford (Himself).

NOTE: Approximately twenty Yankee rookies and other team personnel appear unbilled. Cast as one of the young ballplayers, also unbilled, is David Mantle, Mickey's son.

with *Safe at Home!* featuring "The great M&M playing themselves! Big Buddies to the luckiest kid in the world!" Given Frawley's popularity, he was spotlighted for playing "the tough, gruff, lovable coach."

Unsurprisingly, the film's reviews were at best tepid. *New York Times* critic Eugene Archer summarized the majority opinion by declaring: "Mickey Mantle and Roger Maris came up to bat in unfamiliar surroundings yesterday and went down swinging," adding that *Safe at Home!* was "a whimsical little children's film" and "minor league production."[8] Additionally, in order to be cast in *Safe at Home!* Mantle and Maris were afforded membership in the Screen Actors Guild, which made them eligible to garner Best Actor Academy Award nominations. But they were not members of the Academy of Motion Picture Arts and Sciences, which barred them from voting in the Oscar race. "They must achieve distinction as actors," explained an unnamed Academy expert, adding: "It is not felt that their distinction is in the field of acting."[9]

Almost four decades after the release of *Safe at Home!*, I interviewed a number of the film's participants while researching *Meet the Mertzes*, a double biography of William Frawley and Vivian Vance, his *I Love Lucy* co-star. One was Tom Naud, who explained that Frawley "loved being cast in (the film). He loved calling Ralph, Mickey, Roger, and Whitey by their first names." At the same time, Frawley only palled around with the stars. "I wouldn't have been invited to talk baseball with him," recalled Jim Bouton, then a Yankees rookie, who was one of the extras. "That was for Mickey

Mantle and Roger Maris and the big guys, like Whitey Ford. I was just happy to be asked to be an extra in the movie, for which I got paid the munificent sum of $50."[10] (According to the *New York Times*, the rookies "had [each] received $100 for romping on the field.")[11]

As for Mantle and Maris, Walter Doniger offered a take on the ballplayers that was far-removed from what he told the press during the shoot. Doniger described them as "pretty arrogant and ego-driven." To convince them to respond to his directorial cues, he determined that "the best thing I could do would be to pretend total ignorance of baseball, and not know who they were. One time, I said to them, 'I'd like in this scene for you to run not counterclockwise but clockwise around the bases. 'They looked at me and said, 'You can't do that in baseball.'" Doniger added: "I would deliberately get their names reversed, so that they kept trying to prove to me that they were important. I thought the best thing to do would be to make them ordinary people to me, and not big league stars and world heroes. So I did that, and it seemed to work.'"[12]

Whether the M&M boys were model citizens during the shoot, or haughty superstars, or something in between, what matters today is that *Safe at Home!*, while no *Pride of the Yankees* or *61**, does offer a nostalgic snapshot of a moment in time. (And speaking of *61**, wouldn't Billy Crystal—famed Yankees fan who celebrated his sixtieth birthday by DH-ing in a 2008 spring training game in Tampa—have made a perfect Hutch Lawton?) ∎

Notes

1. Robert Creamer, "Mantle and Maris in the Movies." *Sports Illustrated*, April 2, 1962, 96–108.
2. John Drebinger, "Teamwork on the Citrus Circuit." *The New York Times*, February 25, 1962, X7.
3. John Drebinger, "Toothpick Bat: Weighty Topic in Yanks' Camp." *The New York Times*, February 7, 1962, 59.
4. John Drebinger, "Two Infielders Figure in Plans." *The New York Times*, February 14, 1962, 29.
5. John Drebinger, "Houk Gets Some Coaching, Hollywood Style." *The New York Times*, February 15, 1962, 32.
6. John Drebinger, Teamwork on the Citrus Circuit. *The New York Times*, February 25, 1962, X7.
7. Ibid.
8. Eugene Archer, "Double Bill at Neighborhood Theatres." *The New York Times*, April 14, 1962, 14.
9. Murray Schumach, "Mantle, Maris in Oscar Race." *The New York Times*, February 16, 1963, 5
10. Rob Edelman, Audrey Kupferberg. *Meet the Mertzes* (Los Angeles: Renaissance Books, 1999), 204–205.
11. John Drebinger, "Houk Gets Some Coaching, Hollywood Style." *The New York Times*, February 15, 1962, 32.
12. Rob Edelman, Audrey Kupferberg. *Meet the Mertzes*. (Los Angeles: Renaissance Books, 1999, 204–205.)

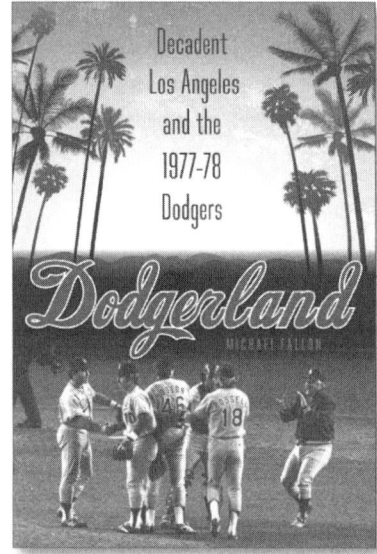
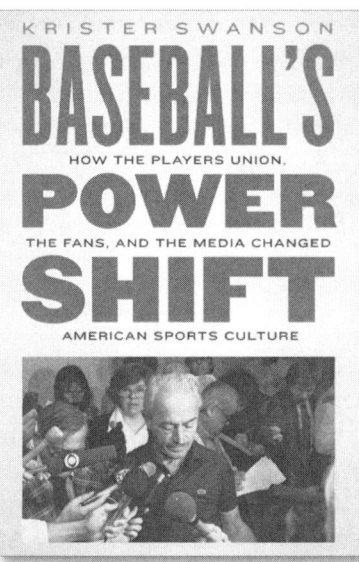

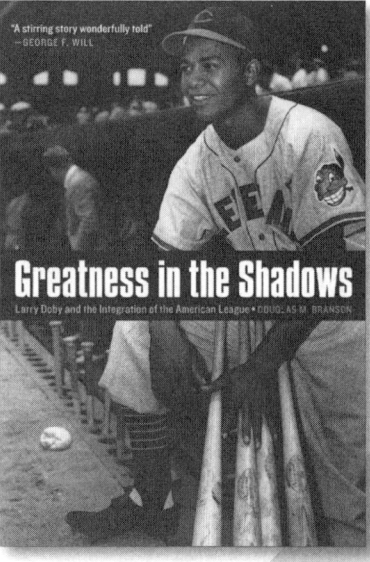

Field of Schemes

The Spring Training Tryout of NFL Star "Jerry LeVias"

Dan VanDeMortel

In 1513, explorer Juan Ponce de Leon arrived in Florida, according to fable in search of the Fountain of Youth. Ever since, Florida's menu of sun, fun, beaches, and citrus has symbolized renewal and regeneration, an "enchanted reality," per state historian Gary Mormino, ripe for second chances amidst a constantly shifting dreamscape.[1]

Since the early twentieth century, Florida has offered the "enchanted reality" of spring training, with players and fans annually migrating to the Sunshine State for salubrious weather guaranteed to banish winter and welcome a fresh start. Dreams abound: a sharper curve, a quicker bat, fleeter feet, fewer aches and pains, a little bit more luck, making the team, a higher finish in the standings. Sportswriters, too, hear this suggestive call, the time when prose contracts the occupational disease "superlativitis," as described by *Sport* magazine.[2] The air tingles with possibility.

In February 1971, it seemed that Houston Oilers star receiver Jerry LeVias sensed that possibility even though he was at the pinnacle of a standout NFL career. The Beaumont, Texas, native had excelled as quarterback for his segregated high school. Upon graduation in 1965, he had blazed a trail as the first black scholarship athlete in the Southwest Conference, joining Southern Methodist University as a receiver in an era of racial turmoil. While there, he had lived alone and experienced racism from opponents and teammates in the form of hate mail, death threats, and on-field racially-motivated beatings. "My trademark was not to get tackled by more than one person so as not to end up under the pile. I tried to survive because I knew the things that would happen," the 5-foot-10, 175-pound speedster later recalled.[3] Encouraged during a brief meeting with Martin Luther King Jr., LeVias graduated in 1969, racking up All-SWC and All-American honors, and most SWC receiving records. Considered the "Jackie Robinson of the Southwest," he was drafted by the American Football League's Oilers, where he made the Pro Bowl as a rookie wide receiver and kick/punt returner. When the AFL merged with the National Football League in 1970, he joined the league of his Detroit Lions cousin, Mel Farr, and finished fifth in all-purpose yards.

LeVias hadn't played baseball since he was an SMU sophomore, but he had been a .305-hitting second baseman. And he had stolen 52 bases in part-time high school ball, which had prompted the New York Yankees to offer a $30,000 bonus and a $12,000 annual contract.[4] San Diego Chargers star halfback Mike Garrett had just cancelled a well-publicized plan to try out for the Los Angeles Dodgers, so the idea of an NFL star contemplating a career change to baseball was not unheard of at the time.

Detroit Tigers farm director Hoot Evers and chief scout Ed Katalinas began to receive calls in February from LeVias about a spring tryout, introducing himself as Farr's cousin, explaining he loved and wanted to play baseball instead of football, which, "wasn't really his game."[5] Katalinas procured an old scouting report on LeVias and conferred with Evers, who told LeVias he was welcome at the Lakeland Tiger Town training site if he could obtain the Oilers' permission. LeVias quickly agreed. Katalinas told the press, "Our club is always looking for speed. He's got two items on his side: unadulterated speed and great body control. He has what we call an infielder's body. We have to find out if he has major league potential. After three weeks or so, he'll know and we'll know."[6]

After obtaining Tigers infielder/pinch hitter Gates Brown's phone number from the club, LeVias contacted him to advise that he was leaving football and would be reporting to Lakeland. Shortly thereafter, he showed up at Brown's Detroit west-side bar under adversity, asking for a $300 loan for the round-trip airfare to Florida to help cover luggage lost on his flight to Detroit, a marriage to a woman in Atlanta, and funds tied up in Houston. Brown loaned the money and the two of them flew together with little additional conversation to Tiger Town on Friday, February 19.[7]

The Tigers team awaiting their arrival was undergoing its own regeneration. The 1968 World Series champions were recovering from a 1970 ordeal beset by more clubhouse drama than wins. To jumpstart

William Douglas Street Jr., shown here in a recent mugshot, has racked up multiple convictions for fraudulent impersonation.

success, Billy Martin had been signed to manage a re-vamped roster. This was the same diminutive but fiery Martin who would be hired and fired with clockwork regularity over his managerial career, as his brawls, alcoholism, and combative personality would repeatedly wear out his welcome.[8] It was also the same Martin who was peerless as a tactician and who would rejuvenate every team he inherited, including the Tigers. He met with every player during the offseason to address problems and boost morale. "I'd play Adolf Hitler nine innings every day if he was the best man I had for the job," he proclaimed, warning during the offseason, "I won't put up with liars, alibi Ikes, or con artists."[9]

In this atmosphere of high expectation, the Tigers rolled out the red carpet for LeVias. He was housed at the team's newly built, three-story Fetzer Hall dormitory.[10] A press release was issued. Potential snags were quickly averted. When LeVias explained that his Oilers' written release was in luggage lost on the flight in from Detroit, along with Brown's luggage, the team relaxed their rule and issued him a gray second-string uniform.[11] Showing up without spikes equally proved inconsequential: a travelling sporting goods salesman handed over a pair of shoes with no payment due until their next meeting.

As LeVias donned his uniform, media, team officials, and players orbited about. In reports that would circulate nationwide, LeVias detailed his disappointment with football: "I've just lost all my feeling for football. I don't ever want to go back. I'm just a little thing, you know, and I'm a little tired of getting belted around all the time. It was a mistake to play in Houston those two years. The players there didn't give it all they've got. It's tough to play when you've got a quarterback who won't throw the ball to you because he's jealous of all the attention you've received. And when I'd get hurt, the people wouldn't believe me. I've been disenchanted with football ever since I got to Houston."[12]

LeVias estimated he needed a half to a full season in the minors to move up to the Tigers and considered returning to school if he failed to make the cut. With camera snapshots exposing his face under a Tigers cap rather than concealing it behind an Oilers facemask, the man the *Detroit News* had dubbed "Speediest Rookie" headed for the field.[13] When he strode toward the plate, the Tigers regulars stepped aside to let him bat.

As LeVias finished his swings and commenced fielding drills under veteran scout Bernie DeViveiros's supervision, however, his skills appeared rawer than expected. "I wasn't too impressed with the way he threw. Once in a while he would pop the ball a little with something on it, but right away I had my doubts. I watched him run and I wasn't at all impressed. I just couldn't see the speed that I was supposed to see," DeViveiros recalled.[14] "Something was clearly wrong with all his fundamentals," added Katalinas, also in attendance.[15] Once the 40-minute workout concluded, DeViveiros left the field muttering, "The fellow doesn't look like an athlete to me."[16] Overall, he looked like "horse feathers," observed another coach.[17] Amidst swirling disappointment, LeVias remained undeterred, announcing he would issue a formal statement about quitting football in a day or two, and even asking for a monetary advance to tide him over.[18]

Meanwhile, an ominous cloud was heading toward his prospects. Once UPI picked up Detroit media coverage, the press contacted Oilers publicity director Jim McLemore for comment. Unaware of LeVias's career change, McLemore called LeVias via the team's contact information. The LeVias he reached was in Texas, though, where he was training for the upcoming football season. "This is a hoax," McLemore quickly claimed to UPI after the workout.[19] "Me quit football?" chimed in LeVias from Texas. "I don't know where a thing like this got started. Biggest hoax I ever heard of."[20]

Despite a tightening noose, the Lakeland LeVias insisted he was genuine to *Detroit News* beat writer Watson Spoelstra over two interviews, claiming papers to prove it were in his lost luggage. Finally, during a third interview with Spoelstra, nine hours after the tryout, LeVias came clean. News flash: His real name was *Jerald Lee* LeVias, not Jerry LeVias. Born in Detroit, the 23-year-old had graduated from Detroit Central High School where he was an All-City high school football player, and had recently gotten out of the Army and married when the imposter idea came to him. As for his raison d'etre at Tiger Town, the self-proclaimed lifelong Tigers fan offered, "I love baseball, that's all. I figured I'd get a better chance if I were somebody."[21] Although of similar build to the receiver and having read about him in a magazine, Jerald Lee had only been to Houston once and had never seen Jerry play.

After quickly being contacted by Spoelstra and conferring with LeVias, and later general manager Jim Campbell, Evers announced, "The boy misrepresented himself and I'm sending him home. I don't fault him that much if he wants to play baseball. But he went about it in a very wrong way. He seems like a very nice young man. He got some publicity he wasn't deserving of and I'm certainly sorry."[22] Evers confessed he was "red-faced" and had erred in relaxing rules regarding the Oilers' permission. "He said both his and Brown's luggage had been lost at the airport...If one suitcase was lost we might have suspected something. But, when he said both were lost, it sounded right."[23] Katalinas was likewise embarrassed, oversold on LeVias showing up to camp with Brown. LeVias, meanwhile, retreated to a darkened room, refusing photographs. "I feel like a heel now...I had no idea the other LeVias was that popular. I just wanted to work out for a few days to show them what I could do. I was going to tell them the truth."[24]

The next morning, LeVias was flown back to Detroit. He recalled, "I began to feel a little guilty when they started taking all those pictures. I just didn't expect to get all that attention. But, things were happening so fast, I didn't know what to do. So I just went along with it."[25] With questionable self-analysis that as a "celebrity" he "shouldn't have any trouble getting a tryout somewhere else now," LeVias boarded with two airline-provided servings of Cutty Sark "hooch" for luggage

Gates Brown was the first Tigers player to be drawn in by Street's scam when he lent the impostor $300 and accompanied him on an airline flight to spring training.

to "get me a little drunk tonight" on the Tigers' dime.[26] Or, rather, on a $93 first-class departure ticket, which combined with Friday's $72 team-covered coach arrival fare meant the Tigers paid $165 to be hoaxed and Brown was $300 lighter for an "airfare loan."[27] "Live and learn," Brown lamented. "I'll have to chalk it up to experience. I didn't even know who Jerry LeVias was. Somebody in the front office gave him my phone number and that's why I thought he was okay."[28]

Before, during, and after departure, Jerald Lee's hoax deepened. With his story publicized in Detroit, he was identified as William Douglas Street Jr. by a friend who recognized his picture. The "nice young man" man in actuality was a 20-year-old west-side Detroiter, the son of a bus driver and homemaker, who "couldn't hit or pick up the ball" and was "equally as bad" at other sports, according to Central High's baseball captain.[29] Recently married to a local woman, not Atlantan, he'd decided that a life like his father's was for "chumps," but spent too much time "partying and goofing off" to obtain a profession.[30] "I guess you can say I was always a man who believed in shortcuts," he later admitted.[31] A 1970 larceny conviction while posing as a Ferris State College student had been one of those short cuts.

Via enchanted reality and despite poor high school baseball skills, Street envisioned being a professional baseball player, his marriage certificate's listed occupation, if given the opportunity. In 1969, he had finagled a summer workout with the Boston Red Sox when they visited Detroit. The following year, he had appeared at the team's Winter Haven camp, fabricating that he had been called for a tryout. His skills were so poor, however, the Red Sox "got him off the field before he got killed" and paid for his return home.[32] Later that summer, Street had appeared in Boston as a *Time* magazine writer covering Carl Yastrzemski, asking for and obtaining a uniform to work out with the team to get a "real feel for the story."[33] He was eventually tossed out after being caught warming up in the bullpen and shaving in the dugout during a game. Over subsequent months, Street had continued pestering the Red Sox, highlighted by receiving $50 while impersonating a Boston farmhand on a Detroit television show.[34]

Once Street's full history hit the light of day, Campbell admitted, "We were taken by a real pro...I'm glad we didn't get hurt more than we did." *Detroit News* reporter Jerry Green, who had not bitten on the phony LeVias since he had seen the real LeVias in action, was amazed that Campbell had been so thoroughly hoodwinked since he was "such a straight-laced guy when it came to rules and regulations."[35]

Street's shenanigans fit perfectly with the Grapefruit League's history of dreamers and schemers, some of whom even progressed to the Cactus League for more action. As Tigers coach Charlie Silvera recalled after Street's escapade, some spent a few weeks drifting from club to club, getting a "sandwich and a coffee" for their efforts, the lucky few obtaining a recommendation letter from one general manager to another club.[36] "You'd get a note saying the player was 6-foot-2, 190 pounds and when you'd get him, he'd be sawed off to 5-foot-1 and 110. Some really think they can play, but what they want most is to go to spring training. We used to have a lot of them, but not so much anymore."[37] "Dippers" who would "steal anything—dip into anything—wallets, clothes, rings, watches" also made the rounds.[38] By 1971, however, sophisticated scouting and the free agent draft had virtually guaranteed that an unknown phenom making a team—like Billy Martin had while working out in unappreciated obscurity in Oakland after his high school graduation—were in history's dustbin.

Street's baseball-related impersonation efforts failed to find that same dustbin. On March 3 he was arrested at an Orlando hotel for passing a bad check on its manager under the guise of being with the Minnesota Twins. Returning to Detroit, he concocted a scam for "easy money" while drinking with friends.[39] Knowing that Tigers slugger Willie Horton was in Florida, just past midnight on March 9, Street delivered a letter to Horton's wife at the couple's Detroit home. Horton's wife recognized Street from his newspaper picture and refused to open the door. Identifying herself as Mrs. Horton's sister, she instructed Street to leave the note. It demanded she withdraw $20,000 from her bank and turn it over to "this man."[40] "This man," in turn, would hand over a briefcase of "pictures, tapes, and records of your husband's criminal dealings," warning her she would be killed if she contacted anyone and that her husband's and children's lives were at stake.[41] Mrs. Horton immediately contacted the police. Shortly thereafter, Street was arrested and sentenced to 20 years' probation for extortion. "That was some troubled times. We had to get security for my kids to go to school. What he put us through, I never wanted to see him again," Willie Horton recalled.[42]

From 1973 onward, Street's schemes veered toward surrealism. After violating his parole, he was sentenced to Southern Michigan prison, from which he escaped. By 2015, his lengthy confidence man resumé featured impersonations of a Michigan football player, a lawyer for the Detroit Human Rights Department, a medical student at Yale University, an Annapolis graduate, and a doctor at an Illinois Hospital, where he came close to

Later in spring training, Tigers slugger Willie Horton became entangled with Street when the con artist delivered a letter to his Detroit home demanding $20,000 and threatening murder if the police were contacted. Undeterred, upon receipt of the letter, Horton's wife contacted the police and Street was quickly arrested.

performing an emergency appendectomy. He had totaled 25 convictions, 11 prison sentences, and numerous aliases, including one as a woman.[43] In July 2015 the Plymouth township resident, living with a wife and special needs step-daughter, was sentenced to 23 months in state prison for issuing falsified checks. On February 8, 2016, he was sentenced to a consecutive term of 36 additional months on federal charges of mail fraud and aggravated theft of a Maryland-based Defense Department contractor's identity used to pick up women and obtain a job. His lawyer describes him as "doing okay" and prepared—in the jailhouse phrase for serving time—to "go lay down for a while."[44] "I'm tired of this nonsense," his client offered in court, "each day we choose who we will serve…and I chose incorrectly."[45]

Street's life has been dramatized in Chameleon Street, which won the Grand Jury Prize at the 1990 Sundance Film Festival. Its director, after meeting with Street extensively, observed, "When he meets someone, he susses out within three minutes exactly who they want him to be, who they are, what hopes and aspirations they might have, how they digest the black persona and he becomes whatever is most advantageous to him."[46]

In a current film industry beset by uninspiring sequels, Street's life more deservedly calls for an updated Chameleon Street, or better yet a well-produced documentary. If Street participated in one, he would likely cite, as he did in a jailhouse interview, his impersonation of LeVias as, "the first time I found out how easy it was to get people to believe whatever you said, so long as you said it right."[47] Asked today the reason for his behavior, he might answer as he did in that same interview: "I don't think of myself as an average guy out to prove something to the world. Sometimes, I think I'm just trying to prove something to myself."[48] ∎

Acknowledgment

Heartfelt appreciation goes out to baseball writer/editor Gary Gillette, SABR-Detroit chair, for his assistance with this article.

Notes

1. Gary Mormino, *Land of Sunshine, State of Dreams* (Gainesville, FL: University Press of Florida, 2005), 2–3.

2. Jonathan Fraser Light, *The Cultural Encyclopedia of Baseball* (Jefferson, NC: McFarland & Company, Inc., 2005), 872.

3. Pro-Football-Reference.com (http://www.pro-football-reference.com/players/L/LeViJe00.htm) lists LeVias at 5'9", 177 pounds. However, 1971 press accounts and his 1971 Topps and Kellogg's football cards list him at 5'10", 175 pounds; consequently, this measurement is relied on.

4. "LeVias Decides to Quit Football," *Wilmington Morning Star*, February, 20, 1971, https://news.google.com/newspapers?nid=1454&dat=19710220&id=FStkAAAAIBAJ&sjid=sQkEAAAAIBAJ&pg=5018,3426816&hl=en.

5. "The Amazing Mr. Street Goes South Again," *Pittsburgh Press*, February 22, 1971, http://tigerlore.blogspot.com/2013/02/the-amazing-mr-street-goes-south-again.html?view=classic; "Tall Tale Grabs Tiger by Tail," *Jet*, March 11, 1971, https://books.google.com/books?id=tjcDAAAAMBAJ&pg=PA52&lpg=PA52&dq=tall+tale+grabs+tiger+by+tail&source=bl&ots=DTHsehWd0E&sig=vA2shwEEtvklZOnAkluoHikzb9o&hl=en&sa=X&ved=0ahUKEwijvbOG0KTKAhVK-2MKHVeGCvoQ6AEIHTAA#v=onepage&q=tall%20tale%20grabs%20tiger%20by%20tail&f=false.

6. Jerry Green, "Baseball's Great Imposter," *Sports Scene*, September 1971.

7. LeVias used a portion of the $300 to pay for Brown's ticket. Brown slept through most of the flight.

8. In true fashion, Martin would guide an improved Tigers team to 91 wins in 1971 and one American League Championship Series win short of going to the World Series in 1972. Despite this success, by 1973 his relationship with general manager Jim Campbell had deteriorated so badly that he was fired in September while the team had a 71–63 record. His repeated etiquettorial remark, "Excuse me, I've gotta go take a Jim Campbell" when he used the restroom likely encouraged that development. Mike Shropshire, *The Last Real Season* (New York: Grand Central Publishing, 2008), 59.

9. Ed Linn, "Billy Martin: A Foreign Body in the Tigers' System," *Sport*, June 1971; Watson Spoelstra, "Martin Warns His Tigers: 'I Hate Alibi Ikes,'" *The Sporting News*, January 30, 1971.

10. Watson Spoelstra, "Tigers Are Red-Faced on Dead-End Street," *The Sporting News*, March 6, 1971; Bill Rufty, "Tiger Town Dorm Getting $1 Million Renovation," *The Ledger*, December 30, 2007, http://www.theledger.com/article/20071230/NEWS/712300465.

11. Brown later explained that his luggage was never lost; LeVias picked up the wrong suitcase at the airport. Once this error was discovered, they drove back and gathered the right one.

12. LeVias Decides to Quit Football," op. cit.

13. Spoelstra, "Tigers Are Red-Faced on Dead-End Street," op. cit.

14. "Tigers Fooled," *Hendersonville Times-News*, February 22, 1971, https://news.google.com/newspapers?nid=1665&dat=19710222&id=a8AmAAAAIBAJ&sjid=TiQEAAAAIBAJ&pg=5208,3447286&hl=en; "Tiger Imposter Feels Like Heel," *Oakland Tribune*, February 22, 1971.

15. Richard Willing, "Will The Real William Douglas Street Jr. Please Stand Up," *Detroit News* (Sunday Magazine), July 14, 1985.

16. Spoelstra, "Tigers Are Red-Faced on Dead-End Street," op. cit.

17. Joe Falls and Jim Hawkins, "How a Kid With a Lot of Guts Pulled a Big Hoax on Tigers," *Detroit Free Press*, February 22, 1971.

18. Jim Hawkins, "Our Man Jim Was Sweet-Talked, Too," *Detroit Free Press*, February 22, 1971.

19. Watson Spoelstra, "'Unitas' Next for Tiger Tryout,'" *Detroit News*, February 22, 1971.

20. "Tigers Are Red-Faced on Dead-End Street," op. cit.; "Tall Tale Grabs Tiger by Tail," op. cit.

21. Spoelstra, "Tigers Are Red-Faced on Dead-End Street," op. cit.

22. Watson Spoelstra, "'Unitas' Next for Tiger Tryout," op. cit.; Green, op. cit.

23. "The Amazing Mr. Street Goes South Again," op. cit.

24. Green, op. cit.

25. "Tiger Imposter Feels Like Heel," op. cit.; Green, op. cit.

26. Joe Dowdall, "'Tigers 'Foul Ball' Strikes Out Here, Too," *Detroit News*, February 22, 1971; Green, op. cit.

27. In 2016 currency, the Tigers paid $967 for LeVias's flights and Brown's loan was $1,758.

28. Spoelstra, "Tigers Are Red-Faced on Dead-End Street," Green, op. cit., see also, Joe Falls, "The Gator Believed 'LeVias'—And He's Out 300 Skins!," *Detroit Free Press*, February 22, 1971.

29. Dowdall, op. cit.

30. Willing, op. cit.

31. "Professional Imposter Poses as Yale Student," *Daily New London*, November 30, 1984, https://news.google.com/newspapers?nid=1915&dat=19841130&id=2y1SAAAAIBAJ&sjid=CDYNAAAAIBAJ&pg=2180,6989111&hl=en.

32. Bill Halls, "Imposter Hit Others," *Detroit News*, February 23, 1971.

33. Ibid.

34. $293 in 2016 currency.

35. Jerry Green, telephone interview, January 14, 2016.

36. Jim Taylor, "No Place for Dreams," *Toledo Blade*, June 20, 1971, https://news.google.com/newspapers?nid=1350&dat=19710620&id=DvNOAAAAIBAJ&sjid=1QEEAAAAIBAJ&pg=7173,4827973&hl=en.

37. Ibid.

38. Ibid.

39. Willing, op. cit.

40. "Warrant Is Sought Against Imposter in Threat to Hortons," *Detroit News*, March 17, 1971; "Arrest Man Who Tricked Tigers for Threatening Horton's Wife," *Ludington Daily News*, March 17, 1971, https://news.google.com/ newspapers?nid=110&dat=19710317&id= bbpNAAAAIBAJ&sjid=FkoDAAAAIBAJ&pg= 1480,4151883&hl=en; "Willie Horton's Wife Gets Imposter's $200,000 [sic] Note," *Jet*, April 15, 1971, https://books.google.com/books?id=jjcDAAAAMBAJ&pg=PA28&lpg=PA28&dq=willie+horton%27s+wife+gets+imposter%27s+jet&source=bl&ots=1boACmZsyw&sig=USz3dc6BJ53u1obiskPMi5PMjNQ&hl=en&sa=X&ved=0ahUKEwjJy7nC56TKAhUY32MKHW9sBHIQ6AEIHDAA#v=onepage&q=willie%20horton%27s%20wife%20gets%20imposter% 27s% 20jet&f=false.

41. "Willie Horton's Wife Gets Imposter's $200,000 [sic] Note," op. cit.

42. Robert Snell, "Game May Be Up for 'The Great Imposter,'" *Detroit News*, June 5, 2015, http://www.detroitnews.com/story/news/local/wayne-county/2015/06/04/epic-con-artist-chameleon-strikes-feds-say/28515197.

43. Ibid.; Willing, op. cit.

44. Joseph Arnone, telephone interview, January 15, 2016.

45. Jennifer Chambers, "'Great Imposter' Who Inspired Film Gets Prison Time," *Detroit News*, February 8, 2016, http://www.detroitnews.com/story/news/local/wayne-county/2016/02/08/william-street-sentencing/80010360.

46. Robert Snell, "'Great Imposter' Pleads Guilty, Faces Almost 3 Years,'" *Detroit News*, September 30, 2015, http://www.detroitnews.com/story/news/local/detroit-city/2015/09/24/longtime-impostor-inspired-film-back-court/72726470.

47. Willing, op. cit.

48. Ibid.

El Presidente

The Life and Times of Dennis Martinez

Danny Gallagher

Dennis Martinez had just lost a heartbreaker of a game, 1–0, tossing 10 innings against the United States, losing to future major-leaguer Rich Wortham.

Martinez, only 17, was hardly displeased with his effort because he had pitched before some 25 major-league scouts in his homeland of Nicaragua against a team of older players in the Federación Mundial de Béisbol Amateur World Series. And not long before that tournament, Martinez had been impressive, too, coming out of the game in the seventh inning in a tournament in the Dominican Republic when Nicaragua beat world-class nemesis Cuba 4–3.

Following the loss to Wortham and Team USA, Baltimore Orioles scout Ray Poitevint sidled up to Martinez and asked him if he wanted to sign with the Orioles. The date was December 10, 1973.

"I signed for $3,000," Martinez said in a phone interview from his home in Miami.[1] "I was looking to come to the US. I was not a homesick kind of kid. It was the last time people in my country would see me pitch."[2]

Earlier in the tournament, Poitevint was told that Martinez wouldn't likely pitch because he was a youngster on a team laden with senior players.

"I was sitting in the first-base dugout and I saw Dennis warming up on the pitchers' mound in left field," Poitevint, 86, recalled in an interview from Palm Springs, California.[3] "I watched him throw a breaking ball. A scout down there by the name of Tony Casanto said it was a hook pitch. Not many people called it a hook. It was a breaking ball like a slider, a little bit stronger than a slider, like an overpowering slider.

"Someone with the Nicaraguan team said I wouldn't have a chance to see him pitch. I then asked if I could work him out. But toward the end of the tournament, one of their starting pitchers got hit in the groin area by a batted ball so they went to another pitcher and it messed up their starting rotation so they put Dennis in."[4]

And it opened up an opportunity for Martinez to pitch three innings. Of course, what Martinez did in the 1–0 matchup with Wortham blew Poitevint away.

At age 20 in 1974, Dennis Martinez spent his first year in the Orioles organization with the Class A team in Miami.

"Dennis pitched outstanding," Poitevint said.[5] "I loved his composure. His natural talent was green as grass but it was there. You could see that he had a chance to be something special. There were 25 scouts there that night and they all were checking to see if I could sign him. When he finished his pitching, I took him from the home-team dugout underneath the stadium to a hotel and I asked his mother to attend.

"In those days, Dennis could be signed by anybody. His mother was a great woman. I tried to do what I could. We didn't have a lot of money to give. The maximum was $3,000. It wasn't very much but the main thing is that I signed a lot of good pitchers and Dennis has done the best. He had two strong attributes I look for in any kind of athlete: mental toughness and emotional control."[6]

1973 was also the year the Orioles signed high draft pick Eddie Murray to a $20,000 contract, as well as the year Martinez got married to the same woman he's with now.

"This girl moved into our neighbourhood across the street from where we lived," Martinez recalled.[7] "She was a little girl. I said to myself, 'Oh, oh, that looks pretty good.' I was like a good scout, I had good eyes. That's my girl. I picked the right woman. I was lucky with Luz."[8]

Martinez was born May 14, 1954, in Granada, Nicaragua, the youngest of seven children raised by his father Edmundo, a farmer, and his mother Emilia, a housewife.

"My dad was a farmer who owned a lot of land," Martinez said.[9] "I was the only one of us born in Granada and my three brothers and three sisters were born in the country. They were joking around that I was the golden boy, that I was born in the city, that I was able to go to a school. We had moved to Granada before I was born.

"We were a poor family but we were able to survive. I helped my parents on the farm. We lived on rice and beans, plantain, vegetables, some meat, some chicken."[10]

A year after signing with the Orioles, the organization decided to place Martinez on the roster of its Class A team in Miami and he was a resounding success with a 15–6 record. In 1975, although his walk ratio worsened, his record improved to 16–5 during stints with Miami, Double-A Asheville, and Triple-A Rochester. The Orioles kept Martinez in Rochester for most of the 1976 season when he went 14–8, prompting a call-up for his major-league debut September 14.

By 1977, Martinez was in the big leagues for good. He was a mainstay of the Orioles' pitching staff until 1986 when he was traded to the Montreal Expos.

Back in 1972, Martinez had been introduced to booze by an amateur teammate in Nicaragua. That started a relationship with the demon alcohol that for many years wouldn't allow him to concentrate.

"I was 17-years-old," Martinez said.[11] "I was 6–0 my first year in amateur baseball. I was undefeated. One day, we went to another town to play a game and we lost 1–0. The catcher, he saw that I was down because we got beat. His name was Roque Zavala. All of a sudden Roque came back to the back of the bus and said, 'Hey man, drink this.'"[12]

The substance was the Nicaraguan specialty rum Flor de Caña, one of the country's most famous exports. Martinez had one, then another and then more. There was no Coke or ice to go with it. Next thing you know, he was drunk and passed out on the two-and-a-half-hour-long trip back to his home.

"We were drinking shots of this rum," Martinez said.[13] "I don't remember how I got home. It got me. Roque really loved me. He always motivated me, always pushed me. He made me feel good. He was the kind of person who was like a mentor to me. He didn't mean to hurt me by offering me the rum. He tried to make me feel okay. From that day onward, I was introduced to alcohol but not every day."[14]

And that introduction spilled into his major-league days, but only on road trips, never at home in the presence of his wife and children. There was always beer in the clubhouse and then he would get invited out to bars by teammates to continue drinking. Funny thing, he didn't develop a passion for rum and was never the big drinker his father was. Ironically, his drinking problem started when he became a regular in the majors in 1977.

"There was beer available after a game and then you would go out for dinner and all of a sudden, it was the lifestyle," Martinez said.[15]

Martinez stopped drinking beer and switched to white wine, which over time got boring, too.

"Beer? I was not a big beer drinker. Somebody told me that beer would get you fat and you would get a belly," Martinez said, chuckling.[16] "I started drinking wine but it gave me a headache. I wouldn't feel good the next day. I changed to amaretto, just with ice. I liked it because it was fruity. Then I went to Grand Marnier, pretty much like amaretto. I liked its sweetness. It was less sugary than amaretto and it was something strong."[17]

What really threw Martinez for a loop, prompting him to quit drinking, was a late-at-night incident after the Orioles won the World Series over the Philadelphia Phillies in 1983. It just so happened to follow his worst season ever in the majors: he was 7–16.

Martinez's drinking and mental deterioration had prompted manager Joe Altobelli to exclude him from use in the American League Championship Series against the Chicago White Sox and the World Series against the Phillies. Altobelli just didn't have the confidence in him.

One night shortly after the World Series ended, Martinez had gone to a gym to work out and ran into a friend coming out of the building. They decided to go for a drink, which turned into several drinks.

"It was five in the afternoon when I came out of the gym," Martinez said.[18] "My friend asked me if I wanted to go for a drink and I said, 'Why not?' I had the first one, the second, the third one and six or seven more. They didn't have amaretto or Grand Marnier at that bar so I drank beer and white wine."[19]

Martinez figures it was nine o'clock when he and his buddy decided to leave the bar. When he was driving toward the expressway to go home, his car had a flat tire. So he pulled over and soon, a state trooper also pulled over, noticed Martinez was under the influence and charged him with intoxication.

"By the next day, it was all over the news," Martinez said.[20] "I was feeling so bad, so shameful, so humiliated, so devastated. When my kids came home from school, I talked to them. Their reaction was, 'Dad, we

After being traded to Montreal, Martinez pitched the highlight of his career, a perfect game on July 28, 1991, at Dodger Stadium.

already know that.' They told me they had heard I was stopped for drinking and driving. I saw the hurt in their eyes. That's what got me. They had a right to be upset."[21]

Martinez knew it was time to quit drinking. He entered rehab and hasn't had a drink for 32 years.

"I turned to God for help," he said.[22] "I was either going to kill somebody or kill myself drinking and driving. I'd become two different people: I didn't drink at home but I drank on the road. It was time for me to overcome my drinking problem and pray with the rosary for the rest of my life.

"I've gone to Alcoholics Anonymous meetings in Miami two or three times a week since then. It's the only way to stay sober. And when I go back to Nicaragua, I go almost every day if I can."[23]

In the three years following sobriety, Martinez was a changed man on the baseball field, not for the good, but for the worse. By 1986, the Orioles gave up on Martinez and traded him to the Expos on June 16, 1986.

The decision to quit drinking took a toll on Martinez's pitching, rather than improve it. In 1984, he was 6–9. In 1985, his record improved to 13–11 thanks to improved run support, but a look at his FIP (fielding independent pitching) he worsened from 4.96 to 5.22. In 1986 prior to the trade, the slide continued.

"I dedicated myself to sobriety, I just focused my mind on not drinking, to change myself and to train myself not to drink," Martinez said.[24] "When I tried to play, it wasn't the same. I wasn't the same pitcher, not the same before I stopped drinking. And it's true, you can't concentrate on the game and on sobriety at the same time. You have to concentrate on one or the other.

"The Orioles were not patient enough. I don't blame them. They didn't see the fire in my eyes anymore. When I heard in the clubhouse that I was traded, I was crying like a baby. One of the players came up to me and said, 'You're hurt and you have a right to feel this way but don't forget this is a business. This team was your livelihood. They may not want you but another team wants you.' That's what I wanted to hear. He encouraged me. I stopped crying and I moved on.

"The Expos had great scouting people and they saw something in me. I was grateful to them. I wanted to prove them not wrong, I wanted to prove them right."[25]

And he proved them right, even though he got knocked around early on. During one particular game when he was being bashed by the Pittsburgh Pirates, pitching coach Larry Bearnarth came to the mound to make him feel better.

"'Okay, kid.' Those were Larry's words," Martinez recalled.[26] "He said, 'You are a veteran, kid, you have been successful, do what you love to do.' He helped turned my life around. That game against Pittsburgh, I got hit so bad. They were hitting the ball hard and I wanted to come out of the game. Larry came with the right things to say. At the end of the season, I started showing signs of pitching better. I won three games [for Montreal], including a shutout."[27] The shutout came on August 5.

After a rough 3–6 stint in 1986 with the Expos, Martinez made progress and more progress. By 1987, after a stint in the minors, he would emerge as the ace of the Expos' pitching staff. This is what he did during his tenure with the Expos: 11–4, 15–13, 16–7, 10–11, 14–11, 16–11, and 15–9.

The highlight of his career came July 28, 1991, on a scorching hot day in Chavez Ravine at Dodger Stadium when he threw a perfect game against the Dodgers: 27 up, 27 down, including shutting down former Orioles teammate Eddie Murray three times.

Martinez did it at age 36 in his fifteenth season as a major-leaguer. It was done in the midst of trade rumours that suggested he was going to the Toronto Blue Jays in exchange for Québec native Denis Boucher.

When the twenty-seventh batter, pinch-hitter Chris Gwynn, hit a long fly to center, Martinez turned around and saw right away that outfielder Marquis Grissom had lots of time to get under the ball.

"He didn't hit it that hard. He'd gotten it on the big barrel of the bat and the ball stayed in the air so it gave Marquis a chance at going after it," Martinez said.[28]

As the ball landed in Grissom's glove, Martinez was whooping it up and turned toward third baseman Tim Wallach. They may have been teammates but they were adversaries, too. Wallach never cared much for Martinez's style of popping off to the media if he felt the team was playing poorly. That day, though, Wallach forgot the past to hug Martinez.

"Eli was showing his emotions," Martinez said.[29] "There was that bond between us despite the past. He hugged me and I hugged him, too. I was happy but my emotions took control of me. I started to cry."[30]

There were some hair-raising moments that put the perfecto in doubt. The closest call came in the seventh when Juan Samuel tried to leg out a hit with a drag bunt down toward the first-base side. Martinez moved in quick, picked up the ball with his bare right hand and threw to first baseman Larry Walker, who had to sprawl in the dirt for the ball and keep his foot on the base at the same time.

"It was risky doing it barehand," Martinez said.[31] "It could have rolled off my finger or something like that. I have a video of the game and it shows I had plenty of time to throw him out."[32]

What Martinez didn't know was that Samuel was unaware that Martinez had a perfect game in the works.

"We were down 2–0 and I thought I'd try to get something going," Samuel recalled.[33] "Then when I got to the bench, I looked up at the scoreboard and noticed that Dennis had a no-hitter going. I didn't know that. I said, 'What if I had gotten a hit on the bunt?' I sat at my locker after the game wondering.

"I wouldn't have wanted to break up the no-hitter that way. If I'd known he had a no-hitter, I wouldn't have bunted. I would have just swung away. I live in Miami like Dennis does and I've helped to raise money for the people in Nicaragua like Dennis does. I told Martinez that it was the biggest play of the game. I told him that he looked like a shortstop the way he sprinted off the mound for the ball."[34]

Martinez said he threw 80 percent fastballs that day. Of the 96 pitches he threw, only 30 were balls. Prior to hitting to Grissom to end the game, Gwynn had hit a line drive foul past third, causing a few hearts to flutter.

"I made no bad pitches. I've watched every single pitch on the video. It was remarkable," Martinez said.[35] "When I went out to the mound for the ninth, I was shaking. The crowd [more than 45,000] was clapping and giving me ovations. I said, 'Please, God, help me.'"[36]

Funny thing, in the fourth inning, Martinez experienced some soreness on his right side and he was tended to by trainers Ron McClain and Mike Kozak. During the course of the game, the trainers also doused Martinez with ammonia to keep him cool in the scorching heat.

"He had such good control," said Dodgers second baseman Alfredo Griffin.[37] "He had good command of his pitches. He had a nasty slider. When you have command, you have a lot of confidence in anything you throw."[38]

When all of the hullabaloo after the game ended, Martinez found his way to a spot in the dugout. He wanted time to himself. His head was in his hands or his hands were clasped as he bowed to the floor.

"There were tears in my eyes because of the joy, what God allowed me to do. I thought of the people in Montreal who treated me so good," Martinez said of his time alone.[39] "I was just praying to me. I was kind of numb. I was dreaming. I was biting my tongue."[40]

The next day, Martinez appeared on NBC's Today show at 4:45 AM Pacific Daylight Time with Bryant Gumbel. A few days later, he sent his uniform top, a ticket stub and an autographed ball from the game to the National Baseball Hall of Fame and Museum in Cooperstown, New York.

At the first game back in Montreal at Olympic Stadium, Expos brass gave him a Chevrolet Blazer and a framed photo of himself. Three weeks later, accompanied by reporters from the *Montreal Gazette*, *La Presse*, and *Le Journal de Montréal*, Martinez travelled to his birthplace in Granada to be feted by his countrymen.

What he remembers more than anything from that time was not so much the perfect game, but that day of recognition in his homeland. It was special because he was the first player from Nicaragua to play in the majors.

"I pitched that game in LA, but to share it with my people in Nicaragua is something I will never really forget," Martinez said.[41] "It was an unbelievable feeling, a great day I will never forget. Every time I look at the video of the game, I'm living a dream. It happened 25 years ago but it feels like yesterday."[42]

When he returned to Montreal from Nicaragua, Martinez arranged to spend over $7,000 with the Royal Canadian Mint in Ottawa to obtain Canadian Maple Leaf coins for his teammates, other uniformed personnel and Expos' staff members to commemorate his special day.

DOUG McWILLIAMS, NATIONAL BASEBALL HALL OF FAME LIBRARY, COOPERSTOWN, NY

Martinez's 245 wins—104 in the NL and 141 in the AL—are the most of any Latin American pitcher, eclipsing Juan Marichal's 243.

Martinez would stay with the Expos through the 1993 season but not before turning down an August trade that year, a proposed transaction that would have sent him to the Atlanta Braves. Martinez would go on to sign a multiyear deal with the Cleveland Indians and later played for the Seattle Mariners and the Braves.

By nixing the trade to Atlanta in 1993, he missed out on playing for the pennant-contending Braves. He wanted to finish the season with the cash-strapped Expos. In what seemed like a bizarre decision on Martinez's part, he used his power as a 10-and-5 (10 years in the majors, at least the last five with the same team) player to veto the trade.

"I had a lot of discussions with my lawyer [Ron Shapiro] to see what was best for me on the field," Martinez told the *Globe and Mail* that day.[43] "We decided on the Expos as the most reliable situation for me because I'd be able to pitch every five days. Going to Atlanta, it sounds like I was going to be more of the insurance man for them. Being the fifth man in the rotation there wouldn't allow to me to pitch as often as I would here. They have the best pitching staff with four solid starters. I didn't want to be in that situation. I don't want to be there just for the hell of it."[44]

Martinez had also used his 10-and-5 power to obtain financial compensation from both the Expos and Braves to make the deal possible.

"We didn't want to give him any compensation because we felt that by sending him to a team that might make the playoffs and the World Series was compensation in itself," Expos GM Dan Duquette said.

"The Braves made it clear right from the start that they would not do anything about a contract extension and that there would be no compensation of any sort whatsoever for going there," Martinez said.[45] "I didn't like that. It's not right. It's not fair."[46]

Both Martinez and Shapiro believed the Braves claimed Martinez to prevent a trade to the San Francisco Giants.

"They were blocking San Francisco on waivers," Shapiro said at the time.[47] "They haven't a darn use for Dennis. They weren't going to put him in a role to win a game because they had guys who could do it. If there was going to be no compensation, it didn't make sense to approve the trade.

"Dennis has 96 National League wins and wants to be a 100-win man in both leagues. That's what it's all about from here on in. With Atlanta, maybe he would have had three or four starts. In Montreal, he might get seven or eight."[48]

Sure enough, Martinez did get his 100th win before the end of the 1993 season. That offseason, though, Duquette and the Expos decided Martinez was too expensive to sign to a new contract so they let him go.

Along the way in his career, Martinez boasted two friends whom he cherished in the majors: Eddie Murray and the late Mike Flanagan.

"Eddie, Mike, and I all came through the Orioles' farm system to the big leagues," Martinez said.[49] "I was able to show them as a Latin kid that I had no preference for any race. I chose a white boy and a black boy. I had good eyes. And here I was a Latino. I was in the middle. You can't go wrong that way."[50]

Since 1989, Martinez has lived in Miami, including the last 24 years in the same house. It didn't hurt that he had lived there briefly in 1974-75 when he played Class A ball.

"I've always liked Miami. First of all, there's the atmosphere, the environment," Martinez said.[51] "There are a lot of Spanish people there. My wife and family, my brothers and sisters, all wanted to stay in Miami. The weather is nice and warm and we're closer to Nicaragua."[52]

Martinez would stay out of baseball for years after his retirement following the 1999 season but he eventually resurfaced as a minor-league instructor for several teams and was bullpen coach for the Houston Astros in 2013.

As a token of appreciation for what he did with the Expos, the voting members of the Canadian Baseball Hall of Fame in St. Marys, Ontario, elected Martinez on February 2, 2016, as one of its new members. In 520 major-league bats, Martinez had gone homerless, but two days prior to his induction on June 18, 2016, Martinez, 62, stunned onlookers when he lined a home run over the left-field fence in the second inning of a celebrity slow-pitch softball game in St. Marys. One inquirer asked Martinez on the conference call what it was like to be swapped to the Expos, a move that turned his career around.

"I was so grateful to be traded to the Expos, to a different country, to a different culture," Martinez said.[53] "That was my second chance in baseball. They treated me so good in Montreal. I was so happy to play there. People took me under their wing."[54]

Martinez finished his big-league career with more than 100 wins in both the American League and National League. His 245 wins, 104 in the NL and 141 in the AL, are the most of any Latin American pitcher, eclipsing the 243 won by Hall of Famer Juan Marichal. Martinez also finished with a 3.70 ERA, 122 complete games, and 30 shutouts in a career that fell just short of 4,000 innings pitched.

Poitevint, a pioneering baseball scout, who spent close to six decades in the game and still remains active as a consultant, just loves Martinez.

"I don't like to broadcast it but Dennis was always first class," Poitevint said.[55] "He's something extra special. He went through a lot of hardships, a lot of problems. He did it on his own. Of all the people I signed, he was the best person and the best pitcher."[56] ∎

Notes

1. Dennis Martinez, telephone interview, January 22, 2016.
2. Ibid.
3. Ray Poitevint, telephone interview, January 27, 2016.
4. Ibid.
5. Ibid.
6. Ibid.
7. Dennis Martinez, telephone interview, January 22, 2016.
8. Ibid.
9. Ibid.
10. Ibid.
11. Ibid.
12. Ibid.
13. Ibid.
14. Ibid.
15. Ibid.
16. Ibid.
17. Ibid.
18. Ibid.
19. Ibid.
20. Ibid.
21. Ibid.
22. Ibid.
23. Ibid.
24. Ibid.
25. Ibid.
26. Ibid.
27. Ibid.
28. Danny Gallagher, *You Don't Forget Homers Like That* (Scoop Press, 1997), 36.
29. Ibid.
30. Ibid.
31. Ibid.
32. Ibid.
33. Ibid.
34. Ibid.
35. Ibid, 37.
36. Ibid.
37. Ibid.
38. Ibid.
39. Ibid, 40.
40. Ibid.
41. Dennis Martinez, telephone conference call, February 2, 2016.
42. Ibid.
43. Danny Gallagher, "Martinez nixes trade to Braves," *Toronto Globe and Mail*, August 16, 1993.
44. Ibid.
45. Ibid.
46. Ibid.
47. Ibid.
48. Ibid.
49. Dennis Martinez, telephone interview, January 22, 2016.
50. Ibid.
51. Ibid.
52. Ibid.
53. Dennis Martinez, telephone conference call, February 2, 2016.
54. Ibid.
55. Ray Poitevint, telephone interview, January 27, 2016.
56. Ibid.

Miami Amigos

Eric Robinson

Ever since the 1963 minor leagues realignment, the leagues that have held the Triple-A classification have been fairly consistent. The International League and Pacific Coast League have been fielding teams annually since then, with the American Association joining in 1969 before being disbanded in 1997 and having its teams absorbed by the other two leagues. Astute fans of baseball being played in other countries will be aware that the nonaffiliated Mexican League has held the Triple-A designation since 1967. What many may not realize is that for several months in the spring and summer of 1979 that there was one other Triple-A league, the Inter-American League (or IAL). The league was the dream of Roberto "Bobby" Maduro, a Cuban exile who was working as Coordinator of Inter-American Baseball for Commissioner Bowie Kuhn.[1] This ambitious league had six teams in three different Latin American countries (the United States, Venezuela, and Panama) with its flagship franchise being the sole team based on the mainland United States, the Miami Amigos.

Maduro had been the owner of the Havana Sugar Kings of the International League since 1954. He had to relocate the team to Jersey City in 1960 due to Fidel Castro nationalizing control of American businesses in Cuba.[2] At the end of the 1961 season Maduro moved the franchise to Jacksonville, Florida, where they became the Jacksonville Suns.[1] In 1963 Maduro sold his 51% ownership stake of the Suns in a sale of stock to the people of Jacksonville but remained with the team acting as it's General Manager.[2] Maduro resigned from his position following the 1965 season but he stayed involved in professional baseball, taking a position in the major league office while working toward his goal of establishing professional baseball league in Latin America.

On December 31, 1978, Maduro resigned in order to prep for the inaugural season of the Inter-American League which was to begin four short months later on April 11, 1979.[3] The Miami Amigos were organized prior to the teams located in the Dominican Republic, Panama, Puerto Rico, and Venezuela.[4] The owners were established South Florida baseball men: Ronald Fine and Joe Ryan who owned the Class-A Miami Orioles of the Florida State League. The cost for the franchise was $50,000.

The duo announced to the public the creation of the team at an event in September of 1978 that also featured Miami mayor Maurice Ferre as a speaker. The mayor stated, "This is one of the most significant developments to happen in Miami in recent years," which proved to an overly enthusiastic prediction of the importance of a baseball franchise that would be defunct before July of the following year.[5]

The team was to play its games at Miami Stadium, the home to Fine and Ryan's other team, the Miami Orioles. The stadium was opened in 1949 in the Allapattah neighborhood and had been used as a Spring Training home for the Brooklyn/Los Angeles Dodgers and Baltimore Orioles, as well as various South Florida minor-league and college teams.[6] When it opened, baseball commissioner Happy Chandler declared that he knew of "no more beautiful park anywhere."[7]

Miami Stadium was no longer in its original splendor but was still a serviceable stadium for a Triple-A team. The stadium had a seating capacity of 9500, down from its original 13,000, when the Amigos began play in 1979. This made it the smallest of the stadiums in use by the teams in the IAL by nearly 5000 seats.[8] Despite this smaller size, the team was second in attendance for the league behind the Caracas Metropolitanos in Venezuela.

The Amigos' uniforms reflected the Latin American influence that was a significant part of both the city of Miami and the IAL. The team's colors were green with red and yellow trim. While the home uniform was a basic white jersey with white pants, the road jersey was a garish bright green V-necked pullover with the team city and name written across the chest in bold yellow letters with red trim. The logo had Miami written above Amigos with the two words sharing a large A. The team's cap was in a pinwheel style that was popular during the time with a red bill, a white front panel with a large red M joined with a pointed green A, and a green back.

The players wearing these uniforms were a motley bunch of ex-major leaguers, young Latin talent, and other assorted players and characters thrown in. The highest-profile person affiliated with the Amigos was future world champion manager Davey Johnson.

The scrappy three-time Gold-Glove-winning infielder had finished his 13-year major league playing career the previous season as a pinch hitter and third baseman for the Chicago Cubs. Johnson was 36 when Fine and Ryan hired him for his first managing job. Even though he was hired to manage the Amigos, he also got 25 at bats for the team playing in limited use. Johnson would later say that his time as Miami's skipper was difficult but when asked to reflect on the experience he stated he learned important skills such as, "putting a team together from scratch, judging talent, putting a lineup together, putting a pitching rotation together…all of that helped."[9]

Johnson described the roster as "probably the best Triple A club in existence."[10] Of the 30 different players who wore the Amigos green and red over the course of the team's 72 games, 17 had at one time played in the major leagues and pitcher Porfi Altamirano would later debut with the Philadelphia Phillies in 1982.

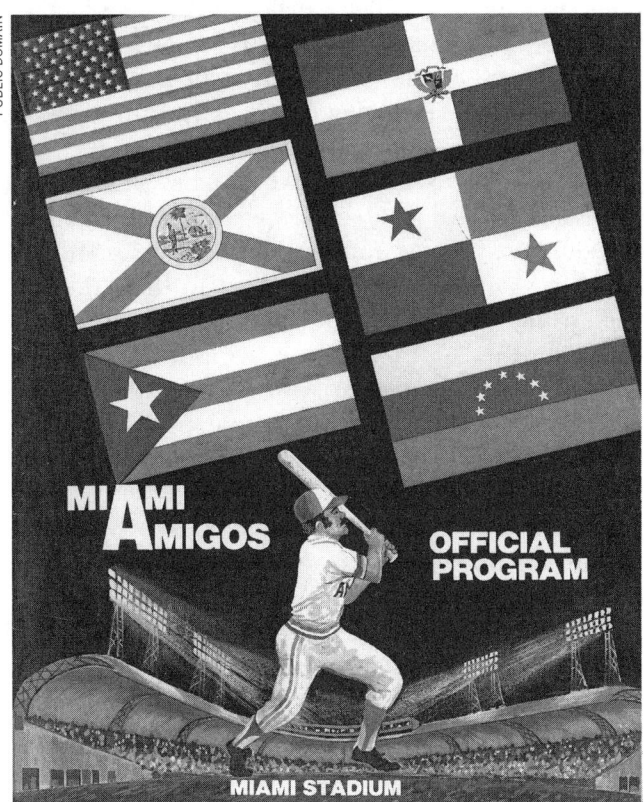

The cover illustration to the Amigos program shows the distinctively cantilevered roof of Miami Stadium, later known as Bobby Maduro Stadium.

The Amigos featured several players with circumstances that were unique to say the least. Oscar Zamora had pitched parts of four seasons in the big leagues with the Chicago Cubs and the Houston Astros. By 1979 he owned a successful shoe factory located in Miami and due to the obligations of that job, the 34-year-old could only travel to away games on the weekends.[11] Despite these restrictions, Zamora was tied for second on the team in wins with eight.

Another player with restrictions on when he could play was outfielder and one-time Milwaukee Brewers top prospect Danny Thomas. Thomas earned the nickname the Sundown Kid due to his affiliation with the Worldwide Church of God and his adherence to their belief of not working between sundown on Friday and sundown on Saturday.[12] His season was cut short following a suspension for an "unnecessary" argument with an umpire which also brought his pro career to an end just three seasons after he had been the Eastern League's Triple Crown winner.[13] The following year he committed suicide in an Alabama jail cell he was in due to allegations of sexual assault of a minor.[14]

The team's top pitcher was Mike Wallace who earlier in the decade had a strong season with the New York Yankees. Wallace would lead both the team and league in wins with a dominant record of 11–1 while also posting a strong ERA of 2.27. The team also featured the Tyrone brothers, Jim and Wayne, who starred as the top hitters in the IAL.[15] Jim, a one-time Cub and Athletic, lead the league with a .364 batting average. His younger brother Wayne hit a league-leading eight home runs that season. His most high-profile moment would come in 1983 when the Texan would appear on *The Price is Right* and win a new car.[16]

Difficulties faced by the Amigos during the season-opening road trips were indicative of the mixture of offbeat snags and serious problems the team and the league would face in its three-month existence. The season began on April 11, 1979, with a game in Panama City against the Panama Banqueros, followed by a series against the Caracas Metropolitanos. However, the team did not get to don their memorable bright green uniforms for these games, nor did they even get to play wearing uniforms with the actual team name on them. Pitching coach Oscar Pena explained, "We got these beautiful new uniforms and somebody stole them out of Miami Stadium so for the first few games we had to wear uniforms that said Miami Marlins."[17]

The trip from Panama to Venezuela revealed the visa complications that would play a part in the downfall of the IAL. The league was playing in four different

Davey Johnson, who would manage the Mets to a World Series championship in 1986, took the helm for the Miami Amigos during their brief existence.

countries and had players from even more, and the teams would encounter hassles as they traveled from country to country. As the team arrived in Venezuela, the authorities refused to admit a player from Nicaragua and Cuban catcher Jorge Curbelo.[18] In addition to Curbelo not being allowed to play the series, the Amigos faced another problem after their series with the Metropolitanos was complete, the team could not find the backstop. After finally reaching his mother on the telephone, Amigos officials found out that he was at his home taking a nap.[19]

Despite these early setbacks, the Amigos immediately proved to be the top team in the league. The talent that team officials assembled and Davey Johnson led went on to finish with a season (and franchise) record of 51–21 and include the IAL's pitching and hitting leaders.[20] The next best team had 14 fewer victories. The atmosphere at Miami Stadium for Amigos games was just as festive as the jerseys the team wore, with the crowd bringing conga drums and other percussion and beating out Latin rhythms throughout the game.[21] In another departure from the staid world of major league baseball, the team had their own cheerleaders that went by the name of the "Hot and Juicy Wendy's Girls."[22]

Their winning ways and party-like vibe in the stands was not enough to bring folks out to the Amigos' games. Despite strong early attendance and a showdown between one-time Cy Young winner Mike Cuellar with the hometown shoe industry businessman/part-time pitcher Oscar Zamora that attracted over 3,000 spectators, the average attendance for the games at Miami Stadium was only 1,350 people.[23,24] Fine and Ryan even offered a promotion where fans could purchase a joint season ticket with Ryan's Miami Orioles for all of the two teams' combined 130 home

games for $250. However, this did not draw out South Florida's baseball obsessives. A major problem that the Amigos and other teams in the IAL faced were lack of both television and radio broadcasts, which cost them a major source of revenue, as well as the opportunity to draw fans to the ballpark. Only one IAL game was broadcast in Miami, and that was on the radio.[25]

And while operations in Miami were run like a Triple-A team, not all franchises were run to that professional level. In Panama, the Amigos had to play one afternoon game without a scoreboard as the operator was only hired to work night games.[26] That game was called early due to rain despite the team having a modern tarp just for any potential rain delays. The problem was the grounds crew consisted of children that had not been instructed on the proper way to cover the infield. One game the Amigos played in Venezuela had to called early when the stadium's lights went out and never came back on.[27]

Another significant problem not just for the team but for the entire league was the cost and scheduling of the air travel between the Caribbean countries. DC-10 planes were grounded following an American Airlines crash which made the already problematic logistics even more difficult.[28] The Amigos had few flights in their entire existence that were less than an hour late.[29] Other problems included the team having to take separate flights, with one of the flights arriving only minutes before game time, games starting at 10:00PM, and others being called early so the teams could reach the airport in time.

By June, the league lost two of its six franchises, San Juan and Panama. The league then divided the schedule into halves and awarded the first half pennant to Miami with their 43 wins in their first 60 games. The Amigos would only play 12 more games following this split. Following two other teams announcing they wanted to suspend operations for a year, Bobby Maduro announced on June 30 that he would be shut downing the IAL. He promised that it would return in 1980, but those plans never came to fruition.

The season began with the team not wearing their own uniforms and ended with the Amigos playing their final games without their manager guiding them. Johnson was still suffering from an injury that occurred from a home-plate collision during his time as a Phillie in 1977 and was in traction following the removal of two disks in his back.[30] This experience managing the Amigos helped Johnson as in 1981 he took a position as the manager of the Mets Double-A team in Jackson, Mississippi, and by 1984 he was manager of the big league New York Mets. In 1986, he skippered that team to a World Series victory over the Boston Red Sox.

For a number of the Miami Amigos, this was their last stop playing professional baseball. Fine and Ryan continued to be involved in Florida baseball. Bobby Maduro never was able to start his dream of a Latin American professional baseball league and when he passed away in 1986 from brain cancer it was still too early to see the Florida Marlins expansion team. He did receive a lasting posthumous honor when in 1987 Miami Stadium, the one-time home of the Miami Amigos, was renamed Bobby Maduro Miami Stadium as a tribute to his being a friend to baseball in the Miami region.[31] ■

Notes

1. John Cronin, "When a Dream Plays Reality in Baseball…," *The Baseball Research Journal* 40 (2011), 88–93.
2. "International League in Cuba:50 Years Later," The International League Historical Scrapbook (2010), 8-9. http://www.milb.com/documents/2010/08/06/13100514/1/Cuba.pdf Date Accessed February 25, 2016.
3. John Cronin, "When a Dream Plays Reality in Baseball…," *The Baseball Research Journal* 40 (2011), 88–93.
4. Bill Colson, "The Over the Hill League," *Sports Illustrated* (June 4, 1979).
5. "Triple A Team Set for Miami," *St. Petersburg Times*, September 15, 1978.
6. Robert Andrew Powell, "Rough Diamond," *Miami New Times*, August 15, 1996. http://www.miaminewtimes.com/news/rough-diamond-6361494 Date Accessed February 25, 2016.
7. Ibid.
8. John Cronin, "When a Dream Plays Reality in Baseball…," *The Baseball Research Journal* 40 (2011), 88–93.
9. Long, Gary, *Miami Herald* "For Johnson…" 3/28/1987.
10. Bill Colson, "The Over the Hill League," *Sports Illustrated*, (June 4, 1979).
11. Gary Long, "For Johnson, Mets a Snap After Amigos," *Miami Herald*, March 28, 1987.
12. Ibid.
13. Bruce Markusen "The Short, Wild Life of the Inter-American League," *Hardball Times*, July 8, 2014. http://www.hardballtimes.com/the-short-wild-life-of-the-inter-american-league/ Date accessed February 25, 2016.
14. Ibid.
15. John Cronin, "When a Dream Plays Reality in Baseball…," *The Baseball Research Journal* 40 (2011), 88–93.
16. Ibid.
17. Sam Jacobs, "A Vanishing League," *Miami Herald*, July 4, 2004.
18. Gary Long, "For Johnson, Mets a Snap After Amigos," *Miami Herald*, March 28, 1987.
19. Ibid.
20. Baseball Reference http://www.baseball-reference.com/register/league.cgi?id=b950ed7f Date accessed February 25, 2016.
21. Bill Colson, "The Over the Hill League," *Sports Illustrated* (June 4, 1979).
22. Bruce Markusen "The Short, Wild Life of the Inter-American League," *Hardball Times*, July 8, 2014.
23. Bill Colson, "The Over the Hill League," *Sports Illustrated* (June 4, 1979).
24. John Cronin, "When a Dream Plays Reality in Baseball…," *The Baseball Research Journal* 40 (2011), 88–93.
25. Sam Jacobs, "A Vanishing League," *Miami Herald*, July 4, 2004.
26. Ibid.
27. Ibid.
28. Markusen, Bruce, *Hardball Times*.
29. Bill Colson, "The Over the Hill League," *Sports Illustrated* (June 4, 1979).
30. Gary Long, "For Johnson, Mets a Snap After Amigos," *Miami Herald*, March 28, 1987.
31. John Cronin, "When a Dream Plays Reality in Baseball…," *The Baseball Research Journal* 40 (2011), 88–93.

One Last Season in the Sun

The Saga of the Senior Professional Baseball Association

William Schneider

As shortstop Ivan De Jesus fired the ball across the diamond into the glove of first baseman Lamar Johnson to retire Toby Harrah for the game's final out, to the casual observer it might have appeared to be little different from any other playoff series-concluding game. Pitcher Elias Sosa raised his hands in triumph on the mound, the players tumbled out of the dugout to converge on the field in celebration, and winning manager Bobby Tolan smiled happily. Across the field, losing manager Dick Williams could be forgiven for scowling at the unhappy conclusion to the efforts of a season just ended.

When you look beneath the surface, however, the details reveal that this game was not just another in the yearly run of major league baseball playoff games, and these teams were not typical playoff combatants. The team names themselves are revealing, as Bobby Tolan skippered the St. Petersburg Pelicans and Dick Williams managed the West Palm Beach Tropics. Additionally, the game was played on February 4, 1990, at the neutral site of Terry Park in Fort Myers, Florida. Finally, Elias Sosa and Lamar Johnson were both 39 years old, Ivan De Jesus was 37, and Toby Harrah checked in at 41.

GETTING STARTED

The Senior Professional Baseball Association (SPBA) may have had roots in nostalgia, but it was organized for a less esoteric reason: to make money for real estate investor Jim Morley.[1] At the time of his inspiration, reportedly on a beach in Australia in the winter of 1989, Morley was aware of the fan interest (and dollars) such golfing legends as Chi Chi Rodriguez, Gary Player, and Jack Nicklaus were generating on the Senior PGA Tour. Why wouldn't the recently retired legends of baseball generate similar interest if fans got another opportunity to see them ply their craft?

Morley decided to find out. He approached the task of organizing a league using a decidedly different approach than other alternate sports leagues have utilized. Morley decided to line up players first. He obtained a list of all players who had ever played in a major league baseball game, highlighted players who had debuted between 1969 and 1978 as a proxy for age, and mailed cards to those players asking of their interest in playing in a league for "players over thirty-five, catchers over thirty-two."[2] Responses far exceeded his expectations, as he ultimately received positive responses from over 700 players.

With players lined up, Morley's next order of business was to find places to play. He decided Florida offered potential in the form of spring training ballparks that sat empty during most of the winter months. Assisted by his brother, he toured the state to meet with the city officials who ran those parks. He found a receptive audience.

By now, the 1989 major league baseball season was fast approaching. Morley had succeeded in creating a buzz in the baseball community. He began to field calls from people interested in owning teams in the new league, and recruited famous reserve clause challenger Curt Flood as league commissioner. Morley selected seven owners from among the 73 inquiries he received, and the Senior Professional Baseball Association was announced with an eight-team lineup (Morley himself owned the eighth).

Morley had accomplished the unlikely, if not impossible, task of creating a baseball league from a crazy idea and his own drive and ambition. He had found players, parks, and owners. Could he find fans?

The initial divisional alignment of the Senior Professional Baseball Association was as follows:

NORTHERN DIVISION
St. Petersburg Pelicans
Bradenton Explorers
Orlando Juice
Winter Haven Super Sox

SOUTHERN DIVISION
West Palm Beach Tropics
Fort Myers Sun Sox
Gold Coast Suns
St. Lucie Legends

The seven other owners, by and large, were thirty-something men with backgrounds similar to Morley's.[3] They each (Morley excepted) committed approximately $1 million for the privilege of joining the Senior League, with the money allocated to franchise fees ($175,000), player salaries, stadium leases, and league expenses.[4] Two of the original seven owners, Joe Sprung of the St. Lucie Legends and Philip Breen of the Orlando Juice, would have a significant impact on the league's fortunes. The league elected to hold an inaugural draft to allocate talent. Each team selected 15 players in a draft on August 9, 1989, with the remainder of the rosters filled out by undrafted free agents.[5] League opening day was set for November 1, 1989, with 72 games scheduled from November through January.

Each team's salary was capped at $550,000 for the season, with individual player salaries ranging from $2,000 to $15,000 per month.[6] The league signed a three-year television contract with Prime Network, a cable provider, to provide additional revenue and exposure.[7] The contract with Prime stipulated a minimum of six teams in the league, a fact that would loom large in the association's second season.[8]

SEASON ONE

The SPBA kicked off Opening Day with a full schedule on November 1. Opening day crowds ranged from 3,304 at West Palm Beach to 1,242 at Orlando, an average of 2,069 fans per game. Morley believed that average attendance of 2,000 per game represented a break-even point, so things appeared on track after Day One.[9] However, the next day's figures dropped ominously to an average of only 639 for the four scheduled games. It remained to be seen whether fans would support the league to a sufficient degree.

After one week of play, the St. Petersburg Pelicans stood in first place in the Northern Division with a 4–1 record, followed by the Orlando Juice at 3–2 and the Bradenton Explorers at 2–3. Winter Haven struggled from the start, winning only one of their first five. Remarkably, the first week effectively foreshadowed the season in this division, as St. Petersburg, Bradenton, and Orlando would fight for the division crown all season while Winter Haven would ultimately slide to irrelevance.

In the Southern Division, Dick Williams's West Palm Beach Tropics started a perfect 5–0. The Fort Myers Sun Sox also started well, going 4–1. The St. Lucie Legends and the Gold Coast Suns, conversely, did not, with the Legends going 1–4 and the Suns 0–5. The opening week was representative of the Southern Division seasons well, as West Palm Beach would end the season with

As third baseman for the West Palm Beach Tropics, Toby Harrah led the league in on-base average.

the league's best record at 52–20. Fort Myers would battle the Tropics for first place throughout the month of November, but lost 11 of 13 after November 28 to fade to a distant second. They finished a nonetheless respectable 37–35. Gold Coast and St. Lucie remained also-rans, with the Legends the league doormat with a final record of 20–51. The Northern Division pennant race did serve up season-long excitement, despite the fact that the Pelicans ultimately led wire-to-wire. The most serious challenge to the Pelicans came from the Juice, who ultimately fell to third place after a late season surge from the Explorers, who won 10 of their last 14 games.

The end of season standings looked like this:

Southern Division	W-L	GB
West Palm Beach Tropics	52–20	–
Fort Myers Sun Sox	37–35	15
Gold Coast Suns	32–39	19.5
St. Lucie Legends	20–51	31.5

Northern Division	W-L	GB
St. Petersburg Pelicans	42–30	–
Bradenton Explorers	38–34	4
Orlando Juice	37–35	5
Winter Haven Super Sox	29–43	13

The league faced a dilemma as the regular season wound down; major league training camps were scheduled to open across Florida. Thus the home stadiums for the most of the teams were unavailable. The only exception was in Fort Myers, as Terry Park was not a training site for a big-league club; the end-of-season tournament would be held there. It was originally announced that the playoff format would consist of games between the Northern Division first place team and the Southern Division second place team and vice versa, with the championship game a matchup between the winners of the first two games. After the announcement, the league decided to revise that plan. The one-game-and-out format had already diminished the importance of the regular season, and the neutral site for the playoffs denied the league's elite the benefit of home field advantage. The revised plan called for a one-game playoff between Fort Myers and Bradenton (the two second place teams), the winner of which would take on St. Petersburg (the first place team with the worse record) in one game. The winner of that second round game would face the West Palm Beach Tropics in the championship game.[10]

Bradenton defeated Fort Myers 4–3 on February 1 to advance to the second round. St. Petersburg handled the Bradenton Explorers 9–2 to set up the championship game between the league's two best teams. St. Petersburg jumped out to a 9–0 lead and would ultimately triumph 12–4, setting up the scene that opened this article.

What follows is a team-by-team capsule summary of Season One:

WEST PALM BEACH TROPICS
Manager: Dick Williams
Team Performance: Finished 1st in Southern Division, 1st in Runs Scored, 1st in Runs Allowed
Most Recognizable Players: OF Mickey Rivers, DH Dave Kingman, RP Rollie Fingers, RP Al Hrabosky
Offensive Highlights: SS Ron Washington batted .359 with five homers and 73 RBIs (led league), and was named league Most Valuable Player. OF Mickey Rivers finished second in the league in BA with a .366 figure. 3B Toby Harrah led the league in OBP.
Pitching Highlights: Juan Eichelberger went 11–5 with a 2.90 ERA, placing second in the league in wins. While Fingers and Hrabosky were ineffective, lefty Will McEnaney had a 1.67 ERA out of the pen.
Fun Fact: Dave Kingman had a lifetime average of .236 in the majors, but batted .271 in the senior league. However, the league BA was .303, so contact hitting still wasn't "Kong's" game at age 41.

FORT MYERS SUN SOX
Manager: Pat Dobson
Team Performance: Finished 2nd in Southern Division, 2nd in Runs Scored, 3rd in Runs Allowed
Most Recognizable Players: DH/OF Amos Otis, P Dennis Leonard
Offensive Highlights: 42-year-old Amos Otis hit 11 homers to go with 52 RBI and a .332 average. SS Tim Ireland led the league in BA with .374. 2B Kim Allen led the league with 33 SB and chipped in a .330 BA.

Pitching Highlights: No pitcher won more than five games, but Rich Gale was the most effective starter (4–5, 3.39 ERA). Dave LaRoche and Steve Luebbers anchored an effective relief corps.
Fun Fact: Tim Ireland pulled off the hidden ball trick three times.

GOLD COAST SUNS
Manager: Earl Weaver
Team Performance: Finished 3rd in Southern Division, 4th in Runs Scored, 7th in Runs Allowed
Most Recognizable Players: SS Bert Campaneris, OF Cesar Cedeño, P Mike Cuellar, P Joaquin Andujar
Offensive Highlights: 47-year-old Bert Campaneris stole 16 bases to lead team. 1B Orlando Gonzalez and OF Cedeño both hit .331 to share team lead.
Pitching Highlights: Most of the staff struggled, as team allowed over seven runs per game. Andujar was very effective (1.31 ERA) but in only eight starts.
Fun Fact: Mike Cuellar was oldest pitcher in the league at age 52. Of course it showed, as he allowed 58 base runners in only 25.1 innings in his combined efforts with Gold Coast and Winter Haven.

ST. LUCIE LEGENDS
Manager: Graig Nettles (2–9), Bobby Bonds (18–42)
Team Performance: Finished 4th in Southern Division, 7th in Runs Scored, 8th in Runs Allowed
Most Recognizable Players: 3B Nettles, OF Bonds, OF George Foster, P Vida Blue
Offensive Highlights: While with St. Lucie, 1B Willie Aikens had 12 HR, 58 RBI, and batted .345 to mount serious challenge for league MVP. George Foster finished third in the league with 11 home runs, giving St. Lucie two of the top three (Aikens was second).
Pitching Highlights: No pitchers were very effective. Blue had a 4.87 ERA in 11 starts. Reliever Al Holland allowed 90 base runners in only 47 innings for a 7.74 ERA.
Fun Fact: As the worst run-preventing team in the league, St. Lucie gave significant innings to pitchers with seriously high ERAs. Roy Branch had a 10.22 ERA in 24.7 innings, Tommy Moore 9.82 ERA in 40.3 innings, and Ed Ricks a 14.47 ERA in 32.3 innings.

ST. PETERSBURG PELICANS **LEAGUE CHAMPIONS**
Manager: Bobby Tolan
Team Performance: Finished 1st in Northern Division, 3rd in Runs Scored, 5th in Runs Allowed
Most Recognizable Players: OF Ron LeFlore, P Dock Ellis
Offensive Highlights: OF Steve Henderson (5 HR, 55 RBI, .352 BA) and OF Steve Kemp (.329 BA) paced the offense. 1B Lamar Johnson hit six HR with 22 RBI and a .372 BA in only 86 AB.
Pitching Highlights: Twin aces Milt Wilcox (12–3, 3.19 ERA) and Jon Matlack (10–2, 4.10 ERA) led team's staff. Swingman Elias Sosa had a 2.90 ERA. 44 year-old Dock Ellis had a 1.76 ERA in 30 innings and served as team pitching coach.

Fun Fact: Pelicans defeated the West Palm Beach Tropics in seven games out of 10. They led the Northern Division wire-to-wire.

BRADENTON EXPLORERS
Manager: Clete Boyer
Team Performance: Finished 2nd in Southern Division, 6th in Runs Scored, 2nd in Runs Allowed
Most Recognizable Players: OF Ron LeFlore, 1B Graig Nettles
Offensive Highlights: 3B Jim Morrison led league with 17 HR to go along with 55 RBI. 1B Graig Nettles came over from St. Lucie in a trade to bat .330. OF Al Cowens batted .390 in 82 AB.
Pitching Highlights: Starter Mickey Mahler went 8–7, 3.49 ERA. Swingman Danny Boone had a 4–3 record and one save with a 3.16 ERA.
Fun Fact: P Danny Boone became one of three former Senior League players to play in the Major League after the inaugural SPBA season. He appeared in four games for the Orioles in 1990.

ORLANDO JUICE
Manager: Gates Brown (9–12), Dyar Miller (28–23)
Team Performance: Finished 3rd in Northern Division, 5th in Runs Scored, 4th in Runs Allowed
Most Recognizable Players: OF Jose Cruz, P Vida Blue, DH Bill Madlock
Offensive Highlights: OF Jose Cruz hit .306 with 10 HR and 49 RBI. OF Jerry Martin hit .326, in 227 AB had 5 HR, 39 RBI. 1B Randy Bass had five HR and a .393 BA in only 107 AB.
Pitching Highlights: Bob Galasso was most effective starter at 9–2, 2.67 ERA. Pete Falcone was 10–3, 4.41 ERA. Forty-year-old Vida Blue had a 7.20 ERA in 25 innings.
Fun Fact: As the 1989-90 season ended, owner Philip Breen disappeared as the FBI pursued him on charges of embezzlement.

WINTER HAVEN SUPER SOX
Manager: Bill Lee (1–6), Ed Nottle (16–17), Leon Roberts (12–20)
Team Performance: Finished 4th in Northern Division, 8th in Runs Scored, 6th in Runs Allowed
Most Recognizable Players: P Ferguson Jenkins, P Bill Lee, P Bill Campbell
Offensive Highlights: OF Gene Richards (.326), Al Bumbry (.340), and Tony Scott (.360) all hit for high average. Player-Manager Leon Roberts hit eight HR to lead team.
Pitching Highlights: RP Bill Campbell led the league in ERA with a sparkling 2.12 in 72 IP. Forty-six-year-old Fergie Jenkins could only manage 5.55 ERA in 86 IP.
Fun Fact: Playing at the Red Sox former spring training site, the team attempted to appeal to fans by employing former Red Sox players such as Butch Hobson, Bernie Carbo, Cecil Cooper, Bill Lee, and Rick Wise. It didn't work, as the Super Sox continually struggled with poor attendance.

Dick Williams would manage the West Palm Beach Tropics to the best record in the league, 52–20, but the Tropics would lose the championship game to the St. Petersburg Pelicans.

SEASON TWO
As Opening Day for the next season approached, it was apparent that the league was in trouble. Franchise instability, always a challenge for fledgling leagues, had reared its head in a big way. St. Lucie and Orlando were history given their issues late in the first season. Winter Haven and Gold Coast similarly folded operations. This left only four of the original eight franchises in place: St. Petersburg, Fort Myers, West Palm Beach, and Bradenton (who relocated to Daytona Beach).

The league countered this attrition by adding two teams in the west. Following the spring training site concept, the Sun City Rays were added in Phoenix, Arizona. Another team was added in San Bernardino, California. The San Bernardino Pride would play on the field utilized by the Seattle Mariners' California League team. The divisional structure of the first season was eliminated, as two divisions of three teams each would not have been a workable setup.

Each of the returning franchises could carry over 15 players from season to season. The minimum age for non-catchers was reduced from 35 to 34, the salary cap was reduced from $550,000 per team to $350,000, and maximum player salary was dropped from $15,000 per month to $10,000. The regular season schedule was reduced from 72 games to 56, and a weeklong break was added at Christmas.[11]

With its Season Two lineup nominally in place, the league was confronted with another challenge. The West Palm Beach Tropics, who had been the winningest, best-attended team in the first season, were unable to reach agreement on a lease for Municipal Stadium. This proved to be too much for Don Sider, Tropics owner, and he folded the team. The SPBA had now dropped below the six-team minimum required

Dave Kingman had a lifetime average of .236 in the majors, but batted .271 in the senior league—still well below the league average of .303.

Bert Campaneris stole 16 bases, the most on the Gold Coast Suns team.

44 year-old Dock Ellis had a 1.76 ERA in 30 innings pitched and served as pitching coach for the league-champion St. Pete Pelicans.

by the Prime TV contract. In response, the league elected to keep the Tropics, now renamed the Florida Tropics, as a traveling team without a home field. The Tropics would be formed from the pool of players not signed or retained by the other teams.[12]

The league opened its second season on November 23, 1990, and reached the Christmas break without any major faux pas. However, the financial red ink had continued unabated from the first season. During the Christmas break, a dispute between Fort Myers owners over responsibility for operating expenses resulted in the disbandment of that team. This proved to be the deathblow for the SPBA, as the league no longer met the terms of its television contract. Jim Morley announced the cessation of league operations on December 26, 1990. Morley discussed plans to reopen operations the next season with a mixture of Japanese League players, rehabilitating major leaguers, and senior players, but the words had to ring hollow to all but the most committed (or delusional) league devotees. The Senior Professional Baseball Association was dead.

WHY DID THE LEAGUE FAIL?

There were several contributing factors to the failure of the senior league. Among these were poor franchise location decisions, the lack of a viable financial plan, and the failure to implement a vetting process for prospective owners.

Other than visiting potential team sites personally in the summer and fall of 1989, Jim Morley did not appear to perform any real analysis of the Florida markets where he would base his teams. As time would prove, some of the cities that served as franchise bases did not demonstrate enough fan interest to support a team due to population and/or stadium location and condition. Additionally, it is questionable whether even with better decisions on franchise locations the Florida market could have supported eight teams.

Morley also lacked a solid financial plan for the league. He frequently referred to a break-even point of 2,000 fans per game, but a simple analysis reveals that number to be insufficient. Each team had a salary cap of $550,000, and television and merchandising revenues of $60,000. That means that just to cover salaries, each team would have to generate $490,000 in revenue from their 36 home games. The Tropics' ticket prices ranged from $3 to $5.50. Using that top figure, a 2,000-person crowd would generate $11,000. For 36 games, that would equate to $396,000, or nearly a $100,000 gap between revenues and player salaries. When management salaries, transportation expenses, per diem allowances, and league overhead are included, it appears even 2,000 fans per game would have been woefully insufficient to approach financial solvency.

The original ownership group also contributed to the league's problems. St. Lucie owner Joe Sprung routinely struggled to generate sufficient cash to pay his team's expenses. Orlando owner Philip Breen's disappearance while being pursued by the FBI at the end of season one also contributed to league instability. Finally, the dispute between Fort Myers' owners became the proverbial straw that broke the camel's back.

In the end, though, the league's failure was in all likelihood not due to any of the above factors. The concept of a senior league for baseball players may be fundamentally flawed. Baseball is a younger man's game. Per renowned baseball forecaster Ron Shandler, "age never regresses."[13] Fay Vincent similarly opined in a 1990 *Sporting News* interview, "I'm always skeptical whether competitive baseball is compatible with the human body at that age (40)."[14] Jim Morley based his premise for the Senior League on the success of the Senior PGA Tour. However, as Peter King of *Sports Illustrated* pointed out in a 1989 article, senior golfers play on easier courses, with shorter holes, wider fairways, slower greens, and thinner rough.[15] Adjustments like this, such as shortening the base paths or bringing in the fences dramatically, are not possible in baseball without noticeably altering the game. Therefore, the idea that a significant population of aged players can play at a level of baseball comparable to, and reminiscent of, their years as major league regulars doesn't stand up to scrutiny. Despite the marked success of some of the senior league players, the idea that the senior league would play a brand of baseball that would resonate with a fan base nostalgic for another glimpse of their heroes on the diamond was probably doomed from the start.

SUMMARY

Jim Morley took the SPBA from concept to reality in only about ten months. By any test, this stands as a remarkable achievement. In so doing, however, he failed to conduct detailed analysis of financial prospects, potential fan interest, qualifications of ownership candidates, and likely standards of play by an aged player population. Each of these omissions contributed to the league's ultimate failure. Ironically, had Morley conducted the aforementioned analyses, it is likely the senior league would never have become a reality. The players who got one last chance to play the game professionally, the fans who followed the teams, and those (like this writer) who continue to revisit this fascinating footnote to baseball history can be glad that Jim Morley energetically (and, yes, foolishly) pursued his crazy vision. ∎

Acknowledgements

Special thanks are due to Jay Walker, who graciously provided access to *The Senior League Encyclopedia*. The comprehensive statistical record documented in this work greatly facilitated the research for this article.

Notes

1. David Whitford, *Extra Innings*, Harper Collins Publishers, 1991, 5.
2. Ibid., 10.
3. G. Jay Walker, *The Senior League Encyclopedia*, Baseball Press Books, 1998, 5.
4. David Whitford, *Extra Innings*, Harper Collins Publishers, 1991, 139.
5. G. Jay Walker, *The Senior League Encyclopedia*, Baseball Press Books, 1998, 6.
6. Ibid., 7.
7. Ibid., 7.
8. Peter Golenbock, *The Forever Boys*, Carol Publishing Group, 1991, 10.
9. Ibid., 2.
10. Ibid., 366.
11. G. Jay Walker, *The Senior League Encyclopedia*, Baseball Press Books, 1998, 9.
12. Ibid., 9.
13. Ron Shandler, *Ron Shandler's 2016 Baseball Forecaster*, Triumph Books LLC, 2015, 18.
14. *The Sporting News*, February 12, 1990, 10.
15. Peter King, "Seniority Run Rampant," *Sports Illustrated*, July 17, 1989, www.si.com/vault/1989/07/17/106780446/seniority-run-rampant (accessed online February 25, 2016).

Take Me Out to the Courtroom

A Look at Baseball Cases in the Florida Courts

Louis H. Schiff

Baseball, more than any other sport, has had a central role in American life and regularly finds itself in court. As a result there are now more than 10,000 published judicial decisions regarding baseball.[1] While many writers have examined these decisions from a national or holistic perspective, this article will discuss many of those cases originating in Florida's courts.[2]

Florida has long been a hotbed of baseball activity.[3] Today, the state is home to two MLB teams, 26 minor league teams, 15 spring training sites, both of the schools that train future big league umpires, and numerous college, high school, and youth teams.[4] As a result, its case reporters are filled with baseball opinions that stretch back more than a century. Collectively, these judicial opinions chronicle the significant impact that Florida's bench and bar have played in the development of America's pastime.

THE FIRST BASEBALL AND LAW CASES

Just as the common law derives from ancient precedents, judges' decisions, rather than statutes, baseball's codes are the game's distilled mores. Their unchanged purpose is to show respect for opponents and the game. In baseball, as in the remainder of life, the most important rules are unwritten. But not unenforced.

—George Will

On June 5, 1905, the Florida Legislature passed a law that banned the playing of baseball on Sunday.[5] The ban on Sunday baseball was not just a Florida issue, it was a national issue designed to encourage church attendance (for the non-religious, the prohibition was justified as ensuring there would be at least one day of peace and quiet each week).[6] When the ban was challenged in Florida, the Florida Supreme Court acted swiftly, and before the year was over, upheld the newly enacted law against multiple constitutional attacks.[7]

However, with local municipalities putting political pressure on legislators to repeal the law banning the playing of baseball on Sunday, the Florida Legislature on June 3, 1911, enacted a compromise and passed a law delegating to cities the power to pass ordinances superseding or repealing the ban on Sunday baseball.[8] The City of Pensacola immediately repealed the Sunday ban, and before the year was over the issue of whether the city could repeal the Sunday ban was in front of the Florida Supreme Court.[9]

The Florida Supreme Court upheld the right of City of Pensacola to repeal the law, and Sunday baseball became a routine activity across the State of Florida. But it would take 64 years after the original statute banning baseball on Sunday for the Florida Legislature to finally repeal the original law.[10]

JUDGES AND BASEBALL

An umpire is in control of the decorum and behavior of those on the field of play. A judge is in control of the decorum and the behavior of those in his or her courtroom, including themselves.

—Judge David Denkin

Judge Kenesaw Mountain Landis, the first commissioner of baseball, is usually the first judge that comes to mind when there is a discussion of the important role judges have played in baseball.[11] After being named commissioner (with an annual salary of $50,000), Landis, to the surprise of many, refused to give up his federal judgeship (with an annual salary of $7,500), leading to a bitter campaign calling for his impeachment.[12] In 1922 Landis finally agreed to resign from the bench, and as a result, in 1924 the American Bar Association (which in 1921 had censured Landis) formulated its Canons of Judicial Ethics (now the Code of Judicial Conduct), which sets ethical standards for judges and warns them to avoid even the appearance of impropriety and forbids outside full-time employment, but allows such activities such as teaching and writing, to name a few.[13]

Discipline of the Florida judiciary rests in the hands of the Florida Supreme Court and the Florida Judicial Qualifications Commission.[14] When a judge is found to have violated the Code of Judicial Conduct, the judge will face consequences which range from a public reprimand to removal from office.[15]

Judge Landis was a lifelong baseball fan and he often left the courthouse early to attend White Sox or Cubs games.[16] However, a judge must be sure that his or her attendance at a baseball game does not lead to ethical violations. Florida jurists are not immune from judicial misconduct when it comes to our national pastime.

The Florida Supreme Court gave a public reprimand to a judge who accepted free Florida Marlins tickets approximately 15 times from 1994 to 1997 from a firm whose lawyers appeared before him on at least two cases.[17] The court concluded the conduct of the judge violated several canons of the Code of Judicial Conduct and was "so egregious to require a public reprimand."[18]

At a 2008 charity auction, Florida Marlins president David Samson jokingly announced he was putting the team up for sale and in jest accepted a bid of $10 million for the sale of the team. After the "sale" Samson refused to transfer ownership of the Marlins to the winning bidder, the winning bidder filed suit to enforce the sale.[19] During the pendency of the litigation, the trial court judge informed the lawyers he was a Marlins fan and regularly attended Marlins games, however, he told the lawyers he paid for his own tickets. The plaintiff sought to have the judge removed by filing a motion for disqualification.[20] The judge denied the motion, and the case was later dismissed by the plaintiff for reasons not in the public records. The denial of the motion for disqualification was never appealed, and in an unrelated matter an appeals court ruled the case should remain closed after the plaintiff filed the dismissal.[21]

THE BASEBALL RULE

Beware of objects leaving the field of play! ¡Cuidado con objectos que salgan del torreno de juego!

—sign posted at Marlins Park in
Home Plate Box Section 9, Row 1
(behind the visitor's dugout)

The "Baseball Rule" was first announced more than 100 years ago in *Crane v. Kansas City Baseball and Exhibition Co.*[22] A fan filed suit after being struck and injured by a foul ball. The appeals court ruled that foul balls are a fundamental part of baseball; being struck by a foul ball is a well-known risk of attending a baseball game; and the plaintiff chose to sit in a part of the stadium that was not protected.[23] Thus, the invention of the Baseball Rule. The rule immunizes stadium operators and owners from liability for injuries caused by baseballs and bats so long as they provide an adequate number of screened seats.[24]

Over the years, courts have narrowed the meaning of the Baseball Rule, but the rule still stands. In *Martinez v. Houston McLane Company*, the court points out that the following jurisdictions have adopted the rule since 2000: Michigan, New Jersey, Nevada, New Mexico, and Virginia.[25] MLB is considering a uniform policy on netting in ballparks for the 2017 season, but for the 2016 season it is allowing clubs to make their own decisions.[26]

Surprisingly, the Florida Supreme Court has not had to construe the Baseball Rule. However, there is a case pending in Miami-Dade County by a woman who has sued the Miami Marlins claiming that she was injured by "Bob the Shark" (a Marlins mascot in the Great Sea Race) during a 2013 baseball game.[27]

ANTITRUST LAW

Judges are like umpires. Umpires don't make the rules, they apply them. The role of an umpire and a judge is critical. They make sure everybody plays by the rules. But it is a limited role. Nobody ever went to a ballgame to see the umpire.

—United States Supreme Court
Chief Justice John Roberts

In 1922, the United States Supreme Court ruled that the nation's antitrust laws did not apply to Major League Baseball, thus granting MLB an immunity and exemption from the Sherman Anti-Trust Act of 1890.[28] Since *Fed. Baseball Club of Balt., Inc. v. Nat'l League of Prof'l Baseball Clubs*, the United States Supreme Court declined to say the nation's antitrust laws apply to Major League Baseball.[29] The Eleventh Circuit of the Florida Federal Court followed Fed. Baseball on two occasions. The first was in a case involving the scheduling of minor league baseball games.[30] The second was a case filed by the Florida Attorney General who was investigating the proposed contraction of MLB by eliminating and disbanding the Minnesota Twins and the Montreal Expos in the early 1990s.[31]

In contrast the Florida Supreme Court has read the exemption as applying only to player contracts, and therefore the Florida Supreme Court is the only state Supreme Court not to recognize Fed. Baseball as it was intended.[32] The Florida Supreme Court has held that baseball's antitrust exemption extends only to the reserve system and not the sale and purchase of the teams, such as the San Francisco Giants.[33] Accordingly,

The Raiford Prison Baseball team in 1939.

a Florida appeals court reinstated a lawsuit in which the plaintiffs claimed that numerous parties had conspired to keep them from buying the Minnesota Twins and moving them to Florida.[34]

In 2012, an umpiring school owned by former major league umpire Jim Evans filed an antitrust action against Minor League Baseball (MiLB) in state court, claiming that MiLB eliminated competition of his minor league umpiring school when MiLB began its own training school thereby shutting down his school.[35] MiLB claimed they ceased doing business with Evans and his school after they learned that some of the employees of the school attended a party wearing costumes that were offensive.[36] MiLB filed a motion to dismiss the suit, but the state trial court judge denied the motion and wrote the court did not have to, "blindly follow the opinions of the lower federal courts, when the Florida Supreme Court believes the federal decisions to be poorly reasoned."[37] The parties reached a confidential settlement.[38] In November, 2014, MiLB hired Evans as Umpire Advisor, a position created by MiLB to serve as a consultant and advisor to the president of MiLB on umpiring-related matters.[39]

CONTRACT LAW AND CIVIL FRAUD

Baseball has the largest library of law and lore and custom and ritual, and therefore, in a nation that fundamentally believes it is a nation under the law, well, baseball is America's most privileged version of the level field.

—former Baseball Commissioner
Bart Giamatti

The game of baseball has led to many disputes involving a breach of contract and civil fraud. The five cases in this section span Florida case law for over 60 years.

In 1949, the City of Miami opened Miami Stadium and hired Florida Sportservice to run the concession stands. For the next five years, the Miami Sun Sox, a Brooklyn Dodgers farm team, called the field home. In 1954, the Sun Sox folded. Following two seasons without baseball, Sidney Salomon Jr., the owner of Sportservice, bought the Syracuse Chiefs and moved them to Miami, where they became the Miami Marlins.[40]

Before Salomon sold the Marlins, he had the Marlins sign a one-sided concession agreement with Sportservice. He then sold them to media mogul George B. Storer. When Storer found out about the sweetheart deal, he filed a lawsuit to void the agreement. The trial court dismissed the suit brought by Storer, but the appeals court reversed, agreeing with Storer that the deal should be set aside because the original contract was not approved by the board of directors and that the Miami Baseball Company had no knowledge of the agreement.[41]

When the engineering company building the Florida Marlins' original spring training complex was fired, that company sued Brevard County to recover the cost of various oral change orders. Because the orders were oral rather than written, the Florida Supreme Court found the change orders unenforceable, and therefore collection on them was barred by sovereign immunity.[42]

In 1997, the Marlins won their first World Series. As a result, a marketing company purchased premium stadium seats and advertising for the 1998 season, not knowing the club was about to hold a "fire sale" of the players. The Marlins finished last in 1998. The marketing firm believed it was duped, so they sued for a refund. The trial court said there could be no guarantee of how well the team would do the year after winning the World Series and there was no promise of future winning years. The appeals court per curiam affirmed the trial judge.[43]

In a twist of the 1998 lawsuit, before the start of the 2013 season, the Miami Marlins threatened to sue a full-season, $25,000 a year, front row ticket holder for not renewing his seats.[44] The Marlins never followed through on their threat to file suit.[45]

The book *The Card* exposed the corrupt and criminal underbelly of the unregulated baseball memorabilia industry.[46] Florida courts have been presented with issues regarding fraudulent baseball memorabilia. In one case, the plaintiff accused an out-of-state defendant of selling him a fake Joe DiMaggio jersey. The defendant moved to dismiss for lack of personal jurisdiction but the appeals court held that because he was conducting an auction over the Internet and he had a highly interactive website, his company could be sued in Florida because it had sufficient contacts with the state.[47]

In another case involving baseball memorabilia, a baseball autograph's owner was in need of a $203,000 loan, and approached a private lender to use his autographs as collateral for the loan. The prospective lender then took the memorabilia and paid to have it appraised, where a professional appraiser valued it to be worth $300,000–450,000. Relying on the appraisal, the private lender made the loan, and shortly thereafter the borrower defaulted. Using the collateral, the lender attempted to sell the autographs to satisfy the borrowers' debt. The lender discovered the appraised autographs were worth no more than $3,000, and so he brought an action against the appraiser. The appeals court found in favor of the lender, placing upon the appraiser the duty to use reasonable care to ensure the accuracy and validity of the appraisal.[48]

CRIMINAL JUSTICE AND THE BENCH

Baseball is almost the only orderly thing in a very unorderly world. If you get three strikes, even the best lawyer in the world can't get you off.
—Baseball Hall of Fame member Bill Veeck

Judges are required to ensure that trials proceed in a timely and fair manner. At times, justice is delayed or the courts err.

Baseball Hall of Famer Ted Williams was a silent partner is a sports souvenir shop owned by Vincent Antonucci. Williams alleged in a civil lawsuit that Antonucci swindled him out of thousands of dollars. While the civil suit was pending, the State of Florida filed criminal charges seeking to convict Antonucci and send him to prison.[49] The trial court judge in the criminal case unilaterally continued the case so the civil case could finish first. The state objected to the court-imposed continuance, arguing that Williams's advanced age would deny and delay justice.[50] On appeal, the trial judge was told he abused his discretion in continuing the matter and was ordered to immediately try the case.[51]

In another case, former Detroit Tigers pitcher Denny McLain asked the court to overturn his federal racketeering conviction because McLain alleged the prosecutor and trial court judge denied him of a fair trial. The conviction was overturned by the federal appeals court.[52]

THE BEST OF THE REST—IF YOU BUILD IT, THEY WILL SUE

You can't grow up in the South Bronx without knowing about baseball.
—United States Supreme Court Justice
Sonia Sotomayor

In 1966 the Florida Supreme Court ruled the City of Deerfield Beach could not build a spring training facility for the Pittsburgh Pirates.[53] Thirty-five years later, with public sentiment regarding such projects having shifted, the Florida Supreme Court held that the City of Clearwater could build a spring training for the Philadelphia Phillies.[54]

When it looked like Orlando would get an MLB expansion team, Orange County pledged to build a new stadium using a 1% tourist tax.[55] A group of hotel owners filed a lawsuit seeking to stop the tax, but the action of the hotel owners was dismissed. The matter became irrelevant when in 1995 Tampa Bay was awarded with a franchise.[56]

After the City of Miami agreed to build a new stadium for the Marlins, two taxpayers sought a temporary injunction stopping the city from selling bonds to pay for the project.[57] In dismissing the appeal of the taxpayers as immaterial, the appellate court pointed out that the failure of the taxpayers to request an emergency stay had resulted in the bonds being issued.[58]

Bob the Shark, pictured here with the author and his wife Leslee.

THE FUTURE OF BASEBALL AND LAW IN FLORIDA

Every lawyer should learn about baseball. If litigation is the nation's real pastime, then baseball comes in a close second.

—Law professor Roger I. Abrams

What sorts of baseball cases can Florida courts expect to handle in the future? Gazing into a crystal baseball and forecasting the winner of the World Series during spring training is an impossible task, and so too is predicting what is ahead for the Florida courts. But picking the winner of the World Series during spring training, and predicating the course of future legal issues, is a time-honored tradition.

First, with the Baseball Rule under attack, it seems likely that actions involving injured fans will continue.[59]

A number of lawsuits may arise if the Tampa Bay Rays make good on their threat to abandon Tropicana Field for a new stadium in Hillsborough County, as at the current time the Rays and the City of St. Petersburg appear to be at a stalemate.[60] This has led some to predict the Rays will remain in Pinellas County.[61] Indeed, if past lawsuits can gauge the future, it is almost certain that a group of taxpayers will challenge whatever funding mechanism is used to finance the project. Moreover, if the negotiations are not transparent, an open-records lawsuit might also be considered. And, of course, at least some Pinellas County residents may seek to force the club to honor its existing lease, which requires the Rays to play at the Trop until 2027.[62] There is also a growing concern about the future of spring training in Pinellas County.[63]

The current litigation in California between minor league players and MLB has enormous potential ramifications for Florida. In two related suits, the players contend they are being grossly underpaid in violation of federal law.[64] If the players prevail, the continued viability of one or more of Florida's minor league teams could be in jeopardy.

Just before the start of the 2015 season, MLB punished Miami Marlins pitcher Jarred Cosart after published reports that he had bet on baseball.[65] Concluding he had gambled on other sports but not baseball, MLB fined Cosart an undisclosed amount of money.[66] Nevertheless, MLB and the country's three other major sports leagues are getting closer to dropping their longstanding opposition to sports gambling.[67] The position of Commissioner Manfred may conflict with that of the Florida Attorney General and may force this issue into state courts.[68,69]

President Obama's decision at the end of 2014 to normalize relations with Cuba and his trip to Cuba in early 2016 will have important consequences for baseball in general and Florida in particular. Already, there is talk of holding spring training games in Cuba.[70] Many baseball fans (especially those in South Florida) will probably travel to such games, and it is not difficult to imagine some of these road trips ending in lawsuits if something goes wrong.

Lastly, baseball seemingly is a topic of conversation every time Florida lawmakers meet. During the 2015 Florida Legislative Session, the legislature helped advance construction of a joint-use facility for the Houston Astros and Washington Nationals in West Palm Beach by approving a needed zoning change.[71] The Atlanta Braves are interested in moving back to West Palm Beach starting with 2018 spring training.[72]

Baseball and the law will continue to be intertwined in Florida. As long as there are new laws, new issues and lawyers filing new lawsuits, Florida courts will be faced with making rulings off the diamond which will affect the play on the diamond. ∎

Author's Note

This article originated as a paper written by Judge Louis H. Schiff and Professor Robert M. Jarvis and a program presented by Judge Schiff and Judge David Denkin at the 2015 Conference of County Court Judges of Florida called "Florida's Judiciary at the Plate: Baseball Cases in the Sunshine State." This article is also adopted from a law review article written by Judge Schiff and Professor Jarvis, "A Survey of Florida Baseball Cases," 40 *Nova Law Review* (2015). *Nova Southeastern University Law Review* has allowed material used in the law review article to appear in this paper. The last component of this article is additional research which was not part of the original paper, program, and law review article. The author is extremely grateful for the assistance and guidance of SABR Publications Director Cecilia Tan, the staff of SABR, Alaska District Court Judge David L. Zwink, and the members of the South Florida Chapter of SABR.

Notes

1. Lexis and Westlaw databases.
2. This article is a survey of Florida judicial decisions. It would take an encyclopedia of Florida Baseball Law to cover every aspect of this topic.
3. Kevin M. McCarthy, *Baseball in Florida* (Sarasota, Florida: Pineapple Press, 1996).
4. Florida's Grapefruit League is Home to Major League Baseball's Pre-Season, Fla. Grapefruit League, http://www.floridagrapefruitleague.com (hover over "Teams"); Team-by-Team Information, MLB.com, http://mlb.mlb.com/team/index.jsp; Teams by Geographical Location, MiLB.com, http://www.milb.com/milb/info/geographical.jsp; Umpire School Information, MLB.com, http://mlb.mlb.com/mlb/official_info/umpires/camp/schools.jsp.
5. Act of June 5, 1905, 1905 Fla. Laws ch. 5436, § 1.
6. Bill Kelly, "Arrested for Playing Baseball! How the National Pastime Became a Church and State Battleground in Nebraska," NPR, June 6, 2013, at http://netnebraska.org/article/news/arrested-playing-baseball-how-national-pastime-became-church-and-state-battleground.
7. *West v. State*, 39 So. 412 (Fla. 1905).

8. The mayor and the city council of Pensacola had, by ordinance, repealed or superseded Chapter 5436 of the Laws of Florida. *Nickelson v. State ex rel. Blitch*, 57 So. 194 (1911).

9. Ibid. The court found the Petitioner Blitch, a local minister, lacked standing to bring such an action in "the name of the state."

10. Act effective July 1, 1969, ch. 69–87, 1969 Fla. Laws 322.

11. Louis H. Schiff and Robert M. Jarvis. *Baseball and the Law: Cases and Materials* (Durham: Carolina Academic Press), 3.

12. Ibid. 104.

13. Ibid.

14. http://www.floridasupremecourt.org/pub_info/jqc.shtml#Information.

15. http://www.floridasupremecourt.org/decisions/ethics/index.shtml.

16. J.G. Taylor Spink, *Judge Landis and 25 Years of Baseball* (St. Louis: The Sporting News Publishing Company, 1974).

17. In re Luzzo, 756 So. 2d 76 (Fla. 2000).

18. Ibid. 79.

19. *Pomeranz & Landsman v. Miami Marlins Baseball Club*, L.P., Fla. 17th Cir. (CACE 12-003405).

20. Ibid.

21. *Pomeranz & Landsman Corp. v. Miami Marlins Baseball Club*, L.P., 143 So. 3d 1182 (Fla. 4th Dist. Ct. App. 2014).

22. 153 S.W. 1076, (Mo. Ct. App. 1913).

23. Louis H. Schiff and Robert M. Jarvis. *Baseball and the Law: Cases and Materials* (Durham: Carolina Academic Press), 576. For a further discussion of Crane, see J. Gordon Hylton, *A Foul Ball in the Courtroom: The Baseball Spectator Injury as a Case of First Impression*, 38 Tulsa L. Rev. 485 (2003).

24. *Coomer v. Kansas City Royals Baseball Corporation*, 437 S.W.3d 184 (Mo. 2014), an excellent discussion on the history and origin of the rule.

25. 414 S.W. 3rd 219 (Tex, Ct. App. 2013).

26. Ron Jenkins, Major League Baseball Approved Extended Netting for 2016 Season, November 19, 2105; http://www.star-telegram.com/sports/mlb/texas-rangers/article45507555.html.

27. *Fedornak v. Miami Marlins*, L.P. Fla. 11th Cir. (2015-013360 CA-01).

28. *Fed. Baseball Club of Balt., Inc. v. Nat'l League of Prof'l Baseball Clubs*, 259 U.S. 200 (1922).

29. Federal Baseball was reaffirmed in *Toolson v. New York Yankees, Inc.*, 346 U.S. 356, reh'g denied, 346 U.S. 917 (1953), and then in *Flood v. Kuhn*, 407 U.S. 258 (1972) the Court gave MLB an exemption to antitrust laws that the Court now felt applied to baseball.

30. *Prof'l Baseball Sch. & Clubs v. Kahn*, 693 F.2d 1085 (11th Cir. 1982).

31. *Major League Baseball v. Crist*, 311 F.3d 1177 (11th Cir. 2003).

32. *Butterworth v. Nat'l League of Prof'l Baseball Clubs*, 644 So, 2d 1021 (1994).

33. Ibid.

34. *Morsani v. Major League Baseball*, 739 So. 2d 610 (Fla. 2d Dist. Ct. App. 1999).

35. *Jim Evans Academy of Prof'l Umpiring, Inc. v. The National Association of Prof'l Baseball Leagues, Inc.*, Fla. 9th Cir. (2012-CA-013001).

36. Gil Imber, Umpire School Receives Baseball's Death Penalty for Racist Party Joke, February 12, 2012; http://bleacherreport.com/articles/1062999-umpire-school-receives-baseballs-death-penalty-for-racist-party-joke.

37. *Jim Evans Academy of Prof'l Umpiring, Inc. v. The National Association of Prof'l Baseball Leagues, Inc.*, Fla. 9th Cir. (2012-CA-013001).

38. In person interview with Scott Poley, Senior Vice President, Legal Affairs and General Counsel, MiLB; June, 2015.

39. Major League Baseball, Evans to Serve as MiLB Umpire Advisor, November 24, 2014; http://www.milb.com/news/article.jsp?ymd=20141126&content_id=102507214&fext=.jsp&vkey=pr_milb.

40. This squad, which played in the International League, should not be confused with the present-day MLB Miami Marlins. Sam Zygner, *The Forgotten Marlins: A Tribute to the 1956–1960 Original Miami Marlins* (Lanham, Maryland: Scarecrow Press, 2013).

41. *Storer v. Florida Sportservice Inc.*, 115 So. 2d 433 (Fla. 3d Dist. Ct. App. 1959).

42. *County of Brevard v. Miorelli Eng'g, Inc.*, 703 So. 2d 1049 (Fla. 1997), appeal after remand, 721 So. 2d 1223 (Fla. 5th Dist. Ct. App. 1998).

43. *CFI Sales & Mktg., Ltd. v. Florida Marlins Baseball, Ltd.*, 837 So. 2d 423 (Fla. 3d Dist. Ct. App. 2002).

44. Tim Elfrink, "Miami Marlins Threaten to Sue Long-Time Season Ticket Holders," *Miami New Times*, Mar. 28, 2013. http://www.miaminewtimes.com/news/miami-marlins-threaten-to-sue-longtime-season-ticket-holders-6391398.

45. Craig Davis, "Marlins at Odds with Fans as Second Season at Marlins Park Begins," *S. Fla. Sun Sentinel*, April 7, 2013, http://articles.sun-sentinel.com/2013-04-07/sports/fl-marlins-home-opener-0408-20130407_1_marlins-park-marlins-president-david-samson-season-tickets.

46. The story of the Honus Wagner baseball card. Michael O'Keeffe and Terri Thompson, *The Card* (New York: William Morrow, 2007).

47. *Pathman v. Grey Flannel Auctions, Inc.*, 741 F. Supp. 2d 1318 (S.D. Fla. 2010).

48. *Blumstein v. Sports Immortals, Inc.*, 67 So. 3d 437 (Fla. 4th Dist. Ct. App. 2011).

49. Ben Bradlee, Jr., *The Kid: The Immortal Life of Ted Williams* (New York: Little Brown and Company, 2013).

50. In person interview with Jim McCune, who was the assistant state attorney who prosecuted Antonucci, June, 2015.

51. *State v. Antonucci*, 590 So. 2d 998 (Fla. 5th Dist. Ct. App. 1991).

52. *United States v. McLain*, 823 F.2d 1457 (11th Cir. 1987).

53. *Brandes v. City of Deerfield Beach*, 186 So.2d 6 (Fla. 1966).

54. *Roper v. City of Clearwater*, 796 So. 2d 1159 (Fla. 2001).

55. *Tamar 7600, Inc. v. Orange County*, 686 So. 2d 790 (Fla. 5th Dist. Ct. App. 1997).

56. Ibid.

57. *Solares v. City of Miami*, 23 So. 3d 227 (Fla. 3d Dist. Ct. App. 2009).

58. Ibid.

59. *Fedornak v. Miami Marlins*, L.P. Fla. 11th Cir. (2015-013360 CA-01).

60. Matt Baker, "Rays Talks on Hold for Now," *Tampa Bay Times*, April. 7, 2015, at 1B, available at 2015 WLNR 10119939.

61. Roy Cummings, "Naimoli Tosses First Pitch, Says Rays are Staying in St. Pete," *Tampa Tribune*, April 6, 2015, available at 2015 WLNR 10086313.

62. Noah Pransky, Shadow of the Stadium, at http://shadowofthestadium.blogspot.com/. Last checked February 21, 2016.

63. Ibid.

64. *Miranda v. Office of the Commissioner of Baseball*, 3:14-cv-5349 (N.D. Cal.), and *Senne v. Office of the Commissioner of Baseball*, 3:14-cv-608 (N.D. Cal.). In May 2015, the court refused to transfer Senne to the Middle District of Florida. See *Senne v. Kansas City Royals Baseball Corp.*, 2015 WL 2412245 (N.D. Cal. 2015).

65. Craig Davis, "MLB Fines Cosart but Finds No Baseball Bets," *S. Fla. Sun Sentinel*, April 4, 2015, at 5C, available at 2015 WLNR 9889375.

66. Ibid.

67. Barry Svrluga, "Unafraid of Change, Rob Manfred Steps to Plate, Faces Pitches on Pace of Play, Gambling," WashingtonPost.com, Feb. 5, 2015, available at 2015 WLNR 3589207.

68. Maury Brown, Grading MLB Commissioner Rob Manfred After His First Year, January 26, 2016, http://www.forbes.com/sites/maurybrown/2016/01/26/grading-mlb-commissioner-rob-manfred-after-his-first-year/#2ac532052001.

69. Dustin Gouker, Florida Set to Introduce Daily Fantasy Sports Bill, Nov. 10, 2105, http://www.legalsportsreport.com/6042/florida-dfs-legislation.

70. Craig Davis, "Manfred Foresees Teams Visiting Cuba," *S. Fla. Sun Sentinel*, Mar. 11, 2015, at 1C, available at 2015 WLNR 7371030.

71. Joe Capozzi, "Scott's Pen Clears Way for Stadium," *Palm Beach Post*, June 11, 2015, at 1B, available at 2015 WLNR 17218341.

72. Tim Tucker, "Braves Eye Palm Beach Again in Search for New Spring Home," *Atlanta Constitution Journal*, Feb. 17, 2016, http://www.ajc.com/news/sports/baseball/braves-eye-palm-beach-again-in-search-for-new-spri/nqRwK.

The Best Baseball Story Ever?

Cecil "Stud" Cantrell, the Tampico Stogies, and Long Gone

David Krell

Had Henry David Thoreau been a baseball fan, his signature quotation might read, "The mass of minor leaguers lead lives of quiet desperation." Such is the wont of the Tampico Stogies in the 1987 HBO TV movie *Long Gone*. "Now the Tampico Nine always has been and always will be an aggregation that knows it's about to suffer another ignominious defeat," declares Cletis Ramey to Cecil "Stud" Cantrell, the Stogies' player-manager.[1]

Starring William Petersen, Virginia Madsen, and Dermot Mulroney, *Long Gone* takes place in the fictional town of Tampico, Florida—home of the La Madera Cigar Company. It is more than a story about baseball, though. It is a tale of corruption, hope, and love.

Stud—played by Petersen—leads the Stogies of the Class D Alabama-Florida League in 1957 through the stagnant labyrinth of the owners' frugality, the team's mediocrity, and the Deep South's racism. Pushing 40, Stud tells rookie second baseman Jamie Don Weeks—played by Dermot Mulroney—that he rivaled Stan Musial for a spot on the St. Louis Cardinals. After the Japanese attacked Pearl Harbor, Stud signed up with the Marines, fought on Guadalcanal, and suffered a mountain of shrapnel in one of his legs; he persuaded the doctors not to amputate. "I never made it, kid. But I would've. Goddammit, I would've."[2]

Packaging from the video release of *Long Gone*.

"I think he's a flawed character," explained Petersen in a telephone interview. "Stud has a tremendous amount of talent. Things came easy, then a bad break happened and he was bumped down the ladder. He's trying to make the best of it. There are analogies in the acting world where the breaks don't go your way. You find yourself making compromises, maybe for your talent and integrity. At a certain point, the light goes off and the world is what you make of it. He's a regular guy who could be any man."[3]

While Stud has experience in the harsh realities of life, Jamie oozes naïveté. With an attitude of sexual indifference that would make Lothario blush, Stud coarsely instructs Jamie that all women have sex—even the religious ones. But Stud lands in an unintended romance that begins as a one-night stand whose name he can't remember the morning after—Dixie Lee Boxx, Miss Strawberry Blossom of 1957, played by Virginia Madsen. A platinum blonde with the looks of Marilyn Monroe and the street savvy of Lauren Bacall, Dixie Lee is 20, almost half Stud's age. "I'm old enough to like Jax for breakfast,"[4] she explains to a bartender in the glow—or haze—of her dalliance with Stud. (Jax beer was a regional brew manufactured by Jax Brewing Company of Jacksonville from 1913 until it went out of business in 1956.)

Long Gone details Stud's resumé of romance, or lack of it. An aura of cockiness buttressed by crudeness gives the impression that the Stogies' manager is carefree about life and careless with women. In Paul Hemphill's eponymous 1979 novel, Stud got a "Dear John" letter from his wife. While he was arguing with doctors to save his leg, she was cheating on him with a coworker at her plant. With visions of a major league career in the rear view mirror, Stud would play for a Class B team in Corpus Christi. "So began a wallowing odyssey that carried him all over America in that limbo called the 'lower minor leagues': Mountain States League, Cotton States, Evangeline, Itty, Big State, West Texas-New Mexico, Ardmore, Eastman, Hopkinsville, Amarillo, Pocatello, Hazard, Thibodaux," the novel reads. "Bad lights, rutted infields, rickety grandstands, swampy dressing rooms, ancient buses, hand-me-down uniforms, drunken fans. Still smarting from what his wife had done to him, he began to drink and to gorge himself on women, as though repeated conquests might blot the memory that he had once been cuckolded by a 4-F. He hit an umpire at Big Stone Gap, contracted gonorrhea in Galveston, and was run out of Waterloo for knocking up the club owner's teenage daughter."[5] There is no mention of a Mrs. Cantrell in the TV movie.

Publicity still from Long Gone showing actors Dermot Mulroney, William Petersen, and Larry Riley as Jamie Weeks, Stud Cantrell, and Joe Louis Brown.

Southern-style racism confronts the Stogies, who mask their black slugger Joe Louis Brown as José Brown, a Venezuelan; Larry Riley plays Brown. On a road trip, Klansmen block the road, brandish whips, and burn a cross. Wise to the Stogies' scheme of protecting Brown, they call for him. Stud orders him to stay on the bus and, in turn, guides his teammates, each one holding a bat, to chase the Klansmen off the road.

After the tumult, Brown gets off the bus to finish the job, metaphorically. When he gets a nod of approval from Monroe, the Stogies' elderly black equipment manager, Brown takes a vicious swing at the cross— when it hits the ground, the flames are extinguished. A bond is forged, eliminating the awkwardness seen earlier when the white players look at Brown in the locker room without talking to him.

Full of optimism, Stud believes that the Stogies can win the championship, a far cry from the dismal 12–23 record the team had before Jamie and Brown showed up. A slow-motion montage of Stogies highlights against the backdrop of the gospel song "I Don't Believe He Brought Me This Far (To Leave Me)" reflects the inspirational tone that seems to be a prerequisite for sports movies featuring an underdog taking on a superior opponent—in this case, it's the Dothan Cardinals.

Here, *Long Gone* presents an obstacle for the fearless protagonist who sacrificed his baseball career for his country. A native Missourian, Stud never lost his desire to work in the Cardinals organization. When the owner of the Dothan Cardinals presents an opportunity to manage the team next season, Stud grabs it. But the job comes with a catch—he can't play in the Stogies-Cardinals championship game.

Dixie Lee leaves him and then deconstructs Stud's hero image for Jamie, who has lately embodied the swagger of the Stogies' skipper. Jamie suffers a letdown with the impact of a Gulf Coast hurricane, consequently. It comes on the heels of a personal

dilemma—his girlfriend Esther is pregnant. Following Stud's love-them-and-leave-them philosophy, Jamie abandoned Esther emotionally as she went to Mobile, Alabama, to stay with an aunt.

For solace, Stud heads to the bar, where he finds Brown. Immediately, Stud realizes that the Cardinals bought Brown's absence as well. Without Tampico's star duo, Dothan will be assured a victory.

"What'd they give you?" asks Stud

"What'd they give you?" responds Brown.

"I get the privilege of managing Dothan next year."

"I guess they know what they gotta pay for white trash, huh?"

"Come on, what'd they give you?"

"I guess they know what they gotta pay for a nigger, too."

"It's just so damn sad. Baseball ain't nothing but a little boy's game played on some grass," mourns Stud. "It shouldn't matter who the pitcher's daddy is or how much money he makes. It shouldn't matter what color a fella's skin is. You just go out there with a bat in your hands, you hit the ball, and you run like hell. That's all. It's just a shame."[6]

When Brown leaves the bar, he takes a bat to his Cadillac—his price for sitting out the game. It's the latter part of a setup-payoff literary device, common in films—Brown eyed the car when he first came to Tampico.

Stud has more than a job in the Cardinals organization at stake. Through the Buchmans, Stud learns that failure to accede to their demands that he not play in the championship game will result in the Cardinals owner, J. Harrell Smythe, informing baseball's power structure about every peccadillo, big and small, resulting in Stud's permanent expulsion from the game.

But Tampico's manager and slugger renege on their deal to sit out the game. In another setup-payoff, Stud faces Dothan hurler Dusty Houlihan with the bases loaded in the bottom of the ninth inning. Bad blood exists between the two because of Stud's relentless

William Petersen and Virginia Madsen as Stud and Dixie Lee.

insults about Houlihan's sister. Stud admitted, earlier, that he's only 2-for-68 against Houlihan in his career.

And so, when Houlihan comes in from the bullpen to face Stud, the ante is raised. A taunt that is vicious at worst and inflammatory at best enrages Houlihan, who beans Stud. After being knocked unconscious, Stud stumbles to first base. The Stogies are Alabama-Florida League champions! Tampico exorcises the ghosts of failure underscored by Cletis earlier in the story, consequently.

"I think Stud had become a lost cause, but only to himself," says Petersen. "Dixie Lee is the one who is straightening him out. When he looks across at Joe Brown and they ask themselves who they are and talk about what they should be, I think Stud saves himself."[7]

Stud marries Dixie Lee, Jamie marries Esther, and the Stogies, for once, have pride.

Notably, two performers known for comedy appear as the father and son owners of the Stogies—Henry Gibson and Teller play Hale Buchman and Hale Buchman, Jr., respectively. They're greedy for money, giddy for victory, and garrulous for explanations about their nickel and dime management. In lesser hands, their characters could have been caricatures.

Long Gone resonates three decades after its premiere, largely because the joy in making the movie comes across in the performances. "I have fond memories of working with Virginia and Dermot," recalls Petersen. "The 1986 World Series was going on while we shot the movie. We'd go back to the hotel after shooting and watch in the bar. I also had friends from Chicago who were in the movie. You have to be close. You can't do a baseball movie and not have the guys be a team. We were just very fortunate. It was like falling off a log.

"Baseball reminds me of my childhood and a time and place when things were more fun and simpler. For many of us, baseball will always be that type of memory. It will always be reflective."[8] ■

Notes

1. Michael Norell, based on the 1979 novel *Long Gone* by Paul Hemphill, *Long Gone*, directed by Martin Davidson (HBO Pictures, Landsburg Company, 1987).
2. Ibid.
3. Telephone interview with William Petersen, March 4, 2016.
4. *Long Gone* (HBO Pictures, Landsburg Company).
5. Paul Hemphill, *Long Gone* (New York: The Viking Press, 1979).
6. *Long Gone* (HBO Pictures, Landsburg Company).
7. Telephone interview with William Petersen.
8. Ibid.

Walking It Off—Marlins Postseason Walk-Offs

Steven Glassman

The Marlins won the World Series both times they qualified for the postseason in 1997 and 2003. This was not accomplished without a little drama: Five of the Marlins 22 postseason victories were walk-offs.[1] Remarkably, they did not allow a walk-off in any of their 11 losses.[2]

NATIONAL LEAGUE DIVISION SERIES
Edgar Renteria (September 30, 1997, Game One versus San Francisco off Roberto Hernandez)[3,4]

Neither team did much offensively for the first six innings. Kevin Brown retired the first 14 hitters before allowing a Stan Javier two-out, infield single to short in the top of the fifth inning. Javier was caught stealing second to end the inning.

In the bottom of the first, the Marlins put together a two-out rally against Giants starter Kirk Rueter. Gary Sheffield walked and Bobby Bonilla's line drive single to left moved Sheffield to third. However, Moises Alou flied out to center fielder Daryl Hamilton to end the inning.

In the top of the sixth, Rueter helped himself with a two-out single to left. "[Jeff] Conine made a diving stab of Daryl Hamilton's ground ball down the line, saving a run and preserving a scoreless tie" wrote Steve Gietschier. Edgar Renteria hit a line drive single to center and Sheffield walked to lead off the bottom of the sixth. However, Bonilla lined out to Hamilton and Alou and Conine flied out to Javier to end the scoring threat. Both teams scored on leadoff seventh-inning home runs. Bill Mueller hit one to right off Brown and Charles Johnson to left-center off Rueter.

Sheffield lined a double to left and Bonilla was intentionally walked by relief pitcher Julian Tavarez with one out in the bottom of the eighth. Alou grounded into an around-the-horn double play to third baseman Mueller to end another Marlins opportunity.[5]

Tavarez started the bottom of ninth inning. Conine singled to left and Johnson was hit by the first pitch. Tavarez was replaced by Roberto Hernandez. Rookie Craig Counsell's sacrifice bunt to Mueller moved Conine and Johnson up to third and second, respectively.

Edgar Renteria started the Marlins' walkoff "tradition" with the game-winner off Roberto Hernandez in the first game of the 1997 NLDS.

Jim Eisenreich, pinch-hitting for Dennis Cook, was intentionally walked to load the bases. Devon White's fielder's choice, Jeff Kent to Brian Johnson, reloaded the bases with two outs for Renteria. The second-year shortstop got ahead of Hernandez 2–1 and singled to right to score Charles Johnson to end the game.[6] It was Renteria's first career postseason walk-off and the Marlins won its first postseason game in franchise history.

According to SFGATE's Henry Schulman, "Hernandez came in with a fastball for strike one, then threw another sinking fastball on the outside corner. Renteria, a fine clutch hitter, slapped the other way into right field." Schulman added, "Renteria hit a fastball from Roberto Hernandez, who is paid to blow pitches by hitters like Renteria. But Hernandez fell behind Renteria in the count, tilting the odds in the hitter's favor. Hernandez knew he had to throw the ball over the plate with the bases full. 'I'm not thinking about giving up a hit,' he said. 'I'm thinking about not giving up a walk. Normally a guy like that is somewhat aggressive and he tries to pull it. Then you get a ground ball to third. But he did the right thing and went with the pitch.'"

Charles Nobles wrote in *The New York Times*: "Ahead in the count, Edgar Renteria shut out the mushrooming delirium around him and decided to guess. With the bases loaded and two out in the bottom of the ninth inning of a tie game, the Florida Marlins shortstop simply looked for a fastball on the outside part of the plate." Renteria said to Nobles that "He got me out on sinkers the last time I faced him. But after he threw two of them for balls, I thought it was a good time to gamble."

Moises Alou (October 1, 1997, Game Two versus San Francisco off Roberto Hernandez)[7]

Game Two was a slugfest compared to the first, with four lead changes. Marlins had led 2–1 after the first inning, but the Giants tied it in the second. Both teams scored in the third. They took a lead in the top of the fourth before the Marlins retook it in the bottom half on a Kurt Abbott ground-ball double play to shortstop Jose Vizcaino. The Marlins left the bases loaded at the end of the fourth. Sheffield extended the lead to 6–4 on a sixth inning, two-out solo home run to left off Tavarez. Barry Bonds's one-out, seventh-inning double to right off starter Livan Hernandez scored Vizcaino and narrowed the margin to 6–5.

The Marlins' ninth-inning defense deserted Florida closer Robb Nen. Hamilton reached on Conine's fielding error as the latter was trying to flip a ground ball to Nen (and bobbled it) to start off the ninth. Javier's infield single to Renteria moved Hamilton into scoring position. Nen recovered, striking out Javier looking and getting Bonds to force Javier at second. However, Counsell's throwing error on the double play attempt allowed Hamilton to score and tie the game.

Giants manager Felipe Alou made numerous changes for the bottom of the ninth, starting the inning again with Roberto Hernandez on the mound. Rookie Dante Powell entered the game, playing center field. J.T. Snow also entered the game, playing first, and Kent moved from first to second, replacing Mark Lewis.[8] Sheffield managed a leadoff single off Hernandez and stole second with Bonilla at the plate. Bonilla walked and Moises Alou was due up for the Marlins. On a 1–1 pitch, Alou lined a single to Powell.[9] The center fielder's throw hit off to the side of the pitcher's mound and Sheffield scored.[10] This was Alou's first postseason walk-off.[11] The Marlins led the best-of-five series, 2–0.[12]

Alou said to SFGATE's Bruce Jenkins: "The guy throws so hard, you've got to think fastball. But he threw me a breaking ball that stayed over the plate.' He added to SFGATE's Nancy Gay that, "This was pretty big, but I think there should be a few more big hits coming in the postseason, hopefully. It just felt great to deliver at the right time." Alou was quoted by

The Times's Nobles: "Those last at-bats didn't mean anything. My thought was 'I have everything to gain and nothing to lose.'"

Ivan Rodriguez (October 3, 2003, Game Three versus San Francisco off Tim Worrell)[13]

The Marlins scored first on a one-out, two-run Ivan Rodriguez home run off starter Rueter.[14] The Giants tied the score in the sixth. Bonds and Edgaro Alfonzo reached on consecutive singles to start the inning. Bonds scored on Jose Cruz Jr.'s fielder's-choice groundout to third baseman Mike Lowell. Pinch-hitting for Rueter, Pedro Feliz singled to left, scoring Alfonzo to even the score. Giants also had opportunities to take the lead.[15]

The Giants took the lead in the eleventh off of Braden Looper. Rich Aurilia walked on five pitches start the inning. Bonds reached on Alex Gonzalez's error on a force attempt. Alfonzo singled in Aurilia for the go ahead run. Neifi Perez was intentionally walked with one out to load the bases. Cruz Jr. forced Bonds at home and Snow grounded to second to end the inning.

The Marlins also took advantage of the Giants' defense in the bottom half. Conine reached on Cruz Jr.'s error on a fly ball to start the inning.[16] Alex Gonzalez walked facing Tim Worrell. Cruz Jr. said to SFGATE's Ray Ratto, "I should have caught it, and I didn't." Schulman wrote, "[Conine's fly] ball hit the heel of Cruz' glove as he closed it too soon." Rookie Miguel Cabrera sacrificed to Worrell, moving the runners up one base, and Juan Pierre was intentionally walked to load the bases. Luis Castillo forced Conine at home, reloading the bases. Worrell got ahead of Rodriguez 1–2, but he lined a single to right, scoring Gonzalez and Pierre to win the game.[17] This was Rodriguez's

Moises Alou had the second walk-off hit in a row off reliever Roberto Hernandez, becoming the hero of NLDS Game Two in 1997.

first postseason walk-off.[18] According SFGATE's Henry Schulman, "Worrell got ahead 1–2 before I-Rod lined a fastball into right field. Gonzalez jogged in with the tying run. Cruz Jr. fielded the ball quickly, but any hope of a redemptive throw home was dashed by the sight of the mercury-quick Pierre rounding third with on his way home with the winning run." *The Times*'s Angel Hermoso wrote: "Rodriguez batted next, aware of Worrell's slider and control. Rodriguez said later that when he fell behind in the count, 1–2, he reminded himself to hang back and try to slap a single. He did, hitting a line drive single to right." Hermoso added, "Cruz's throw had a high arc and was off-line."

WORLD SERIES
Edgar Renteria (October 26, 1997, Game Seven versus Cleveland off Charles Nagy)

The Marlins had an opportunity against Indians rookie starter Jaret Wright in the first inning.[19] Renteria hit a ground-ball double to right and Sheffield walked with one out. However, Darren Daulton grounded to second baseman Tony Fernandez, and Sheffield was automatically called out for running out of the baseline, ending the scoring threat.

The Indians opened the scoring in the third off of Leiter. Jim Thome's full-count walk and Marquis Grissom's ground-ball single opened the inning. Wright's sacrifice bunt to Daulton moved Thome to third and Grissom to second. Fernandez's line drive single to center scored Thome and Grissom to give the Indians a 2–0 lead. Right fielder Manny Ramirez's walk moved Fernandez into scoring position, but David Justice struck out swinging to end the inning.

The Indians had another opportunity in the fifth. Omar Vizquel reached on an infield single to Renteria with one out and stole second. Ramirez was intentionally walked and Vizquel stole third with two outs. Justice ended another Indians scoring chance looking at a called third strike.

Meanwhile, the Marlins went hitless off of Wright between the second and sixth innings. Daulton reached third on Ramirez's error with two out in the sixth, but Alou flied out to Grissom to end the inning. The Marlins knocked out Wright in the seventh. Bonilla hit Wright's first pitch of the inning to right-center to cut the lead in half, 2–1. Indians manager Mike Hargrove pulled Wright from the game after a one-out walk to Counsell.

The Indians opened up the ninth with Antonio Alfonseca walking Matt Williams. Catcher Sandy Alomar Jr. forced Williams at second. Marlins manager Jim Leyland brought in left-handed pitcher Felix Heredia to face the left-handed hitter Thome. Thome singled to right, advancing Alomar Jr. to third. Leyland replaced Heredia with Nen to face Grissom. Grissom hit a ground ball to Renteria, who threw Alomar Jr. out at home. Nen retired rookie pinch-hitter Brian Giles on a flyout to Alou end the ninth.

Hargrove went to Jose Mesa for his second straight save opportunity and a chance to clinch the Indians' first World Championship since 1948. Alou led off the inning with a line-drive single to center and Johnson's single to Ramirez advanced Alou to third with one out. Counsell's sacrifice fly to Ramirez scored Alou to tie the game.

Renteria and Sheffield reached on consecutive singles with one out in the tenth. However, Mesa struck out pinch-hitter John Cangelosi looking and Charles Nagy induced Alou to fly out to Ramirez to end the tenth.[20]

In the eleventh, Williams led off the inning again with a walk, but Alomar Jr. bunted into a fielder's choice to pitcher Jay Powell. Thome ended the inning with a double play ground ball to Counsell.

Bonilla singled up the middle to Grissom leading off the bottom of the eleventh. Gregg Zaun popped up a bunt to Nagy. Counsell reached on Fernandez's fielding error with one out and advanced Bonilla to third. Replays showed that Bonilla was trying to avoid getting hit by Counsell's ground ball and it may have shielded Fernandez. *The Times*'s Jack Curry wrote, "Fernandez declined to blame Bonilla for screening him and said that the ball did not take a bad hop. He just missed it." Fernandez said about his eleventh-inning fielding error: "I didn't want to make the error, but the Lord allowed it to happen" (Cleary 1997). Eisenreich was intentionally walked to load the bases. Center fielder Devon White's ground ball to Fernandez forced Bonilla at home for the second out and reloaded the bases with Renteria due up for the Marlins.

After taking a called strike to start the at-bat, Renteria lined a single to center field past Nagy's glove to score Counsell and dramatically end the World Series.[21,22] It was Renteria's second career postseason walk-off.[23] Indians broadcaster Herb Score said: "Line drive, base hit, game over. And so that's the season for 1997" (Terry Pluto).[24] *The Times*'s Murray Chass quoted Hargrove: "I thought Charlie had good stuff tonight. He made a great pitch to Devon White to jam him and get a ground ball out at home plate. He made a great pitch to Renteria and he hit it where nobody was standing. Those are the breaks of the game." Renteria said, "I have been in those situations before so I wasn't nervous." He added: "'I felt relaxed"

(Perrotto 22). Renteria also said, "that Nagy made a tactical mistake in the fateful 11th: 'He threw me a slider on the first pitch. I took it for a strike. I knew he was going to throw me another slider and I hit it. Too many breaking pitches'" (Carter and Sloan 198). "'The [Edgar] Renteria line drive,' [Nagy] said. 'It tipped off my glove. I really wish I could have caught it'" (Pluto).

Alex Gonzalez (October 22, 2003, Game Four versus New York Yankees off Jeff Weaver)[25]

The Marlins took the early lead in the first inning off starting pitcher Roger Clemens, scoring three runs on five hits.[26] Cabrera hit a one-out, two-run home run, scoring Rodriguez. Derrek Lee's two-out single to right scored Conine.

The Yankees responded in the top of the second with three straight singles off starter Carl Pavano. Aaron Boone's two-out sacrifice fly to Pierre scored Bernie Williams. The Yankees got Jason Giambi into scoring position with two outs in the third and the Marlins got Lee to second in the fourth with two outs, but neither scored. Neither team had any scoring opportunities between the sixth and eighth innings.

Marlins manager Jack McKeon called on Ugueth Urbina for his second save opportunity of the series. Williams singled to Pierre and Hideki Matsui walked on six pitches with one out. Jorge Posada forced Matsui at second and moved Williams to third with two outs.

Yankees manager Joe Torre made a pair of moves. He had Ruben Sierra pinch-hit for Karim Garcia and David Dellucci pinch-run for Posada. Torre's moves paid off for the Yankees. Sierra's line-drive triple to right easily scored Williams from third and Dellucci from first base to tie the game at three. Pierre led off with a walk and moved to second on a Castillo sacrifice bunt to pitcher Jose Contreras in the bottom of the tenth. However, Contreras struck out Rodriguez and Cabrera swinging to end the threat.

The Yankees loaded the bases with one out in the top of the eleventh on a Williams double, Matsui walk, and an intentional pass to pinch-hitter Juan Rivera. Looper relieved Chad Fox, struck out Boone swinging, and induced catcher John Flaherty to pop up to Lee to end the inning.

Yankees pitcher Jeff Weaver was in his second inning of relief in the bottom of the twelfth and Gonzalez was leading off the inning, entering the at-bat 1-for-13 (.077) in the series with six strike-outs.[27,28] Gonzalez worked a full count and lined Weaver's eighth pitch of the at bat, curving into the left field corner for a home run.[29,30] This was Gonzalez's first postseason walk-off. Gonzalez was quoted

In 2003, Jack McKeon had retired from managing in the big leagues, but was enticed to take over the Marlins after their dismal 16–22 start. The result was not only the wild card but the eventual World Series championship.

by the Associated Press after the game: "I had a feeling" (Wilkins 2003). Gonzalez said in Jack Curry's Game Four recap for *The Times*: "When I hit the ball, I said, 'Get up ball, get up ball.'" *The Times*'s Dave Caldwell wrote that "Gonzalez worked a full count against Weaver, who then tried to throw a sinker, down and away. It caught too much of the plate, and Gonzalez sent it down the left-field line and over the fence." Weaver said in Caldwell's article: "He did what he was supposed to do, I guess. I feel like I was making good pitches. One just got away." Weaver added: "I felt fine. After not throwing to a lot of hitters for a long time, it was nice to get in there." Curry also wrote that Weaver, "was in the game because Manager Joe Torre wanted to use a long man for extra innings." Caldwell also noted that "Torre had to use Jeff Weaver, the seldom-used right hander who had such a disastrous regular season that Torre had not used him in a month." Caldwell added, "Weaver is—present tense—his long man, Torre said after the game." Torre himself said afterward, "If he is not in the game there, he shouldn't be on the roster."[31] ∎

Notes

1. Most National League Postseason Walk-Offs (Five or more): St. Louis Cardinals 7, Boston-Milwaukee-Atlanta Braves 6, Brooklyn-Los Angeles Dodgers 5, Cincinnati Reds 5, Marlins 5, Houston Colt .45s-Astros (National League) 5, and New York Mets 5. In the American League, the Yankees have 19 walk-offs and the Boston Red Sox have 11.

2. Most NL Postseason Walk-Offs Allowed (Five or more): Brooklyn-Los Angeles Dodgers 11, Boston-Milwaukee-Atlanta Braves 9, St. Louis Cardinals 9, New York-San Francisco Giants 7, Philadelphia Phillies 6, and Houston Colt .45s-Astros (National League) 5. The Marlins and the Milwaukee Brewers are the only NL franchises who have not allowed a postseason walk-off. The Yankees have allowed 14 walk-offs and the Red Sox have allowed eight. The Brewers and the Toronto Blue Jays are the only AL teams who have not allowed a postseason walk-off.

3. The Giants' first postseason appearance since 1989.

4. The Marlins' first-ever postseason appearance.

5. Altogether, the Marlins had runners in scoring position in the first, sixth, and eighth innings.
6. The last time Renteria faced Hernandez, he walked and scored on a Sheffield home run on September 14, 1997. He never struck out in six regular season plate appearances against Hernandez.
7. The Marlins led the best-of-five series, 1–0.
8. Powell came in because Hamilton "hurt his left groin muscle running the bases and had to come out" (Schulman 1997).
9. Alou was hitless in eight at-bats in the series before the hit.
10. The Marlins came back from three one-run deficits (1–0, 3–2, and 4–3).
11. Hernandez became the first Giant since Jack Bentley (1924 versus the Washington Nationals) to allow multiple walk-offs in the same post-season. Hernandez also was the first to do it since Twins relief pitcher Ron Perranoski in the 1969 American League Championship Series versus the Orioles. Hernandez also joined Bentley, Dennis Eckersley (1988 WS and 1990 ALCS), Tug McGraw (1978 and 1980 NLCS), Tom Niedenfuer (1981 NLDS and 1985 NLCS), Alejandro Pena (1991 and 1995 WS), Perranoski, and Jeff Reardon (1981 NLDS and 1992 WS) with multiple postseason walk-offs allowed. This group was later joined by Steve Kline (2001 NLDS and 2002 NLCS), Dan Miceli (2004 NLDS and NLCS), and Rick Porcello (2013 ALDS and ALCS). Eckersley is the only one so far who was inducted in the Hall of Fame (2004).
12. Marlins won game three, 6–2, to sweep its first postseason series in franchise history.
13. Best-of-five series tied, 1–1.
14. The Marlins left runners in scoring position in the third and sixth innings. They also wasted a Castillo lead-off walk in the eighth and left the bases loaded in the tenth.
15. The Giants were unable to convert lead-off singles in the seventh (Grissom) and the eighth (Benito Santiago).
16. Cruz Jr. won the 2003 Rawlings NL Gold Glove as an outfielder.
17. The Marlins led the best-of-five series, 2–1, and won Game Four, 7–6, to advance to the NLCS.
18. Rodriguez also contributed defensively in the series. He threw out Grissom trying to steal third with one out in the seventh inning and Alfonzo at the plate in a tie game. In game four, he tagged Snow out at home plate (on a Conine throw) to preserve a 7–6 win and end the series.
19. Nagy, the Game Three starter, was scheduled to start Game Seven, but Hargrove chose Game Four starter Wright instead, after game six. Wright was also working on three days' rest. Nagy received a no decision in Game Three, allowing four walks, five runs (all earned), and six hits in six innings. He also had started five September games with a 5.18 ERA.
20. Nagy's first relief appearance since September 1, 1990, versus the Blue Jays.
21. At the time, the second NL Game Seven World Series walk-off (Mazeroski in 1960) and the fourth Game Seven Series walk-off (first since Gene Larkin in 1991). Furthermore, it was also, at the time, the fifth Game Seven postseason walk-off (first since Larkin in 1991) and the first Series-ending walk-off since Joe Carter in 1993.
22. The Marlins won its first world championship in franchise history and became the first Major League expansion team since the 1992 Blue Jays to win its first World Series on its initial attempt. They were also the first overall, expansion, and NL team since the 1969 Mets to win the WS in its first postseason. The Marlins were the first Wild Card team to win a WS.
23. Renteria became the first NL batter with two walk-offs in the same postseason. At the time, he was second player with multiple walk-offs. Tigers' Goose Goslin accomplished this feat (one in 1934 and another in the 1935 WS). Renteria and Goslin were later joined by Bernie Williams (one in 1996 and another in the 1999 ALCS), Alfonso Soriano (one each in the 2001 ALCS and WS), and David Ortiz (one in the ALDS and two more in the 2004 ALDS). Goslin is the only one so far who was inducted in the National Baseball Hall of Fame (1968).
24. It was Score's final radio call for the Indians after 35 seasons.
25. The Yankees entered the game, leading best-of-seven series, 2–1.
26. This was Clemens's final game prior to his announced retirement, however he returned to pitch for the Houston Astros in three additional seasons—2004, 2005, 2006—and then appeared in 18 games for the Yankees in 2007.
27. Weaver made two relief appearances (September 22 and 24 versus the White Sox), pitching one inning since September 14. Altogether, he made seven appearances (one start) since August 19).
28. Juan Encarnacion pinch-hit for him in game three. Gonzalez was 1-for-16 (.063) in the NLDS with one walk and three strikeouts. He was 3-for-24 (.125) in the NLCS with two doubles four RBIs, and six strikeouts. Altogether, Gonzalez was 5-for-53 (.094) in the postseason with two doubles, four RBI, one walk, and 15 strikeouts before this at-bat.
29. This was the first Yankees walk-off allowed since Bill Mazeroski's Game Seven home run in 1960.
30. The best-of-seven series was tied, 2–2 and the Marlins won the next two games to win its second world championship in franchise history.
31. Weaver pitched in his first and only 2003 postseason game. It was also his last Yankees' appearance. He was traded with pitcher Yhency Brazoban and minor league pitcher Brandon Weeden to the Dodgers for pitcher Kevin Brown on December 13, 2003.

Bibliography
Books
Gietschier, Steve, 1998. "Year in Review: Marlins Win World Series." In *The Sporting News Baseball Guide: 1998 Edition*, edited by Craig Carter and Dave Sloan, 155–56. St. Louis: The Sporting News.
_____, 1998. "Year in Review: Marlins Nip Indians In Seven." In *The Sporting News Baseball Guide: 1998 Edition*, edited by Craig Carter and Dave Sloan, 158. St. Louis: The Sporting News.
"N.L. Division Series: Florida Vs. San Francisco." In *The Sporting News Baseball Guide: 1998 Edition*, edited by Craig Carter and Dave Sloan, 174–77. St. Louis: The Sporting News.
Perrotto, John, 1997. "World Series." In *Baseball America's 1998 Almanac*, edited by Allan Simpson, 17–22. Durham: Baseball America, Inc.
_____, 2004. "World Series." In *Baseball America Almanac 2004*, edited by Allan Simpson, 25–30. Durham: Baseball America, Inc.
White, Paul, Bill Koenig, and Pete Williams, 1998. "'Break up the Marlins!:' Game 7: Florida's Dramatic 11th." In *USA Today Baseball Weekly 1998 Almanac*, edited by Paul White, 55–56. New York: Henry Holt and Company.
"World Series: Game 7." In *The Sporting News Baseball Guide: 1998 Edition*, edited by Craig Carter and Dave Sloan, 197–99. St. Louis: The Sporting News.

Online Articles
Caldwell, Dave. 2003. "Baseball; Playing His Hand, Torre Wins Once But Loses Later." *The New York Times*, October 23. http://www.nytimes.com/2003/10/23/sports/baseball-playing-his-hand-torre-wins-once-but-loses-later.html.
Chass, Murray. 1997. "'97 World Series; Marlins Win World Series." *The New York Times*, October 27. http://www.nytimes.com/1997/10/27/sports/97-world-series-marlins-win-world-series.html.
Cleary, Dennis. 1997. "The Week in Quotes: October 20-November 2." *Baseball Prospectus*, November 10. http://www.baseballprospectus.com/article.php?articleid=23.
Curry, Jack. 1997. "'97 World Series; A Bitter Ending Frustrates Fernandez." *The New York Times*, October 27. http://www.nytimes.com/1997/10/27/sports/97-world-series-a-bitter-ending-frustrates-fernandez.html.
_____. 2003. "Baseball; Gonzalez Homers and Marlins Walk Off." *The New York Times*, October 23. http://www.nytimes.com/2003/10/23/sports/baseball-gonzalez-homers-and-marlins-walk-off.html.
Dickey, Glenn. 1997. "Glenn Dickey – Heartbreaker Likely Dooms The Giants." SFGATE, October 1. http://www.sfgate.com/sports/article/GLENN-DICKEY-Heartbreaker-Likely-Dooms-The-2803642.php.

Gay, Nancy. 1997. "Crushing Loss for Giants/Marlins win tight Game 1 in 9th inning." SFGATE, October 1. http://www.sfgate.com/sports/article/Crushing-Loss-for-Giants-Marlins-win-tight-Game-2826961.php.

_____. 1997. "Giants Confident They Can Bounce Back." SFGATE, October 1. http://www.sfgate.com/sports/article/GIANTS-NOTEBOOK-Giants-Confident-They-Can-2826381.php.

_____. 1997. "Giants in Real Trouble/Marlins seize upper hand." SFGATE, October 2. http://www.sfgate.com/sports/article/Giants-in-Real-Trouble-Marlins-seize-upper-hand-2803766.php.

Hermoso, Rafael. 2003. "Conine and the Marlins Relive the Past." *The New York Times*, October 4. http://www.nytimes.com/2003/10/04/sports/baseball-conine-and-the-marlins-relive-the-past.html.

_____. 2003. "Baseball; Two Unlikely Heroes Save the Marlins." *The New York Times*, October 23. http://www.nytimes.com/2003/10/23/sports/baseball-two-unlikely-heroes-save-the-marlins.html.

_____. 2003. "Baseball; Unsung Penny Lifts The Marlins." *The New York Times*, October 24. http://www.nytimes.com/2003/10/24/sports/baseball-unsung-penny-lifts-the-marlins.html.

Jenkins, Bruce. 1997. "Unassuming Players Have a Banner Year." SFGATE, October 1. http://www.sfgate.com/sports/article/MARLINS-STARS-Unassuming-Players-Have-a-Banner-2803944.php.

_____. 1997. "Marlins, Miami Giddy About 2-Game Lead Over Giants." SFGATE, October 2. http://www.sfgate.com/sports/article/Marlins-Miami-Giddy-About-2-Game-Lead-Over-Giants-2826174.php.

Keown, Tim. 1997. "Tim Keown – Postseason The Time to Second-Guess." SFGATE, October 1. http://www.sfgate.com/sports/article/TIM-KEOWN-Postseason-The-Time-to-2826842.php.

_____. 1997. "Page One – Backs Against the Wall/An unlucky bounce – Giants face elimination." SFGATE, October 2. http://www.sfgate.com/sports/article/PAGE-ONE-Backs-Against-the-Wall-An-unlucky-2826225.php.

Knapp, Gwen. 1997. "Lemke clones add panache to postseason." SFGATE, October 1. http://www.sfgate.com/sports/knapp/article/Lemke-clones-add-panache-to-postseason-3329153.php.

_____. 1997. "A bitter taste of their own medicine." SFGATE, October 2. http://www.sfgate.com/sports/knapp/article/A-bitter-taste-of-their-own-medicine-3328894.php.

Manoloff, Dennis. 2009. "Ex-catcher Sandy Alomar Jr. reflects on joy, heartache of time as he enters team Hall of Fame." cleveland.com, July 31. http://www.cleveland.com/tribe/index.ssf/2009/07/excatcher_sandy_alomar_jr_refl.html?FORM=ZZNR3.

New York Times. 1997. "'97 World Series; Wright Was a Well-Taken Risk, October 27. http://www.nytimes.com/1997/10/27/sports/97-world-series-wright-was-a-well-taken-ris.k.html.

Nevius, C.W. 1997. "C.W. Nevius – One That Slipped Away/Tough loss in the 9th – a must-win today." SFGATE, October 1. http://www.sfgate.com/bayarea/nevius/article/C-W-NEVIUS-One-That-Slipped-Away-Tough-loss-3317864.php.

Nobles, Charles. 1997. "Division Series Playoffs; Renteria Outguesses The Giants in the 9th." *The New York Times*, October 1. http://www.nytimes.com/1997/10/01/sports/division-series-playoffs-renteria-outguesses-the-giants-in-the-9th.html.

_____. 1997. "Division Series Playoffs; Alou's Bat Wakes Up Just in Time." *The New York Times*, October 2. http://www.nytimes.com/1997/10/02/sports/division-series-playoffs-alou-s-bat-wakes-up-just-in-time.html.

Pluto, Terry. 2009. "Team to honor old friend and 'neighbor' Herb Score: Terry Pluto." cleveland.com, April 10. http://www.cleveland.com/pluto/blog/index.ssf/2009/04/team_to_honor_old_friend_and_n.html.

_____. 2014. "Former Tribe pitcher Charles Nagy always felt at home in Cleveland." cleveland.com, June 22. http://www.cleveland.com/pluto/index.ssf/2014/06/former_tribe_pitcher_charles_n.html.

Ratto, Ray. 1997. "The Plot Thickens." SFGATE, October 1. http://www.sfgate.com/news/article/THE-PLOT-THICKENS-3098063.php.

_____. 2003. "A defeat that was properly earned." SFGATE, October 4. http://www.sfgate.com/sports/article/A-defeat-that-was-properly-earned-2584298.php.

Schulman, Henry. 1997. "Renteria's heart at home plate, not home in the 9th inning." SFGATE, October 1. http://www.sfgate.com/sports/article/Renteria-s-heart-at-home-plate-not-home-in-the-3239768.php.

_____. 1997. "Marlins have solved mystery of Hernandez." SFGATE, October 2. http://www.sfgate.com/sports/article/Marlins-have-solved-mystery-of-Hernandez-3098077.php.

_____. 2003. "Giants drop the ball, face elimination/Cruz error, blown chances doom them in 11 innings." SFGATE, October 4. http://www.sfgate.com/sports/article/Giants-drop-the-ball-face-elimination-Cruz-2584219.php.

_____. 2003. "Giants Notebook/Nathan Unhappy with short appearance." SFGATE, October 4. http://www.sfgate.com/sports/article/GIANTS-NOTEBOOK-Nathan-unhappy-with-short-2554750.php.

Sheehan, Joe. 2003. "Prospectus Today: Give it Away." *Baseball Prospectus*, October 4. http://www.baseballprospectus.com/article.php?articleid=2375.

_____. 2003. "Prospectus Today: Game Four." Baseball Prospectus, October 23. http://www.baseballprospectus.com/article.php?articleid=2437.

Verducci, Tom. 1997. "Happy Ending." Sports Illustrated Vault, November 3. http://www.si.com/vault/1997/11/03/234198/happy-ending-the-marlins-stirring-11th-inning-come-from-behind-defeat-of-the-indians-in-game-7-redeemed-an-otherwise-lackluster-series.

Wilkins, Ryan. 2003. "The Week in Quotes: October 20-26." *Baseball Prospectus*, October 27. http://www.baseballprospectus.com/article.php?articleid=2436.

Online Box Scores

http://www.baseball-reference.com/boxes/FLO/FLO199709300.shtml
http://www.baseball-reference.com/boxes/FLO/FLO199710010.shtml
http://www.baseball-reference.com/boxes/FLO/FLO199710260.shtml
http://www.baseball-reference.com/boxes/FLO/FLO200310030.shtml
http://www.baseball-reference.com/boxes/FLO/FLO200310220.shtml
http://www.retrosheet.org/boxesetc/1997/B09300FLO1997.htm
http://www.retrosheet.org/boxesetc/1997/B10010FLO1997.htm
http://www.retrosheet.org/boxesetc/1997/B10260FLO1997.htm
http://www.retrosheet.org/boxesetc/2003/B10030FLO2003.htm
http://www.retrosheet.org/boxesetc/2003/B10220FLO2003.htm

Online Videos

http://m.mlb.com/video/v25557593/nlds-gm1-marlins-win-first-playoff-game-on-walkoff/?c_id=mlb
http://m.mlb.com/mia/video/v25550193/sffla-alous-walkoff-single-gives-marlins-20-lead/?c_id=mia
http://m.mlb.com/video/v37184415/ws1997-gm7-renteria-nails-alomar-at-home-in-9th/?c_id=mlb
http://m.mlb.com/video/v3251279/bb-moments-97-ws-gm-7-marlins-take-title-in-11/?c_id=mlb
http://m.mlb.com/video/topic/54053166/v36896173/ws1997-gm7-fish-win-first-ws-on-renterias-walkoff/?c_id=mlb
http://m.mlb.com/video/v13062983/97-ws-gm-7-renteria-wins-it-for-fish/?c_id=mlb
http://m.mlb.com/video/v20852253/2003-nlds-gm3-pudge-lines-walkoff-single-in-extras/?c_id=mlb
http://m.mlb.com/mia/video/topic/54053166/v20081227/2003-ws-gm4-gonzalez-wins-it-with-a-walkoff-homer/?c_id=mia

Contributors

JOHN J. BURBRIDGE JR. is currently Professor Emeritus at Elon University where he was both a dean and professor. While at Elon he introduced and taught Baseball and Statistics. A native of Jersey City, he authored "The Brooklyn Dodgers in Jersey City" which appeared in the 2010 *Baseball Research Journal*. John has also presented at SABR conventions and the Seymour meetings. He is a lifelong New York Giants baseball fan (he does acknowledge they moved to San Francisco). The greatest Giants-Dodgers game he attended was a 1–0 Giants' victory in Jersey City in 1956. Yes, the Dodgers did play in Jersey City in 1956 and 1957, as did the Havana Sugar Kings in 1960 and 1961.

BRIAN CARROLL is professor and chair of Communication at Berry College in Mount Berry, Georgia, where he has taught journalism since 2003. He is author of *When to Stop Cheering? The Black Press, the Black Community and Black Baseball* (Routledge, 2007); and *The Black Press and Black Baseball, 1915–1955: A Devil's Bargain* (Routledge, 2015). Before joining the professorate, he was a sportswriter for 10 years covering minor league baseball for The (Greensboro, NC) *News and Record*. He serves on the editorial board of *Black Ball*.

ALAN COHEN is a retired insurance underwriter who has been a member of SABR since 2011. He has written more than 30 biographies for SABR's BioProject, and has contributed to 13 SABR books. He serves as Vice President-Treasurer of SABR's Connecticut Smoky Joe Wood Chapter and contributed to the chapter's recently published *100: The 100 Year Journey of a Baseball Journeyman—Mike Sandlock*. His first game story, "Baseball's Longest Day – May 31, 1964," has been followed by several others. His ongoing research into the Hearst Sandlot Classic (1946–1965), an annual youth All-Star game which launched the careers of 88 major-league players, first appeared in the Fall 2013 *Baseball Research Journal*, and has been followed with a poster presentation at the SABR Convention in Chicago. He serves as the datacaster (stringer) for the Hartford Yard Goats of the Class-AA Eastern League. A native of Long Island, he now resides in West Hartford, Connecticut, with his wife Frances, two cats and two dogs.

ROB EDELMAN teaches film history courses at the University at Albany. He is the author of *Great Baseball Films and Baseball on the Web*, and is co-author (with his wife, Audrey Kupferberg) of *Meet the Mertzes*, a double biography of *I Love Lucy*'s Vivian Vance and famed baseball fan William Frawley, and *Matthau: A Life*. He is a film commentator on WAMC (Northeast) Public Radio and a contributing editor of *Leonard Maltin's Movie Guide*. He is a frequent contributor to *Base Ball: A Journal of the Early Game* and has written for *Baseball and American Culture: Across the Diamond, Total Baseball, Baseball in the Classroom, Memories and Dreams*, and *NINE: A Journal of Baseball History and Culture*. His essay on early baseball films appears on the DVD *Reel Baseball: Baseball Films from the Silent Era, 1899–1926*, and he is an interviewee on the director's cut DVD of *The Natural*.

DANNY GALLAGHER of Bowmanville, Ontario, started covering Major League Baseball in 1988 when he became a Montreal Expos' beat writer for the *Montreal Daily News*. Since then, he has written four books on the Expos, including two he co-authored with Bill Young, the latest of which is *Ecstasy to Agony* about the 1994 squad. He won a Saskatchewan Baseball Association award in 1985 for a series of stories on that province's contributions to the big leagues. He also played competitive sandlot, adult baseball from 1968–94 in various Canadian provinces.

STEVEN GLASSMAN has been a SABR member since 1994 and regularly makes presentations for the Connie Mack Chapter. 2016 will be his 11th SABR convention. "Walking it Off—Marlins Postseason Walk-Offs" will be his third SABR published article. "Philadelphia's Other Hall of Famers" and "The Game That Was Not—Philadelphia Phillies at Chicago Cubs (August 8, 1988)" were published for the SABR43 and SABR45 online journals, respectively. The Temple University graduate in Sport and Recreation Management is currently the volunteer Director of Sports Information for Manor College. He has attended Phillies games since the 1970s. Steven serves as first base coach/scorekeeper for his summer league softball team. He currently resides in Warminster, Pennsylvania.

JOHN ROCKWELL HARRIS is a writer, photographer and producer of the B&H Photography Podcast. In addition to writing on baseball history, he has written extensively on photography and camera technology. His photographs have appeared in *The New York Times* and have been exhibited at the International Center of Photography, Museum of Modern Art, and Victoria & Albert Museum. A lifelong Indians fan, he had a short stint with the baseball team of his alma mater, Fordham University. John can be reached at harrisfoto@gmail.com or @jrockfoto10 on Twitter.

LOU HERNÁNDEZ is the author of several baseball histories. He resides in South Florida and roots for the Marlins.

STEPHEN R. KEENEY is a lifelong Reds fan and a new SABR member, joining in early 2015. He graduated from Miami University in 2010 with degrees in History and International Studies, and from Northern Kentucky University's Chase College of Law in 2013. After passing the bar exam he moved from his hometown of Cincinnati to Dayton, where he works as a union staff representative and lives with his wife, Christine.

FRANCIS KINLAW, a member of SABR since 1983, has contributed to 16 convention publications. He resides in Greensboro, North Carolina, and writes extensively about baseball, football, and college basketball. When the North Carolina Tar Heels won the NCAA basketball championship in March of 1957, he was certain that a World Series victory by "his" Detroit Tigers would follow later that year. He was to learn, however, that one utopian dream per year was his limit.

DAVID KRELL is the author of *Our Bums: The Brooklyn Dodgers in History, Memory and Popular Culture* (McFarland, 2015) and the co-editor of *In the Arena: A Sports Law Handbook* (New York State Bar Association, 2013). David has spoken at SABR's Frederick Ivor-Campbell 19th Century Base Ball Conference, Jerry Malloy Negro League Conference, and Annual Convention. He has also spoken at the Cooperstown Symposium on Baseball and American Culture, Queens Baseball Convention, Mid-Atlantic Nostalgia Convention, and Hofstra University's New York Mets 50th Anniversary Conference. David's writing has appeared in *Black Ball: A Negro Leagues Journal*, *Base Ball: A Journal of the Early Game*, the *Baseball Research Journal*, *The National Pastime*, and the *New York State Bar Association's Entertainment, Arts and Sports Law Journal*, and thesportspost.com.

ERIC ROBINSON is an educator and writer in Denton, Texas. He has presented his research on Central Texas Negro League history and other topics to groups ranging from the SABR National Conference, regional SABR conferences, elementary schools, Nerd Nite, and on Central Texas NPR. He can be contacted at ericrobinson1776@gmail.com and his website can be visited at www.lyndonbaseballjohnson.com.

LOUIS H. SCHIFF has served as a Broward County (Florida) Court Judge since 1997, and has been a member of the Florida Bar since 1981. He is the co-author of the first baseball and law textbook, *Baseball and the Law: Cases and Materials* (Carolina Academic Press, 2016). He serves as an Adjunct Professor of Law teaching baseball and law courses for The National Judicial College (University of Nevada: Reno); Mitchell | Hamline School of Law (St. Paul); and the Florida College of Advanced Judicial Studies (Tallahassee). He regularly gives baseball and law presentations to various bar associations and community groups. He is full-season ticket holder for the Miami Marlins. He has been a SABR member since 2013. You can contact him at: Schiff@baseballandthelaw.org

WILLIAM SCHNEIDER has been a baseball fan since receiving his first pack of baseball cards in 1974. An engineer by profession, Bill recently began writing about baseball in addition to avidly reading about and watching the game. He has a particular interest in the strategic aspects of team building and roster construction.

STEVE SMITH is a retired CPA who has been a SABR member since 2000. His primary passion is researching the baseball history of his hometown, Keokuk, Iowa. Since moving to Florida, he has researched the long forgotten Florida International League co-writing an article with SABR member Sam Zygner on the 1952 Florida International League pennant race. He has also published in the SABR Biography Project. He now lives in Englewood, Florida, near the Tampa Bay Rays spring training site in Port Charlotte.

DAN VanDeMORTEL became a Giants fan in Upstate New York and moved to San Francisco to follow the team more closely. He has written extensively on Northern Ireland political and legal affairs, and his Giants-related writing has appeared in San Francisco's *Nob Hill Gazette* and *The National Pastime*. An investigation into the shooting of a spectator at the Polo Grounds will be published in 2017 in a Polo Grounds anthology. He is currently writing a book and related articles on the 1971 Giants and welcomes feedback at giants1971@yahoo.com.

ROBERT D. WARRINGTON is a native Philadelphian who writes about the city's baseball history.

SAM ZYGNER is the author of the book *The Forgotten Marlins: A Tribute to the 1956–1960 Original Miami Marlins*. He has been a member of SABR since 1996 and is the Chairman of the South Florida Chapter of SABR. He received his MBA from Saint Leo University. His writings have appeared in the *Baseball Research Journal*, *The National Pastime*, *NINE: A Journal of Baseball History & Culture*, and *La Prensa de Miami*. A lifelong Pittsburgh Pirates fan, he has shifted some of his focus to Miami baseball history.